A Very Narrow Bridge

Reflections of a Psychologist

RICKEY MILLER, Ph.D.

A Very Narrow Bridge: Reflections of a Psychologist
by Rickey Miller Ph.D.
ISBN 978-1-0691008-0-1

Text design and layout: www.WeMakeBooks.ca
Cover design: Kim MacKillop Monteforte

To my daughter and son
who make the journey worthwhile

וְדַע, שֶׁהָאָדָם צָרִיךְ לַעֲבֹר עַל גֶּשֶׁר צַר מְאֹד מְאֹד, וְהַכְּלָל וְהָעִקָּר שֶׁלֹּא יִתְפַּחֵד כְּלָל

Know that a person needs to pass over on a very, very narrow
bridge and the greatest rule is not to be overwhelmed by fear.
Rabbi Nachman of Breslov, 1772–1810

"Homo sumi, humani nihil a me alienum puto"
I am human. I consider nothing human alien to me.
Terence, c. 195/185 BCE – c. 159 BCE

Author's Note

My memoir is a story of my life and includes patients' stories. It is written about events from my perspective. I acknowledge that my memory of events may be different from those of others. I am relating my recollection to the best of my knowledge. Some names, identities, and events have been changed or have been fictionalized to protect the identities of individuals, companies, and institutions.

Acknowledgements

To my patients: Over the years you have taught me the true meaning of resilience, courage, and personal growth. I am honoured and humbled by the trust you put in me. Your stories naturally intertwined with mine and enabled me to write this book.

Terry Poulton and Tamara Handler, thank you for the invaluable feedback you provided in your memoir writing classes at Metropolitan University in Toronto. Both of you consistently encouraged me to keep writing and to continue to be courageous in sharing my story.

Drs. Linda Gruson, Patricia DeFeudis, and Rosemary Barnes, my dear friends and fellow psychologists, thank you for taking the time to read the manuscript and for your helpful recommendations. Thank you also, Dr. Peter Bernstein, for providing a thoughtful review and encouragement.

Andrea Lemieux, your editing of my first draft was superb. You helped me tighten up the text and made my story so much more engaging.

Debbie Moskovitch, thank you for the helpful advice you provided about revising my website and tips for publishing. Your encouragement and recommendations were greatly appreciated.

Howard Shrier, thank you for sharing your experience and for your editing suggestions to produce a more concise and compelling narrative.

Paula Mandel, thank you for your excellent suggestions, which helped me revise the back cover.

William Taberner, thank you for your interest in my manuscript. Having worked with you on a number of legal cases over the years, I have a lot of respect for you. It meant a lot to me that when I mentioned that I was writing the manuscript, you took the time to ask me about it and make suggestions.

Gina Fusco, of Re:word Content Co., thank you for your proof-reading and for your positive feedback. It meant so much to me that you said that reading the manuscript made you think and reflect on your own journey, and offered perspective about certain situations in your life as this is one of the major goals that I had in writing my book.

Heidy Lawrance, thank you for all your help and advice about publishing and promotion. Kim Monteforte, thank you for the beautiful cover that you created. Beth Crane, I am grateful for your excellent and efficient typesetting.

To my son: Thank you for your insights when I read portions of my memoir to you and for your encouragement to keep writing. Your tenacity and continuing to reach for goals no matter how difficult they are to achieve encouraged me to pursue my goal of completing this manuscript.

To my daughter: I am grateful for your generosity in sharing your brilliant and creative insights and your literary talents when critiquing portions of the manuscript. Thank you, especially, for introducing the idea of combining patient's stories with my own. Even though you were often stressed by multiple demands on your time, you were loving and kind enough to put time aside to give me your honest feedback.

1

In an Empty Office

Sitting in the only chair left, my high-back leather chair, the psychologist's chair, I am looking out upon the sea of banker's boxes arrayed before me. Every box is bursting with files, each one telling the unique story of a person who I had the privilege to try to help. The boxes wait patiently for their lids and the movers who will soon carry them away into storage.

The chair will soon revert to being the chair of a previous practising psychologist, and I am about to revert to being just an ordinary person.

The silence of the empty office is strangely deafening. I miss hearing the familiar sounds drifting through my slightly opened door while I prepare for my next patient; the classical music from the radio in the waiting room; the ringing of the telephone; the soft tones of Cathy, my secretary; the muffled conversations coming from the hallway as the front door opens; the footsteps of patients arriving and departing. These sounds that I had taken for granted are now lost friends.

The quiet amplifies the rumbling thunder of intense and conflicting emotions gathering within me. I am humbled by how surprised I am by this storm. Despite all my years of practice, I still have limited insight into my own psychology.

For over forty years the 'me' I had known was a full-time clinician. When I lock the door for the last time, I will be leaving a huge part of me behind. Who will be left? Will I recognize and embrace that new person? How is it that I had not contemplated the pain of a loss of one of my most cherished identities?

I recall my immediate change in attention as soon as patients entered my office. The minute details of their behaviour provided a window into their thoughts and feelings. At the same time, I was aware of the emotional impact that their behaviour had on me. Both observations were essential in shaping effective treatment. "Evenly hovering attention" was one of the core principles of my training, as was appreciating that every interaction, whether regarded as assessment or therapy, was a treatment intervention, an invitation to help, an opportunity to promote change.

The names on the file folders staring up at me bring to mind my patients' stories and my own as they spontaneously and freely weave an intricate and beautiful tapestry of our common humanity.

I picture the way my office looked before everything had been donated or sold. My large oak desk was topped with a neat pile of folders, one for each patient I would be seeing that day. A pad of lined paper and an assortment of pens lay on top of the little glass table that sat between the two chairs for patients. The telephone, with its permanently disabled ringer, sat on my desk along with my treasured pen and pencil holder labelled "Chief Psychologist." It celebrated the position I had held for five years at a community hospital before Amani and I embarked on our private practice together.

Amani was the first psychologist I hired. We had worked together for five years and became close friends. I recall Amani's amazing skill in the kitchen. Her Indian dishes, which she always made from scratch, and all other food that she prepared were not only delectable, but left those fortunate enough to enjoy them with sweet and long-lasting memories.

Amani and I were terrified and excited when we took our gigantic leap of faith into the unknown of private practice. We joked that our workdays might be filled with Amani teaching me how to knit.

The first time our telephone rang, we joyfully and loudly shouted in unison, "Oh!!" We jumped out of our chairs with glee like little children surprised by ice cream cones that were suddenly handed to us. Amani took that first call and employed her most professional voice while trying to hide her joy. I covered my mouth to stifle my laughter. It was our first patient.

I look down at the carpet under my feet. It is the same wall-to-wall low-pile broadloom that we had chosen together in 1990. The tiny rainbow specks still brighten the dark blue background. I can scarcely see the old coffee stains or any evidence of all the shoes and boots that travelled on it during the past thirty-two years.

Although Amani and I attended different graduate programs, the layout of our offices reflected our common approach to treatment. We both worked most effectively when we sat face to face with our patients. We chose not to include a couch in our offices although we often lamented the absence of having a comfy place to lie down and rest in between sessions.

Our desks were placed near a window, so that our swivel chairs could be rolled out from behind the desk to directly face our patients. We chose comfortably padded low-back chairs with oak arm rests for them.

The oak credenza sat against the opposite wall from my desk. Just above it my seven diplomas and certificates proclaimed that I knew what I was doing. I smile as I recall all those moments when I wasn't sure about that at all.

The windows looked eastward and caught the cheerful rays of the sun that greeted me most workday mornings. My many plants crowded the windows and seemed to shoot out new branches and blossoms as I looked. I can picture the bright red flowers of the crown of thorns, the broad green leaves of the dieffenbachia and schefflera, and the variegated greens and whites of the spider plant's clones, cascading down to the floor from my desk. My plants warmed the room, giving it a cozy feel. I was aware of the research data suggesting that plants in offices had a calming effect, encouraged creativity, cleaned the air of carbon dioxide, making it easier to breathe, and helped to mute sounds. However, Amani and I added plants to our offices simply because we loved them and shared a passion for gardening.

How cold and empty my office feels now without Amani! Memories flood my mind as I recall the times we laughed together, consulted about difficult cases, shared stories about our children and everything else. Our friendship and partnership enriched my life for over thirty years.

Just then, a name on one of the file folders catches my eye. I see Mukondi striding into my office with confident, determined steps and turning to look directly, almost fiercely at me as she takes a seat. She is slender and very tall. In each session she wore a strikingly beautiful head wrap. The colours of her scarf blended with the bright patterns of her blouse and skirt. The bold blues, reds, and yellows struck me as clear announcements of inner strength.

Although Mukondi was in her thirties, her face was wrinkled and worn. She looked more like fifty. There was a large, diagonal scar on her forehead and deeper scars encircling her wrists and proceeding up her arms. Her eye contact with me was intense. From time to time, she grimaced.

"Would you prefer Ms. Kimani or Mukondi?" I asked softly.

"Mukondi."

"Nice to meet you, Mukondi. Please make yourself as comfortable as possible. Stand and walk around if you wish."

Mukondi began speaking as soon as my usual introductory remarks ended. There was urgency in her tone. "I was doing my job in the warehouse packing heavy boxes with electronic equipment." She continued angrily. "A man drove a forklift loaded with heavy boxes toward me. As he passed me, he came to a sudden stop for some reason and all the boxes fell on top of me." She placed her hands on the top of her head and grimaced. "I fell down and banged my head on the floor. I heard another worker shout 'You killed that lady!' I felt that I was going to die. Some of the workers took the boxes off of me. It took them a while. A supervisor and another worker helped me to stand up and took me to an office. They put an ice pack on my head."

Mukondi, who had been looking down as she spoke, suddenly looked at me straight in the eyes. "They didn't call an ambulance but a taxi and told the driver to take me to the hospital. I am angry that they didn't call an ambulance. I was at the hospital overnight. They did a CT scan and told me that I had a concussion. They said that my brain had moved when I hit the floor and that I should rest for two days." Mukondi paused and slumped into the chair. "I was sent to a rehab place after that for three weeks. It didn't help. I have so many headaches and pain in my neck, shoulder, and back. The rehab people pushed me to walk more and do exercises and my pain got a lot worse. I stopped going. I haven't been able to work for the past six months. I can't even do housework. My three kids do it all. I'm in bed most of the day."

Aware of my sadness and compassion for her, I turned my attention to which path would be best to connect with her emotionally. Her communication was rich in opening up many possibilities—validating her pain problems, her grief about the loss of her lifestyle, her anger about the accident and outrage with the forklift driver, her resentment about the inadequate care that she felt she received from her employer, her resentment that the staff at the rehab clinic were not helpful, and her mixed feelings she had about her dependence on her children. The challenge was to find the most strategic entry point to begin to forge a close and trusting working relationship. Almost always it was returning to the first emotion the patient had displayed. For Mukondi, it was validating her anger with the forklift driver whose sudden stop had caused the boxes to fall.

I recall how automatic these first steps had become over the years; how I would cast aside my tendency to feel empathy. I understood from early on that empathy blocked emotional connection. Imagining how I would feel in my patient's situation brought my focus to me and carried me far away from my patient. My goal was compassionate understanding.

In those precious first few minutes of interaction, nothing was more important than building a genuine connection. I learned that lesson when I worked with my first patient during a summer practicum at a psychiatric hospital.

2

First Intelligence Test

"Pair off. One of you is the clinician. The other is the patient. I will walk around the room and help as required." Dr. Stevens was one of my favourite first-year graduate-school professors. He was teaching us how to administer an intelligence test. The first time around, I acted the part of a patient while Michelle, my fellow first-year student, practised saying the instructions and scoring my answers. It appeared to be a simple exercise. The instructions were printed in the manual. We were not to deviate from them. Scoring was simple. Answers were either right or wrong.

As I recall this exercise, my heart warms with memories of Dr. Stevens. He was confident about his clinical skills and, more remarkably, proud of them. In a Department of Psychology that was approved by the American Psychological Association, publications in peer-reviewed journals were celebrated. We were given the consistent and clear mission to complete high-quality research and publish papers. Even though it was a clinical program, learning clinical skills was considered inferior to learning research skills. We were strongly discouraged from disclosing our intention to become practising clinical psychologists in this highly acclaimed clinical psychology program.

I was confused by the deep divide between academics who engage in research and clinicians who help patients. It was obvious to me that critical thinking and microscopic observation were essential for both. As I became more skilled as a scientist, I became more skilled at understanding and helping patients.

We watched Dr. Stevens as he conducted therapy sessions behind a one-way mirror. It seemed like magic to me that he knew how to respond to the patient. He was always drawn to raw emotion and reinforced any constructive coping strategies that he observed. I noted his unwavering attention to subtle nuance, tone, choice of words, and body language exhibited by the patient. Week after week, his patient became less distressed and more hopeful. Could I ever be as skillful?

Dr. Stevens taught us to appreciate the complexity of administering an intelligence test. It was not obvious how to obtain the patient's best performance. We learned that standardized instructions and our patient's performance are easily influenced by rapport and by our verbal and nonverbal cues. A positive rapport with our patient was elusive and challenging to achieve. It was certainly not automatically the result of simply repeating standardized texts. Dr. Stevens taught us to carefully monitor the multiple channels of communication occurring between us and our patient.

Dr. Stevens enlightened us as to the limited information conveyed by the final Intelligence Quotient numbers that we obtained. He challenged us to investigate the possible reasons a patient did not do well on a certain subtest without compromising the standardized administration. Did the score reflect poor motivation, fatigue, distraction, depression, or anxiety? Did anything that we conveyed put the patient off? Or did it appear likely that this score actually reflected an area of cognitive weakness? This functional analysis that resulted in qualitative data was far more complex and meaningful than simply counting up the correct answers and arriving at a quantitative result.

One day each week Dr. Stevens drove us to a psychiatric hospital for our first practicum. Each of us was assigned to a senior psychologist.

On my first day my supervisor directed me to administer an intelligence test to a patient on the men's unit. Dr. Bateman reviewed the patient's history without a pause. I tried to note down everything he said.

"Mr. Meltzenberg is in his forties. He has been in the hospital for two months with a diagnosis of psychotic depression. He has a history of emotional and physical abuse as a child. His mother physically abused him but not his two younger sisters. His mother was sexually and physically abused by her boyfriend, Mr. Meltzenberg's father, and was forced to move into a shelter with Mr. Meltzenberg when he was an infant. Later, she remarried and had two daughters. Alerted by his school, Children's Aid removed Mr. Meltzenberg from his mother due to the abuse and he was placed in a foster home. When he was sixteen, he went into a group home for the mentally ill where he's been up to now. He's been depressed for many years but it all came to a head a few months ago when he stopped talking to others, stopped taking care of his basic hygiene, and became anorexic. I suspect that he has brain damage due to the physical abuse that he suffered as a child. That's the reason we want you to administer an intelligence test. He's responded a little to medication. He's talking to others now and eating again. You can use the small examination room down the hall from my office."

I was overwhelmed by the heartbreaking story that I had just heard. Thinking about the terrible abuse and rejection that Mr. Meltzenberg had endured as a child knocked the wind out of me.

Thinking back, I feel compassion for my young, inexperienced self who felt deep sorrow for Mr. Meltzenberg's suffering. There was only a frail, crumbling wall around my heart, making it difficult for me to focus intellectually on the steps that I needed to take. I think about my struggle over the years to build a more solid wall but at the same time keep myself from becoming jaded and unmoved by my patients' sad stories. My heart was always ready to become hardened, to protect myself from the pain. Balancing genuine compassion with emotional distance enabled me to be effective. Too much of either obstructed therapy. It was never an easy balance to achieve.

I did not like walking into the men's unit. The odour of sweat and urine was repulsive. I much preferred the smell of bleach that greeted me on the women's unit.

I was anxious around the men. Not that they acted any differently from the women. In their common areas at times there would be tears. At times there would be cries of anger and the flailing of arms. At times there would be arguments. But most of the time, the men and the women sat quietly in their straightjackets of sedation and stared at the television without watching it.

I shuddered inside to think about asking one of the men to come with me. I pretended that I was a psychologist with many years of experience. *I must act confidently.* Underneath the façade, I was trembling with fear that I would be attacked. Feeling vulnerable as a female had been reinforced since childhood.

Many times Mom would tell me to turn around and look behind me when I was walking and to avoid saying anything to men I did not know. This fear was reinforced by frequent reports on the news of men assaulting women.

I entered the little examination room and set up the test materials. I hung a sign on the doorknob to indicate that the room was in use. Then I walked towards the lounge area and, in as confident and professional voice as I could muster, called out his name. "Mr. Meltzenberg?" No response. I tried again, a little louder. "Mr. Meltzenberg?" Still no response.

At the nursing station I asked a nurse to point out Mr. Meltzenberg. She pointed to a man who was slumped over in his chair. I took a few moments to review his chart, not to find out more about him but to catch my breath and get up the courage to approach him. When I looked back, I noticed that he was a tall man. He looked unkempt. His hair was long and straggly. A black beard and moustache framed his expressionless face. His eyes were only partly open when I walked over to him. I began in a soft voice, once again, feigning confidence.

"Mr. Meltzenberg, my name is Rickey Miller. I am a psychology student and work with Dr. Bateman. Please come with me to the room down the hall where we can talk in private."

While I spoke, Mr. Meltzenberg opened his eyes a little more but did not look at me. I wondered if he had heard me. I was relieved when he stood up and followed me, shuffling down the hall and into the examination room.

I took a seat opposite Mr. Meltzenberg and set up the test materials on the desk between us. Taking out the manual and the response sheet, I was all set to go. Mr. Meltzenberg sat slumped over in his chair, his arms dangling by his side. He was looking at the floor. He had assumed the same posture that he had in the lounge and his face remained expressionless. I became aware of his strong body odour and wondered how I would cope in such a small room. I quickly made notes about his appearance as I had been taught.

I proceeded with the introductory speech that I had memorized from the manual. As I spoke, Mr. Meltzenberg looked up at me momentarily. His gaze returned to the floor. He did not say a word. His silence triggered anxiety. *Would he cooperate? Would he get up and leave? If he did that, what should I do?*

Mr. Meltzenberg glanced up at me a few more times. I was sure that he could see how nervous I was. This awareness triggered more anxiety.

"Who is the current prime minister of Canada?" I was pleasantly surprised when Mr. Meltzenberg answered quickly and correctly. *This is encouraging. He is engaged. This should be fine.* I began to relax.

"What is the …" I heard my words suddenly stop. There was a vague awareness of something moving upwards that shouldn't be. I heard myself gasp and felt a shock wave moving with lightning speed across my entire body. Then I saw what I was looking at.

"PUT THAT AWAY!"

My shout split the silence as I pointed down at his member, which was standing up to me in proud defiance, like a soldier ready to do battle. My test manual slammed itself shut with a loud, shocking bang. We both jumped.

Mr. Meltzenberg's member instantly deflated like a balloon that had been popped. It collapsed in shame as it was quickly packed away. He could not bear to bring his eyes to meet mine. There was no longer a vacant stare. A timid, embarrassed expression swept across his face. He was sitting up straight in the chair, his hands covering his mouth.

I felt my body relax as his stiffened.

"Mr. Meltzenberg," I began, "this must be one of the reasons you are here." My tone was soft, calm, and confident. There was no pretense. "You cannot do this kind of thing to people without having bad things happen to you. I startled you a few minutes ago, didn't I?" He nodded and looked at me, his gaze and mine meeting for the first time. "I know a little about the hardship you've been through—well, hardship is probably too mild a word to use." I slowed the pace of my speech and continued softly. "I know that you feel angry and hurt and want to upset others—maybe especially women." Mr. Meltzenberg nodded and looked down again. "There are better ways to let your feelings out, Mr. Meltzenberg. Exposing yourself will only get you into trouble and cause you more pain. Can we agree that you've suffered enough?"

"Yes, I have," he muttered.

I remember the warmth that flowed through my body at that moment; the warmth that comes when we feel a genuine, caring connection with another soul. Now there was the potential for meaningful change for Mr. Meltzenberg and for me.

The test manual sat closed on the desk for the rest of the hour while we talked about his life, how he came to be hospitalized, his anger about those who had caused him pain, and the help that he was seeking.

My thoughts drift across the years, focusing once more on a session with Mukondi. I stand and walk to the window, watching the grey autumn clouds slowly float across the blue sky. Once again I hear the soft tones of her voice.

Mukondi was telling me about her struggle to implement the plan that we had drawn up to pace herself more consistently, to break up each hour she spent lying down by walking even if only for a few moments. She was telling me that it was hard to hold herself back on her good days and to leave her bed on her bad days. "Your goal is to be as active on the good as on the bad days. Remember to compliment yourself every time you take a step. It is a real achievement. The easiest thing is to stay the same. Change is always a huge challenge for all of us. You should be proud of yourself for taking that challenge on."

"It means a lot to me that you believe that I'm in pain all the time."

"I have no reason to doubt your report, Mukondi. Of course, I believe you."

"Other doctors have told me it's all in my head. I should be better by now. They told me to see a psychologist because they thought I am a crazy woman."

I feel sad that it is still common for people to believe that a referral to a psychologist means that they are crazy. I feel frustrated that the reality of pain is so often invalidated by health care professionals, especially when the results of medical tests do not correlate with a patient's pain report.

I responded to Mukondi with words that I have repeated to many patients. "Your pain is as real a perception as are all your others. Choosing to work with a psychologist doesn't mean you are crazy. It means that you have the courage to look inside yourself and learn better ways of coping. Good for you that you have taken on this project, the hardest one of all—improving yourself."

Mukondi's brief smile suddenly transformed into a grief-stricken expression. She walked to the window. She was standing exactly where I am now. The glow of the morning sun illuminated the dark tones of her skin and the deep scars on both of her arms. Mukondi wept for a long time, standing by the window. I waited. I offered her a tissue.

After a few minutes, Mukondi began softly. "I told you that I was born in Kenya. You asked me for my birth date the first time I met you. The truth is, I don't know when I was born. No one knows. My husband made it up so we could come to Canada. I think I'm thirty-nine. I never went to school. I can barely read.

"After the British left Kenya, there were soldiers who went around killing people that they thought had collaborated with the British. The British tortured and killed a lot of people in Kenya who were fighting for independence. I saw a lot of people killed. There was always blood in the lanes between our homes. We never knew who would be killed next." Mukondi paused to catch her breath. She sighed deeply.

"One day, soldiers came and made us walk a long way to a camp. I was maybe six or seven and walked with my mom, my two older sisters, and my dad. We had to leave everything behind. We lived in a tent. Not long after we got there, the soldiers came and beat my dad. They punched and kicked him and he fell to the ground, bleeding, and crying loudly. After the soldiers left, my mother was so scared that we would all be killed that we ran away—all of us except my dad. He couldn't walk with us."

My heart was breaking for the little girl who had witnessed so much pain and cruelty and feared for her life.

While Mukondi was speaking, a familiar thought entered my mind—surely this will be the saddest story I will ever hear. Alas, there was no such thing as the saddest story. There was always another story that was more heartbreaking.

"Mom led us back to our village. It took us days. We were all so hungry and thirsty. Once we got there, we saw that our house was gone. We stayed by a big tree and some people in our village brought us food and water. Mom was very sick. I prayed to Allah—please save her. My sisters and I tried to care for her. Mom stopped eating. I prayed to Allah—please help her eat. Save her. Please. I tried to get her to eat my food. I tried to get her to drink my water. But it just ran out of her mouth. She got weaker and weaker every day." Mukondi sighed and began to weep. "People from the village told us that they asked my father to help us but he never came. One day as I sat beside her, Mom stopped breathing. People in the village carried her body to a grave. I watched her go into the ground. Allah went into the ground with her, Doctor." Mukondi punched the fist of one hand hard into the open palm of the other. "That was the end of her and the end of Allah."

I hear the finality of Mukondi's words spoken so many years ago echoing through time as clearly as if she had spoken them moments ago. I feel her aloneness in a cruel, heartless, brutal world. I feel the agony of her faith and her mother abandoning her. Then, all at once I see myself at my synagogue at age five—as clearly as if I had been there moments ago.

3

Touching God

It was a regular Shabbat service at synagogue. Mom, Dad, and I attended every Friday night since I was four. I was five years old. I looked forward to all the songs and especially the treats afterwards in the sweets room. After the service, I ate some cookies with jam in the centre and enjoyed sucking on sugar cubes. I watched Dad as he bit on a sugar cube, somehow holding it firmly between his front teeth, and then sipped the tea so that it flowed through the cube. He told me that this was drinking tea "Russian style." Whenever I tried to do that, the sugar cube would just dissolve in my mouth before I even started to drink the tea. That was fine with me. I loved the pure, sweet taste, and savoured the luscious tiny bits of sugar dissolving on my tongue.

I sat with my parents in the sweets room as they spoke to each other about something that the rabbi had said in his sermon. Those sermons were the most boring part of the service. I always tried to understand but the words were just too long and complicated. I looked forward to the end of his talking and to the songs that followed. The songs were the best part of the service for me. I enjoyed it each time Dad pointed to the Hebrew words of the prayers and songs and whispered the translation to me. "There is no point in singing songs and saying prayers in Hebrew if you don't know what you are saying," he would say. I looked forward to going to Hebrew school when I was older.

I followed my parents to the library. They returned the books that they had read in the past week and signed out new ones. Dad took a book off the shelf and said something to Mom about it. A large group of people were gathering in the library.

I turned to look across the hall as I did every Friday. The entrance to the bimah was there. The rabbi and cantor used this entrance. It led to the holy ark that was on the centre of the bimah. They would walk out from behind the holy ark to start the service. I thought that they must be very holy to walk through that door and onto the bimah with the holy ark that contained the Torah.

Every week when I looked at that door, I felt an almost irresistible urge to open it and walk onto the bimah when no one was looking.

There was no one in the hall and my parents were still discussing the book. No one noticed when I slipped out.

I hesitated to open the holy door. *Was I good enough? Would God allow me to stand before Him like the rabbi and cantor? I am not special and I am not holy.*

I summoned the courage and opened the door. I climbed the stairs and walked slowly behind the white lattice that was the backdrop of the sanctuary. When I stopped to peer out through the lattice, I was surprised to see the sanctuary in darkness. I had never seen it like that. The stained-glass colours of the windows were only dim hues.

The silence startled me.

I could hear my heart beating rapidly.

My footsteps became slower and softer as I moved forward, for I knew that I was approaching the holy ark. It was drawing me closer and closer.

I trembled with fear but did not resist the urge to move forward.

I wanted, more than anything, to feel the holiness, to be as close to God as I could be. Nothing could make me feel closer to God than standing on the bimah and looking into the ark where the holy Torah scrolls stood, even though Dad had told me that God was everywhere. Still, He seemed to be more here than anywhere else.

As I came to the front of the ark, I knew that I was standing on holy ground. The wooden doors to the ark were closed. I dare not open them. There was a crack between them. I stood on tiptoe to catch a glimpse of what was inside.

My eyes were met with a brilliant white light shining down upon the Torah scrolls, their golden plates and decorations gleaming. The wondrous light warmed my entire body and touched me to the very core of my soul. I felt comforted and safe. My fear evaporated. I was filled with awe. I put my hand on the crack to touch His light. The peace and love that caressed me set off a burning desire to bring the same feelings of peace and love to others.

Suddenly it occurred to me that I might be missed. *Someone might catch me here.* I turned and quickly walked back to the library, relieved that my parents had not noticed my absence.

I left the synagogue that Shabbat evening, transformed. God's light from the ark was shining from within me, challenging me to be as good as I could be and sending me on a mission to spread light to others. More than anything, I wanted to be one of God's angels.

4

The Unanswered Question

"Peggy and Stephen are going like they do every Sunday. Peggy is twelve and will make sure I'm safe. Please let me go." I was seven and had asked every Sunday morning to be allowed to go.

Mom and Dad were silent at first and then went into another room. I heard them speaking in Yiddish so that I would not understand.

I wanted to join my friends at the church that they went to every Sunday morning. It sounded like a fun place.

"Okay," Mom said. "Stay with Peggy."

I left the house and crossed the street to Peggy's house. She answered the door. "I'm so happy. I can go with you, Peggy!" I peeked in the door and saw Stephen sticking his fingers into a jar of strawberry jam and sucking them with delight. He was seven like me.

"Come on, Stephen," Peggy called. The three of us hopped down the stairs and when we got to the sidewalk, skipped over cracks. "Step on a crack, break your mother's back," we chanted.

In the yard in front of the church a girl had a skipping rope. Peggy grabbed one end and the girl held the other. I skipped double-dutch until I tripped, then I let Peggy have a turn.

When we were tired of skipping we sat down by the tree and clapped hands with each other to the song, "Who stole the cookie from the cookie jar? Was it you, number one? Who me? Yes you. Couldn't be. Then who? Number two? Who me? Yes you. Couldn't be. Then who? Number three ..." Some other girls sat down and joined in. We were able to sing all the way up to ten.

A lady came out of the church and asked us to come inside. There was a table set up with chocolate-chip cookies on a plate and little paper cups filled with apple juice. The apple juice was warm and sweet. The only apple juice I had ever tasted was from the refrigerator, but this juice tasted altogether different. It was delightful. So were the cookies. They were freshly baked. The chocolate chunks were still melting when I broke the cookie in half. *How lovely!*

Overlooking us as we enjoyed the treats was a big picture of a man. He had a long beard and straggly hair. His eyes looked soft and gentle and very kind. In the picture, lots of little children were standing around him looking up at him, smiling. I knew that his name was Jesus because Dad told me that Peggy and my other friends prayed to Jesus and that he was a man. Dad said that he was Jewish. He looked like a very nice Jewish man.

A tall lady came up to me and asked me my name. She looked very happy to see me. "Welcome, Rickey!" she said. "So glad you came. You should come every Sunday."

"I will!" I said joyfully.

The lady led us in songs and I joined in after hearing each one a few times.

"Jesus loves me. This I know. For the Bible tells me so. Little ones to him belong. They are weak but he is strong. Yes, Jesus loves me. Yes, Jesus loves me. Yes, Jesus loves me. The Bible tells me so."

"God sees a little sparrow fall. It meets His tender view. If God so loves the little birds, I know He loves me too. He loves me too. He loves me too. I know He loves me too. Because He loves the little things, I know He loves me too."

The song blended into another one, but the image of the sparrow remained clear. I felt sad. A little sparrow fell to the ground and God did nothing. The little sparrow must have been sick or it would have flown away and not fallen. I put up my hand to get the lady's attention. She came over to me right away.

"Why didn't God save the little sparrow? Why did He only watch it fall?" The lady smiled but did not answer. She joined the others who were singing another song. It was as if she hadn't heard my question.

The picture burned into my mind; a little sick bird falling to the ground with God only watching. *What good is it just to watch and do nothing? God could have saved it. That wasn't nice of God.*

After a while, Mom and Dad said that they would be taking me to religious school at our synagogue on Sundays. I was very sad not to be able to join my friends at church. But I knew that Mom and Dad weren't happy when I came home every Sunday singing about Jesus loving me. I didn't see any problem with that. It was about a kind Jewish man and it was about love.

When I went to religious school, I sang the song about the sparrow to my teachers. They had never heard that song before. I asked them why God didn't save the little sparrow but only watched it fall. None of them answered my question.

I would have to figure that out for myself.

5

He Just Watched

The handsome face of my "funny uncle," Natie, comes clearly into view. He was Mom's closest brother and I loved everything about him. Although he was in his fifties, Natie was a big grown-up kid who pursued pleasure and loved to make people laugh. He was a strikingly good-looking man, with sparkling eyes, and a generous smile that invited everyone to smile with him. He never took himself or life seriously. Whenever he visited, his laughter blended with my mom's to create sweet, joyful music that filled the house and my soul. Natie was warm and cuddly. His hugs were long and tender. At every one of his frequent visits, Natie brought me a package of red licorice. Whenever I missed one of his visits, upon coming home, I would find it lying on top of my bed. As I chewed on the candy while completing my homework, I felt Natie's love as if he was beside me.

I picture the last package of red licorice that Natie left me when I was seventeen. The package still lies unopened in my dresser drawer. The day I found it on my bed, I knew it would be his last. I never had the heart to open it and, even after all these years, cannot bring myself to throw it away.

I remember all the times Natie arrived at the house on the weekend when Mom was out. I was doing homework or practising the piano. His cheerful "Hello, Rickey!" would burst through the house like sunshine parting the clouds. Interrupting me gleefully, he would entice me to go out with him to one of his favourite restaurants.

"Come on, Rickey," he said in his usual enthusiastic tone. "You can do the rest of your work afterwards. We won't be long." How could I resist his charm? On our way to the restaurant, he entertained me with his many jokes and kept me laughing all the way.

One time, when we were at his favourite fish and chips diner, he took out a plastic worm and placed it on the floor near our table. I started to laugh at which point Natie put his finger to his lips, and smiling, said, "Shhh, Rickey. Don't laugh." When the waitress approached, he said, very calmly and quietly "Marjorie, there's an unwelcome guest that's come to pay us a visit," and he pointed down at the worm. The waitress jumped and then looked at Natie with an expression that said, "I should have known!" She bent down, picked up the worm, and flung it at Natie. "You can't fool me with your pranks," she said. Turning to me she said, "Your uncle is always fooling around with us. That's why we love him." Before she could say another word, Natie began to tell her a series of jokes, leaving her and me doubled over in hysterical laughter.

One day, I heard a strange guttural but cheerful voice saying, "Hi Faye!" from the front door. I came out of my room and was shocked to see Natie standing in the vestibule. I rushed into his arms for a hug.

"When did you get a cold?" Mom asked.

"I feel fine. I'm just a bit hoarse," Natie replied as he drank a few glassfuls of cold water. He was just as hoarse after he was done.

A few weeks later, I was alarmed when Natie arrived at our house in a somber mood. I had never seen him like that. It was terrifying to see the heaviness in his face and the slowness of his steps as he walked into the kitchen. An aura of sadness and fear filled the room. It frightened me to see the reflection of Natie's tension in Mom's face. I had never seen her that way.

Natie told us matter-of-factly that he had cancer of the larynx. He said that he was scheduled to undergo surgery in one week. He turned to me and, with his tone rising at the end, said, "I know that you will always support me." His statement contained both a plea and a question. I immediately nodded. I could not bring myself to speak. *How could this be?*

Please, God, save him.

I did not go to school on the day of Natie's surgery. I knew that he had to check in at the hospital very early in the morning. I took a bus and subway downtown to make sure that I was there to meet him in the hall as he entered the admissions' department. He was there alone. I was surprised that Natie's wife, Sheila, his daughter, Naiomi, and son, Paul, were not there with him. Mom had been unable to be there as she had a cold and did not want to risk making Natie ill. A flicker of a smile lit his face when he saw me. Once he was in his hospital room waiting to be taken to the operating room, a patient in the bed beside him spoke ominous words. "You'd better say whatever you want now because after your operation, you won't be able to say another word."

How horrifying!

Natie had nothing to say. I held his hand in silence. How could there be words at a time like this?

God, please save him.

In the days that followed, after school I went to the hospital where I met Mom. She was with Natie for hours every day. Aunt Sheila and Naomi were often there and would catch us up on how Natie was progressing.

It was agonizing to watch his recovery. The hole in his throat had to be suctioned often, and this caused him terrible pain. His suffering was even greater because he could not make any sound. He could not call out to ask the nurse to stop. He could only ring his bedside bell if he needed something and then write a message to communicate. Every night I was unable to sleep, fearful that he might need help and no one would come because he could not call out. What if he was unable to reach the bell?

Dad could not tolerate watching Natie's suffering. He seldom visited. As time went on, he became more and more sullen and angry when Mom and I returned from the hospital. Dad resented being left alone every evening and especially having to make his own meals. I knew that he was feeling abandoned. He shouted at us when we returned. "You can't go there every single day!" But Mom and I did. There was no question that Natie's needs were our priority. Dad's resentment toward us and his cigarette butts piled up as the weeks dragged on.

Knowing for a long time that cigarettes were harmful to his health, Dad's smoking was always repugnant to me. I now felt that way about Natie's smoking as well. The cancer that had stolen his voice and threatened his life was, in my mind, the result of his smoking cigarettes.

After Natie became ill, Dad's cigarette smoking choked me whenever he lit up. For me, his smoking was a hostile act and a betrayal. How dare he taunt death? How dare he risk causing us pain? I pleaded with Dad to quit smoking. I provided him with pamphlets that I obtained from the hospital when I visited Natie. Nothing I said, nothing he read, made any difference. The butts kept piling up in the ashtray as did my fear for his life.

During his recovery, Natie received treatment from a speech therapist who taught him how to make sounds by controlled belching from his esophagus. Eventually he mastered the method. The sounds that he produced were nightmarish grunts that were challenging to understand. He became agitated when people could not make out his words. When I failed to correctly interpret his sounds, we cried together.

One day I made out that Natie wanted me to accompany him to the Woodbine Race Track. He told me that he enjoyed betting on horses. I had never been there. When he went to the wicket to place his bet, he was unable to make himself understood. It took a few minutes for me to understand his request, which I conveyed for him. Natie refused to write it down. He wanted to speak like a normal person. His struggle to communicate was heartbreaking.

I do not know if his horse won. He didn't seem to know either.

A few months after his recovery, Natie told us that the cancer had returned. He said that he wanted to remain at home for as long as possible. *Please, God, save him.*

One weekend afternoon, Dad asked me to stay home with him, a very unusual request. Mom was at the hospital with Natie. Dad surprised me further by announcing that he would be taking me out to dinner. This had never happened before. He reserved a table at a French restaurant in our neighbourhood. Neither of us had ever eaten there. I couldn't imagine what had happened to Dad that he wanted to dine at a restaurant. He disliked eating out and always complained about the food no matter where we went.

The last thing on my mind was food. I feared for Dad's life. I feared for Mom's life, watching her suffer along with Natie. She rarely ate and I could hear her wandering around the house at night while I struggled to sleep. Dad, Mom, and Natie seemed to be standing on a precipice that I had never known before, with the very real threat of all of them falling into oblivion. For the first time in my life, I questioned the stability of the ground beneath my feet.

I scarcely noticed the taste of the food that I ate that night. Dad and I did not exchange many words. At one point during the meal, without any introduction, Dad looked up and announced solemnly, "I've stopped smoking. I won't smoke another cigarette. I promise." I left my seat immediately, rushed over to him, and hugged him. Burying my face into his chest, I cried tears of immense gratitude and relief. Finally, he had seen the light. Moved by my reaction, Dad wept too. He was proclaiming his deep love for us, a love that I had doubted with each cigarette he had lit up.

Dad kept his word. Even so, as Natie slid down ever so slowly towards death, my anxiety about Dad's health intensified. In my nightmares, Dad's face transformed into the horribly disfigured face of my dying funny uncle.

Not long after, Natie was hospitalized on a palliative unit.

Please, God, save Natie. Keep my dad and mom alive.

I was an utterly helpless witness to the torment of Natie's suffering, which increased day after day. The hole in his throat was blistered and always oozing around the metal pipe that was sticking out of it, allowing him to breathe. In desperation, he often grabbed the pipe in an effort to pull it out. Was this his desperate attempt to die or to end the pain? Did he understand that if he took the tube out, he would suffocate?

One morning when a nurse arrived at his bedside, Natie asked him for his scissors. I knew that he was planning to cut the bandages in his neck that held the tube in his throat.

The nurse took out the scissors and was about to hand them to Natie. Feeling compelled to prevent him from suffocating, I said quickly, "The nurse can't give you the scissors."

The nurse withdrew the scissors and Natie looked at me with an angry glare that severed my heart in two. Overwhelmed with guilt, I could not find the words to explain to him that he would die if he removed the tube and that I could not bear to watch him suffocate to death.

Every day for weeks, Mom and I watched as Natie battled with death, and kept winning, thus prolonging his suffering. His fighting spirit did not flag. There were moments when the physician told us that he was dying and would not last for long. Each time, Mom and I would sit by his bedside until he regained consciousness.

One afternoon I was with him alone. Mom, Aunt Sheila, and Naomi were taking a break to eat lunch. I was holding Natie's hand. His breathing suddenly became laboured. His pupils became very large. His gaze was piercing through me but I knew that he was not seeing me. Panic began to surface from within me. I searched his wrist for a stronger signal. I was still not ready for him to leave.

Would I ever be?

The beats were becoming slower and fainter and fainter still, and with them, his breathing harder and harder to hear, until, suddenly, everything in the world stopped. The enormity of death brought with it the deepest, darkest silence I had ever heard. I don't know how long I sat frozen in place holding his warm hand in mine. A nurse happened to enter the room and, although she said it in a warm tone, her words were devastating. "He went peacefully."

How does she know that he went peacefully? What is peaceful about dying at age fifty-five? How is any of this peaceful?

I feel compassion as I recall the young me who was sitting in my bedroom that evening, sinking into the deepest grief I had ever known and crying with tears that I thought would never stop. I had been trying desperately to focus on essays that I had to write for my first-year university classes but I could not write a single word.

I felt very much alone in my grief. My sister, Terry, who was seven years older than me, was married and living in the United States. She had travelled to Toronto for Natie's funeral and returned to her home after the seven days of shiva. She was close to Naomi, and had stayed at her home so that she could provide her with emotional support.

My sister and I grieved separately. It would be years before I would begin to understand the reasons there was such a chasm between us. Back then, all I knew was that I was alone in my grief.

Mom's grief was profound. Her throat tightened so much that only a faint squeaking sound emerged when she tried to speak. I continued to fear for her life. Every moment she struggled to keep the dam that held back her ocean of tears from bursting. I did my best to comfort her by sitting in silence beside her and holding her hand.

My grief turned to rage. *How could this be? Where was God? Why did He let this happen? I had prayed and prayed. What good was that?*

All He did was watch my dear funny uncle fall, just like the little sparrow. He just watched.

$$6$$

Across a Crowded Room

*I*n the weeks that followed, my fears about losing Dad intensified. I panicked when he was late coming home from work. The familiar smoker's cough under my bedroom window that woke me at five-thirty every weekday morning was a comfort. I knew that he was still alive.

When he saw me crying for Natie, Dad tried to comfort me. I overheard his frequent question to Mom, "I wonder if she will feel that way about me?"

One day as I wept in my room, Dad reminded me that ten thousand people had died in an earthquake in Managua a few months earlier. Was his intention to comfort me? He failed. "I will cry for all those people as well!" I said through my sobs. I wept bitter tears for all those who had perished and for all those who were dying in the world. It felt as though my tears would never stop.

I was in my second undergraduate year. I struggled to attend lectures and complete assignments, spending much of my time sitting in grief alone in my room every evening and during weekends. I had picked up a pamphlet at a table at the university that advertised upcoming social events. Late one Friday afternoon, I turned to the pamphlet and read through the list.

We would be going to synagogue as usual for Shabbat services. Even though my relationship with God was extremely tenuous, I still accompanied my parents every Friday evening. I was searching, questioning, struggling. Had He been buried with Natie? Or maybe He never existed and my prayers were nonsense; the pleas of a weak child too afraid to face the godlessness of the universe.

I noticed that there was a Jewish get-together on Friday night taking place at the Hillel House downtown.

Should I go? I looked at my face in the mirror and counted the acne pimples that had sprouted in the last few weeks. I looked awful. Despite this, I was seized by the strong urge to depart from our usual routine. I asked Mom and Dad if they would mind if I went to the Hillel event downtown rather than to synagogue. They readily agreed. I didn't pay much attention to the clothes I was wearing and decided not to care about the pimples or sadness that were both clearly visible on my face. I was miserable and needed to do something about it.

After I parked near the Hillel House on St. George Street, I hesitated for a moment before going inside. I did not know anyone. *Just do it.* I propelled myself forward and walked in. There were about twenty people sitting in a large room, talking and enjoying pretzels, potato chips, and Cheezies that filled bowls on little tables.

Almost immediately, I noticed a handsome man with reddish-blond curly hair and a moustache sitting across the room. He was looking at me. I walked over to him and sat down on the vacant chair beside him. He told me that his name was Luke Eisen and that he was a student at a university outside of Toronto. He said that he was visiting his parents. We talked easily and naturally for hours and hours, long past the time when everyone else had left.

As he had taken transit, I drove Luke home. I was surprised to see that his home was not far from mine. Our conversation continued during the trip. He asked me for the name of the street that I lived on. I thought it odd that he did not ask for my phone number. *How disappointing!*

I chuckle now recalling the many times I had counselled my female patients to act assertively and contact a gentleman if they wanted to get to know him. Back in the days when I met Luke, I felt that there was no question about it. It was up to him to contact me if he was interested.

Luke later told me that as soon as he entered his house, he ran into the den and opened the telephone book. He searched through all the Millers to find the one on my street.

I went home, lifted from grief and fear, sailing on hope. Maybe we would meet again.

The next day I was thrilled when Luke called and invited me to go to a movie with him. Afterwards we delighted in another long conversation about everything and anything that came to mind. There was a beautiful ease in sharing that went both ways. Whenever we went out and it was time to pay, Luke insisted on treating me, even though I always offered to pay for myself. He was a real gentleman.

One day before going out to a restaurant, Luke told me that he had asked his father for money for our date. I was surprised by his nonchalance. I would have been ashamed to admit if I had to ask my parents for money to go out. What surprised me more is that he told me that his father questioned him about where he was planning to take me and why he needed the amount that he requested. It sounded as though Luke had to beg for the handout.

Throughout my teens I worked part time as a secretary and saved my money with the goal of paying for as much of my university tuition as I could. It was important to me to earn my own money.

When Luke told me about asking his father for money, a still, small voice deep inside me whispered something that I did not want to hear. I made it disappear.

After a few dates, Luke invited me to visit him on a Saturday at his apartment. The city in which he lived was not far from Toronto. He said that he would prepare supper for me. I counted down the days until the weekend.

I baked a chocolate cake, packed it up carefully, and set off on the highway. Luke introduced me to the two friends who shared his three-bedroom apartment. They were taking their girlfriends out for the evening and left shortly after I arrived.

The smell wafting through the apartment from the oven triggered a memory that I could not identify. There was an unmistakable aversion building in my awareness. I tried to ignore it.

Luke told me that he had attended a dissection class as part of his biology course on Friday. He said that he had felt sorry for all the lab rats that were killed.

"I love animals too. I hate killing anything, even insects," I told him. "They should never have given you lab rats to dissect. They could have taught you about body parts in other ways. Imagine how many are killed year after year. Those poor rats!"

"I totally agree," Luke said. "That's why I refused to dissect my rat. I put it in my backpack and brought it home."

"That's wonderful! Can I see the rat you saved?" I was exuberant and impressed. *Luke is surely a kind-hearted person.*

Luke escorted me to his bedroom. He pointed to a shoe box on the floor with some books on top of the lid. "I put a dish in there with water and some rat food that I got from the lab. I will buy a cage in Toronto. I'm going to keep the rat as a pet," he said proudly. We squatted down. Luke removed the books and opened the lid just enough for me to peek in to see the rat as it jumped around the bottom of the box. It was pure white and very lively. Luke quickly shut the lid and put the books back on top.

"He looks happy and healthy," I said. "He's glad to be alive."

Back in the kitchen, Luke opened the oven door and announced, "Supper's ready." The table was covered in a white cloth and was nicely set. The smell in the kitchen grew more distasteful after the oven door was opened. "I made us a beautiful roast beef!" Luke held the roasting pan with oven mitts, his face shining with pride as he showed off his creation. He waited for an appropriate response.

'Yuck!' threatened to pop out but was quickly smothered by my hope that Luke's roast beef would taste altogether different from Mom's. She made it often and each time, I couldn't bring myself to eat it.

"Oh, that looks absolutely delicious!" was my exaggerated exclamation. I surprised myself. I did enjoy Luke's roast beef.

I am struck now with our obvious hypocrisy. While we were compassionate about the rat, we had no compassion at all about the cow that had been slaughtered for our meal. I reflect with amazement and shame that Luke and I did not allow ourselves to see the inconsistency. For us, the beef was just another inanimate product to be used, not at all like the rat, whose little life we both treasured and sought to protect.

How easy it is for us humans to treat some lives as precious and others as expendable, whether human or animal. We can so easily see another person as non-human and an animal product as never having belonged to a living creature. We possess the terrifying power to distort reality and prevent ourselves from considering whether our choices are ethical.

The next day Luke called me, "I have some sad news about the rat. My roommates came back to the apartment with their girlfriends last night, and while one of my buddies was making out with his girlfriend in his bedroom, my rat jumped out of the shoe box somehow. I don't know how it got out with all those books piled on the lid. The rat ran into his bedroom. His girlfriend screamed. They both climbed up on his bed and watched the rat running frantically around on the floor. The poor thing! My friend finally got down and shooed the rat out of his room. It ran towards the front door and outside just as he opened it. I'm worried that it might not survive when the weather gets cold."

"At least you tried to save it," I said. "Maybe it will make it somehow, Luke." Our conversation was a warm embrace of two kind and compassionate hearts.

I was basking in the warmth of the first glimmers of love.

7

Crushed

*L*oving feelings come in all different shades and intensities and continuously blend with other emotions on a moving canvas. It is difficult to make any sense of them as we delight in the warm glow they bestow upon our world.

David Bloom loved my sister, Terry. He was smitten.

David came into my life when I was eleven years old. He had a slender build, a handsome face, a wonderful sense of humour, infectious laughter, and, always, a beautiful, warm smile for me that lit up his whole face and felt like a hug.

David was at our house often. Many times, he presented Terry with a bouquet of roses. David was an only child. Each time he greeted me as if I was his beloved younger sister.

To me, he was much more than a beloved older brother.

David majored in history. He knew the details of every historical event that I asked him about. I marvelled at his intelligence and his incredible memory. I treasured every word he said to me and kept the birthday cards that he sent me each year.

I was smitten.

Many nights I was kept up until one or two o'clock in the morning by the sound of Terry and David's endless conversations in the kitchen. Their voices echoed down the hall and straight into my bedroom. I didn't mind. Although I was unable to make out what they were saying, their exchanges were peppered with laughter. I heard David's voice most of the time. I longed to be in the kitchen with them.

David's command of English was astounding. When Terry or I used a word that was not exactly accurate, David would always correct us.

"Say what you mean and mean what you say." It was as if the error was a personal affront.

Terry and David graduated together, both achieving their bachelor's degrees. Mom, Dad, and I attended their convocation ceremony. Mom and Dad gave Terry a huge bouquet of red roses. David came over and kissed Terry. Then he told us that he had changed his career goal. Rather than applying to teacher's college, he was applying to law school.

Mom and Dad often spoke highly about David. They told me that David's father had died years ago and that his mother loved Terry just as much as they loved David. They told me that David's mother treated Terry as her future daughter-in-law. They would surely be engaged soon. I was thrilled that David would become my brother-in-law.

One day Terry showed me a professional photo of the two of them that was taken just before their graduation. They were the perfect couple, standing side by side, beautiful, happy, so obviously in love.

"Here," she said. "You keep it."

"Why? Don't you want it?" I was shocked when she handed it to me.

"I told David that we should split up."

I couldn't believe her words. "How come? Don't you love him?"

Terry was unusually open with me. "He's a hypochondriac," she began. "He's always worried about his health. And then he likes his peas separate from his meat. I mean, if the food isn't just a certain way on his plate, he won't eat it. We are just not compatible."

I thought those were flimsy reasons to break up with David.

It didn't matter what I thought. David was suddenly gone from my life. Never to return.

I put the graduation photo in the desk drawer near my bed and looked at it that night. The photo ensured that I would never forget David's handsome face. I missed the sweet sound of his voice that no longer drifted into my room to lull me to sleep. I told myself that I will never again be greeted by that beautiful, warm smile and those sparkling eyes.

As I look at the boxes in front of me again, I reflect on how easy it had been for me to convince myself that it would be "never again." My patients and I often comforted ourselves with the illusion that we know the unknowable future.

8

Cataclysms

Thoughts about the unpredictability of the future bring me back to Luke. Our love blossomed in the months that followed our first date. We wrote letters to each other every day. Each time the phone rang, my heart jumped in excitement, anticipating that it would be Luke. I had dated other boys, but this marvellous, overpowering ecstasy was entirely new. Every moment was filled with thoughts of Luke and memories of the conversations that we had shared.

One Friday night, Luke and his parents took up my invitation to join us at synagogue for Shabbat. I had met his parents a few weeks earlier.

Tom, Luke's father, was warm and welcoming. The first time I met him, Tom pointed to a front tooth and told me that it had been loose. "I fixed it myself. Crazy glue worked fine. See? It is cemented to the next tooth, so now I can eat without any problem." I told him that he should see a dentist. At the same time, I admired his ingenuity and motivation to take care of the problem himself. Luke told me that his father had survived Auschwitz.

Lauren, Luke's Mom, was colder. She spent a lot of time looking me over and hardly said a word. Her examination made me feel uncomfortable and insecure.

After the service, I introduced my parents to Tom and Lauren. Mom and Tom instantly hit it off. They discussed the differences between their Conservative and our Reform service. They discussed the rabbi's sermon. Their conversation flowed easily. Lauren looked on and said very little. Dad was sipping tea through the sugar cube in his teeth. He was casually observing the conversation. On the way home, Dad told us that Tom did not know much about the Torah. Mom commented that she liked him a lot.

One weekend, Luke invited me to spend another day with him at his apartment. I baked a macaroni-and-cheese lunch for us in the morning. As I was getting ready to leave, Dad came into the kitchen.

"Where are you going?!" he shouted angrily.

"Why are you angry, Dad?" I asked innocently. "You know that I'm going to spend the day with Luke. I mentioned this yesterday."

As I turned to cover the baking dish with foil, Dad became furious.

"You are not going today!" he yelled as he stood directly in front of me. His eyes were flaring.

"Why not?" I asked. "What's the problem?" My voice was loud and indignant.

"You see him enough. You are on the phone with him for hours at a time. You write letters to him every day. You spend every weekend with him. It's enough already."

What was Dad's problem? He liked Luke. Stepping forward, I said with less anger, "Dad, I am nineteen years old. I want to spend the day with Luke. There is nothing wrong with my spending the day with him. I am leaving now and will be back later in the evening."

At this, Dad exploded. The intensity of his shouting frightened me. Mom came into the kitchen and told him to calm down. Her comments only fuelled his rage. He kept shouting at me not to go. I grabbed the macaroni-and-cheese dish and my purse and walked past him. I drove away as fast as I could. Several blocks later, I parked the car to stop my trembling. I was in no condition to drive onto the highway. I struggled to understand Dad's reaction. This had not happened any other time that I had visited Luke. Why now? When I arrived at Luke's apartment, I sank into his arms and told him what had happened. He could not understand it either.

When I returned home, late that night, Mom and Dad were already asleep. After a few days, Dad and I slowly began to communicate normally again. Fearful that it would trigger another explosion, I did not dare to ask the reasons for his rage.

All these years later, I can only speculate that Dad was not prepared for his relationship with me to change. He perceived a threatening loss on the horizon.

The following Saturday evening I invited Luke to my house. Luke and I watched TV and kept the volume down so as not to disturb Mom and Dad who were asleep. It was a cold February evening. We delighted in cuddling on the couch. Soon we were hugging and kissing. Suddenly, I heard the sound of footsteps in the hallway. Luke and I instantly let go of each other and moved apart. I could see Dad in the darkness making his way to the washroom. He didn't look right to me. I strained to see him more clearly as he walked back to the bedroom. In the shadows, he seemed larger than usual.

Although we had been dating for five months, Luke and I were not ready to do more than hug and kiss. Luke told me that his father had advised him that if he was serious about me, he should preserve my dignity by having sex with other women. He should have sex with me only when we marry, if we marry.

"How absurd! Does your father really believe that if you have sex with another woman, that would preserve my dignity? It would certainly not preserve yours, especially if you did not love that woman and only used her body for sex." I looked at Luke for his immediate agreement.

"Yes, Rickey. His advice makes no sense. I have no interest in having sex with another woman, let me assure you!" We fell into each other's arms again and snuggled.

For Luke and me, the idea of an open relationship was untenable. Had Luke said that he was thinking about having sex with another woman, I would have been demolished and would probably have broken off the relationship. As for me, I would never have allowed myself to even consider becoming sexually involved with another man while I was dating Luke.

Mom woke me the next morning. She announced that she would be making an appointment for Dad to see his physician as soon as possible. I got up and rushed into their bedroom. Dad's entire face was swollen. So were his arms and legs. It looked as if his body had been pumped up with air. Was this some kind of allergic reaction? Dad said that he didn't feel too bad. He went about the day's activities. I hoped that over the course of the day, the swelling would go down. It did not. My fears about his health increased.

"The doctor says that I have some kind of allergic reaction," Dad told us. "These swellings are hives. He prescribed an antihistamine and wants me to go to the lab for blood work." I was relieved to hear that it was nothing serious.

At the lab, Mom and I waited a long time for Dad to complete the blood work. He told us that it had taken over thirty minutes for the bleeding to stop even though he had pressed down hard on his arm afterwards. As he showed us his arm, we saw that blood was continuing to ooze from under the bandage. He asked the receptionist for another one, sat down in the waiting room, and pressed hard on his arm again.

Over the next few days, Dad's swollen body slowly deflated. *Good. He is healthy again.*

Two weeks passed. It was Valentine's Day. Luke and I were planning to enjoy a romantic dinner out.

That morning as we ate breakfast, I noticed that Dad had a pronounced rash on his arms. He told me that the rash had spread over a lot of his body.

"Does it hurt you?" I asked.

"No. It doesn't hurt and it's not itchy."

I went over to Dad and felt his skin. Tiny pimples clustered underneath his skin. Dad was frightened. "I think I should go to the emergency department of a hospital to find out what is causing this," he said. "I'm thinking that this is related to the allergic reaction that I had a few weeks ago." We were all frightened.

We did not wait long to be seen in the emergency department. Mom and I waited anxiously by Dad's bedside. He had blood drawn and I saw first-hand that there was a problem. He said to the nurse, who was more alarmed than he was, "What are you going to do now that the bleeding is not stopping?" She pressed down on his arm for more than fifteen minutes, checking each time to see if the bleeding stopped. It took much longer than that before it did.

Hours later, a nurse ushered Mom and me out of his cubicle and motioned for us to go down the hall. "What's wrong with him?" Mom asked.

The nurse responded, "It looks like Gerard's Disease." I had never heard of this disease. "He will be okay. We will treat him. Try not to worry." She told us to go home and get some sleep and come back in the morning. We kissed Dad goodnight and reassured him that his problem had been diagnosed and would be treated. Dad had sad eyes as he said good night.

As soon as we returned home, I went to my big Webster's dictionary and flipped through the tissue-paper pages. I could not find 'Gerard's Disease' listed. I wished that the library was open so that I could have searched through medical dictionaries to find out more about this disease.

Mom called Terry to give her the news about Dad. She reassured Terry that Dad would make a recovery from this illness, whatever it was. She told her that Dad was being treated at a major teaching hospital in Toronto.

Back in my empty office, surrounded by my boxes, I walk over to the window. I think about how distant Terry had become by the time Dad was ill. I felt like Terry belonged to a different generation. Our relationship had always been complicated and challenging.

Terry moved into a room in Toronto during her undergraduate years, more than five years before Dad became ill. I never understood this as we lived near the bus stop and it would have been easy for her to travel to the university by transit. Much later I realized that Terry was so unhappy living with us that she needed to move away.

After she graduated with her B.A. degree, Terry moved to the United States where she studied for her Master's Degree. She married Jerome in 1967 and settled in the United States permanently.

I reflect sadly that for most of my life, I have felt like an only child. It took me many years of introspection and heartfelt compassion before I reached any understanding about the possible causes of our estrangement and before I could imagine the feelings and thoughts that Terry might have.

The next morning Mom and I were back at the hospital. A nurse in the emergency department told us that Dad had been admitted. There was a sign on the door to Dad's room stating that he was in isolation and instructing us to put on gowns and masks before entering. A nurse met us there and showed us how to put them on. Mom and I were alarmed.

"Does my dad have some kind of contagious disease?" I asked.

"No," she said. "This is for his protection."

"What exactly is wrong with my husband that he needs protection?" Mom asked.

"I'm not sure of the diagnosis," she said, looking down at the floor, obviously avoiding eye contact with Mom. "You should speak to his physician."

"Where is his physician, then?"

"He will be doing rounds in about one hour," was her response. At that, she walked quickly back to the nurse's station.

We entered the room and kissed Dad. He said that he was feeling okay for the most part. The same sad eyes greeted us that had wished us good night. Mom said that she needed to leave for a few minutes. I joined her. After disrobing, I told Mom that I had never heard of 'Gerard's Disease' and could not find it in our dictionary.

"Mom, I'm desperate to learn more about Dad's illness. Why is isolation for his own protection?"

"I don't know," she said in a trembling voice.

"Mom, why don't you call Dr. Simonston? He saw Dad two weeks ago. He must know what is wrong with Dad. We don't have to wait another hour for Dad's physician to do rounds."

Mom used the pay phone in the hall to make the call.

"Hello, Dr. Simonston. This is Faye Miller. My husband is Al Miller. You saw him two weeks ago because he was swollen all over his body, do you recall? Good. Al is in the hospital. He's in isolation for his own protection, which I don't understand. Doctor, do you know what is wrong with my husband?" Mom's tone was a desperate plea.

Suddenly, Mom's body swayed from side to side, as if she was about to fall over. I had to hold her up. The colour faded from her face. She looked as if she was going to pass out. The receiver slipped through her hand and was dangling by the cord. I heard a voice coming from the receiver. "Are you okay, Faye? Faye, are you still there?" There was a look of horror and panic in her face. Mom was silent. The voice from the receiver continued. "Mrs. Miller, are you okay?"

Many minutes passed before she grabbed the phone and spoke, "Yes, I'm still here." Then, without saying anything more, she hung up the phone.

I helped Mom move to the closest chair. She collapsed. She looked as though she had been shot through her heart. I was terrified to ask her what was wrong but more terrified not to ask.

"What did the doctor say, Mom?"

"He has cancer, Rickey. It's acute leukemia. He said that he doesn't have long to live." We both held each other and cried. My worst nightmare was coming to pass.

The head nurse found us holding each other and weeping.

"You are Al Miller's family, aren't you?" she asked gently.

"Yes," I said, wiping my face. "Has something happened to my dad?"

"No. His condition is the same."

Mom looked up. "Does my husband know the diagnosis?"

"Yes, he does. We told him last night."

Why had we not been told? Why were we told that he had some other disease? Were they too afraid of our reaction to tell us the truth? These questions fled to the back of my mind as I focused on Dad. He needed all the love and care we could provide. Time with him was now precious, more precious than ever.

"He's living on borrowed time now," Mom said. After a few minutes, I called Terry. I promised her that I would keep her informed about Dad's condition. Terry did not say much in the conversation. I am sure that she was also shocked to hear the diagnosis.

Mom and I gowned up and spent the day with Dad. A medical student came into his room later on and said that he was doing research. He asked Dad if he could ask him some questions.

"Anything I can do to help science," Dad said.

There were questions about Dad's diet. Did he smoke? How much alcohol had he consumed? Did he exercise? Where did he work? What kind of chemicals was he exposed to there? And finally, did anything particularly upsetting occur recently?

The last question seared my soul like a torch. The memory of our big argument flashed through my mind.

"No. Nothing particularly upsetting occurred recently," Dad said.

This was not true. Was he trying to protect me from the devastating guilt that was already overwhelming me?

It was my fault. I had caused him to get cancer because I had argued with him about seeing Luke. I should have cancelled that visit.

Dad's condition rapidly deteriorated. He was given transfusion after transfusion of platelets. The chemotherapy caused him to retch for hours at a time. He lost all of his hair. He became pale and was covered in rashes and deep purple bruises. He was growing thinner every day as he was unable to eat.

Holding onto Dad's hand in the hospital room, I reminded him of happy times we had shared. I recounted the trips we had made to farmer's markets out of the city because Mom wanted to buy fresh produce. He smiled. "Remember how we would stop at a chip truck along the way?" My mouth watered as I recalled the crisp French fries that we ate from paper cones. "After carefully inspecting the fresh produce at each market, Mom would return to the car with nothing."

Mom chirped in, "The prices were always highway robbery!"

"After visiting more farmer's markets, you would drive back to the grocery store near our house where Mom would buy vegetables and fruits. Remember, Dad?"

Mom and I did our best to keep Dad's spirits from sinking.

As I looked at his rash and bruise-covered body and the devastation in Mom's face, the fear of losing her overtook me. Would she survive without him? How would I cope if she died?

In the weeks that followed, I applied for and received aegrotat standing from the university. I would pass my third-year courses even though they would be incomplete.

Mom and I spent every day from morning until late at night by Dad's bedside. Terry and Jerome drove to Toronto and joined us. We all did our best to care for Dad. I wiped his forehead with wet washcloths. I propped up his pillows. I told him how much we loved him and that we believed that the chemotherapy would work. In between retching episodes, he said bitterly, "The cure is worse than the illness." It was heartbreaking to watch him suffer. Every night when I kissed him and said good night, I thought it might be the last.

I deeply appreciated the support that our rabbi and cantor provided during those dark days. One time, our cantor stopped me in the hall before visiting Dad.

I told him, "My dad is dying. We were told that the prognosis is poor. There is no hope."

Our cantor simply said, "Where there is life, there is hope. Do not give up." I heard in his words echoes of my parents' voices and my own. *Never give up.* I promised myself to keep hope alive as long as Dad was alive.

God, please save him.

One day soon after, our rabbi came into Dad's room. He hugged me. Then I walked out into the hall to allow Dad to have some time alone with him. I knew, after all their debates, that they had a great deal of respect for each other. After about half an hour, I walked back towards the room and peeked in to see whether the rabbi was still there. He was holding Dad's hand. I was about to walk out again when their conversation caught my attention.

Dad said, "I have to tell you the truth now that I am near death. I'm really not sure that there is a God."

Our rabbi's response was immediate and startling. "To tell you the truth, Al, I'm not sure either."

Was there even a God watching?

A few weeks later, a miracle happened. Dad started to look better. The colour began to return to his face. The rashes and bruises started to recede. Dad was entering a period of remission.

When Dad was first diagnosed, I told Luke that he might not want to stay with me. "This is going to be rough, Luke," I said. "I am going to spend a lot of time at the hospital with Dad. I won't have much time to go out with you. I'm going to be upset a lot."

Luke did not hesitate. "I understand. I will come as often as I can. I will be here for you. I'm not going anywhere."

This was true love. Luke was comforting each time he came to the hospital where he sat with me for hours.

One afternoon, sitting in the lounge, Luke and I spoke about our love for each other and how happy we were to see that Dad was improving. We had been going out for seven months and, since my Dad's illness, we had spent a great deal of time together at the hospital. It was March 1974.

Getting up the courage and feeling a sense of urgency in light of Dad's illness, I turned to Luke and said, "Luke, why don't we get engaged?"

Luke's response was instant. "I have felt that we have been engaged for a long time already."

Pleased and relieved with his answer, I said, "When should we get married?"

I planned to apply to the university that Luke attended for graduate studies after completing my B.A. degree in the spring of 1975. That would be our first opportunity to live together as Luke would be continuing his studies at the same university. We tentatively planned to marry in May 1975. I told Luke that it would mean a lot to Dad if he asked him for his blessing.

We walked into the hospital room.

"Mr. Miller," Luke began. "I would like to marry your daughter. I am asking you for your permission."

"You have to ask her for permission not me but I can give you my blessing," Dad said with tears of happiness in his eyes.

"I agreed, Dad," I quickly said. I hugged Dad tightly and we wept tears of joy.

All of us smiled for the first time in a long while.

Dad was discharged home. He had another few courses of chemotherapy. I drove him to and from the hospital on the days of his treatments.

Our wedding plans progressed in step with Dad's recovery. He was able to return to work and we began to go to Shabbat services every Friday night. Luke and I spent each weekend together.

One evening at supper, Dad turned to me and made a very serious announcement, "I've decided not to keep kosher anymore. It isn't rational. What I eat doesn't make me a good person. I've always told you that God gave us brains to use." He stared at me for a long time. I could see tears in his eyes.

I was surprised at Dad's announcement. His silent, intense stare made it clear. He was not making an announcement to me. He was making it to God. It was a bargain he was proposing. *If I stop keeping kosher, will You save me?*

I knew in my heart that Dad would not be able to keep his end of this deal. *And as for God?*

Faced with death, we become little children, crying out to be saved, willing to make any deal we can with God. That was Dad at the kitchen table that evening. It was also me in bed every night, crying out to God. *Please save him.*

In the fall of 1974, I began my fourth undergraduate year. As the winter term approached, I applied to three graduate programs in clinical psychology. Of course, my first choice was the same university that Luke attended. *What good fortune!* This university had a clinical psychology program with the distinction of being approved by the American Psychological Association. One of my professors told me that many students applied each year but only five were accepted. Confident that high marks guaranteed my acceptance, I worked as hard as I could and achieved A and A+ marks in all my courses.

Terry and Jerome were at our Seder table on March 27, 1975. As he had at all the previous Seders of my life, Dad officiated. He asked each of us to read a portion of the Haggadah in English so that everyone could understand. Then he provided his usual thoughtful commentary. He encouraged questions and enjoyed answering them. He invited everyone to add their ideas, even though Mom was growing impatient to serve the food. That night I cherished every word he spoke. Although I tried desperately to convince myself otherwise, I could see clearly that Dad did not look well again.

Almost immediately after the two Seders, the monster inside Dad's body woke up from its one-year sleep. The rashes and bruises reappeared. Disheartened and fearful, I drove Dad to the hospital where he was quickly admitted and put in isolation again. Once more, he received massive transfusions of platelets. Once more, he was subjected to the torment of the nauseating chemotherapy. Once more, his hair fell out. Once more, he was unable to eat and began to waste away.

I was at the hospital with Mom early every morning and then drove to the university to attend my classes. As soon as they ended for the day, I drove back to the hospital. I did my best to complete my homework in Dad's hospital room, taking breaks to provide him with whatever comfort measures I could.

I enquired about obtaining aegrotat status and was told that I could not do this a second time.

Dad's condition improved to the point that he could go home again. Dr. Gold said that he was going into a second remission. The first evening when he was home again I was sitting with Dad in the kitchen after dinner. Mom was resting in her bedroom. He looked at me very seriously and said, "Rickey, I like the name Elijah." Tears rolled down my cheeks. Aleyahu, his Hebrew name, in English was Elijah. I knew right away that he was requesting this name for the child that I might have in the future. "Elijah," he repeated. "I like that name."

"Yes, Dad. Elijah," was all I could manage to say.

A few days later I picked up my wedding gown from the bridal shop. When I brought it home, I immediately tried it on and showed Mom. Then I walked into my parents' bedroom where Dad was resting.

"You look just beautiful," Dad said. His face lit up. He was elated to see me in my wedding gown. He asked me to walk down the hall and back again. I knew he was imagining that he was walking with me down the aisle at synagogue.

By the second week of April, Mom and I could see that Dad was not well. He was barely able to stand and walk to the washroom. Exhausted, he fell back into his bed. He looked at me with bitterness in his eyes and in his voice. "Rickey, I'm peeved."

"Yes, so am I, Dad." I said, believing him to be referring to the resurgence of his symptoms.

"No," he said loudly. "I am peeved that your wedding is May 11th."

A wave of guilt surged through me. I recalled our reasons for setting that date. Luke and I wanted to wait until we could live together in the same city. Mom and Dad had agreed with this plan. I felt the deep pain of regret. We should have scheduled the wedding earlier.

Despite Dr. Gold's assertion that Dad had entered a second remission, reality came crashing down on all of us. Dad was sinking closer and closer towards death. He knew the truth. "The patient has entered a remission and he is dying," Dad said to us, bitterly.

Through it all, Luke was a consistent source of empathy and comfort and love. I slid into his arms every time he visited and once there, felt safe to cry my heart out. I felt secure in our commitment to be lifelong partners, just like Mom and Dad.

Dr. Gold came into Dad's room every day, put his hands on his waist, and looked pained by his helplessness as he watched his patient deteriorate hour by hour. Dad turned to me and said clearly, "The wedding must go on. Promise me. The wedding must go on."

"I promise," I said, without thinking about the wedding. I wanted only to please him.

All day on April 14, Mom, Terry, and I sat in his isolation room, listening to Dad's laboured breathing. His pupils were tiny. I heard him whisper over and over again for "Momma." Dad appeared to be suffering a great deal of pain. He was agitated and restless even though he could barely move. I held his hand, never leaving his bedside. We were all waiting and just watching.

Sometime in the evening, Dad took his last breath, while still whispering, "Momma. Momma."

"Please breathe!" was all I could say while sobbing loudly.

"We've lost him," Mom said. She was crying as well. Terry was sitting, frozen in her chair.

The nurse came back a short time later with a physician. In the meantime, Luke came into the room. "He's gone," I said.

"No, maybe not. Let's wait and see." Luke's response angered me even though I understood that he was desperate to save me from the inevitable grief.

The physician pronounced Dad was dead. He removed all the tubes that had been attached to him. The nurse returned with two pills.

"These are valium and will help you," she said, turning to Mom and me. She gave each of us a pill, which we swallowed without thinking about it. While my Aunt Susan and Uncle Benny held Mom and me and Luke rubbed my back, it was Terry who went to the locker in the hospital room and packed up Dad's clothes and slippers in preparation for our trip home.

No one offered Terry valium. Looking back now, I feel sad for her.

The physician came back into the room with paper and pen. "Would you give us permission to do an autopsy for medical research purposes?" he asked Mom. She looked at me for direction. I thought that Dad would want to contribute to medical science if he could. Perhaps, this will give his death some purpose. I suggested that she sign it. In a state of shock, Mom could only do as I directed.

When we arrived at home, it was after one o'clock in the morning. The three of us got ready for bed as usual. Mom went into her bedroom. After she turned the light off, she cried out in fear. She was staring out her bedroom window where she saw the branches of our cherry tree blowing in the wind, swaying from side to side, against the backdrop of the moonlight. Terry and I rushed to her side. The branches moving back and forth looked ghostly.

"He's trying to get back inside," she cried. "Look at his arms!" Mom became hysterical.

The branches did look like arms pleading to come into the bedroom and I cried with Mom. It was Terry who was able to bring us back to reality. "They are only branches. They are not arms or hands. It's just the cherry tree, Mom. Those branches are swaying in the wind, that's all," she said calmly and tenderly. I thought she was wise not to turn the light on but rather encourage us to see the branches in the dark for what they were.

A few weeks after the shiva, we received the autopsy report in the mail. When I read it, I was ashamed of myself. I felt horrified knowing that Dad's body had been dissected. I felt totally responsible for the indignity to his body that I had caused by advising Mom to sign the consent form.

The searing guilt would torment me for years.

Sitting back in my chair, I am weeping. Then, quite suddenly, the face of another patient comes into view and carries me away from my guilt and grief.

Lorenzo was a handsome man in his early fifties, tall and slim, with dark, wavy hair. He was proud of his Italian heritage. His sessions were interspersed with details of his favourite Italian recipes that he loved to make from scratch. I respected his need to lighten our often emotionally heavy discussions arising from his irrational guilt.

"What would your dad say to you if he was still alive?" It was a question I had asked numerous times over the many months of Lorenzo's treatment. Lorenzo did his best to convince himself and me that his thirty-five years of guilt-inducing thoughts were impossible to dispel. His desperation to be relieved of his suffering was equally intense.

Looking back, I see how similar we were.

"My dad was digging the garden, overturning the soil, getting it ready for the vegetables. It was early morning. He woke me up and asked me to help. I was too lazy. I was too self-centred. After all he did for me, I could not make myself get up and help him. What a lazy, good-for-nothing son I was! Moments later, out by the garden, he dropped dead. They said it was a heart attack. That would never have happened if I had helped him."

Lorenzo was fifteen years old when his father died.

Although he was married and had two sons, Lorenzo's primary relationship was with alcohol. There was an element of pride in his frequent claim that no one in his family and no one at work knew that he drank alcohol heavily every evening. "Even if you are right about that, Lorenzo, *you* know that you drink a lot every evening. *You* must know that you are harming your health by continuing this addiction."

"Yes, I know, but I'm in good health," Lorenzo immediately replied, brushing aside any reason to feel concern, as swiftly as he would brush away a fly in the air.

In session after session, Lorenzo expressed rage with himself for failing to help his Dad that fateful morning. He created an endless pattern of torment for himself on a daily basis. He suffered the miseries of perfectionism, endless self-criticism, and a pervasive, intense fear that his wife and children might die at any moment, often leading to panic. The only respite that he afforded himself was when he played with his children. Those precious moments were a constant reminder to both of us that when he chose to do so, Lorenzo could turn away from his inner tyrant and soften his heart enough to allow for play and love.

I felt confident that Lorenzo could motivate himself to move towards self-care and forgiveness.

I wasn't so sure that I could do the same for myself.

When I worked with Lorenzo, it was fifteen years since Dad had passed away. I was still plagued by frequent nightmares that I knew were triggered by my guilt. In many of the nightmares I would see images of dead bodies that were first blurry but as I drew near, they would come into focus as the decaying bodies of Dad, Natie, and Mom. These dreams always left me with the strong feeling that I was responsible for their deaths. Once I awoke in terror, I would be unable to fall asleep again.

"Imagine that you were digging in your garden and you asked one of your sons to help. Who would that be?"

"I'd ask Francesco. We're close."

"And he says, 'Dad, I'm too tired.' You would feel?"

"Frustrated with him."

"Naturally, even though you understand how he feels. Imagine you go out to the garden and start digging up the soil. You feel a sudden pain in your chest and you collapse. As you lie there dying from a heart attack, you condemn Francesco to a lifetime of guilt."

"No. I wouldn't want Francesco to live the life of pain that I live."

"You mean the life of pain that you've *chosen*." I paused after emphasizing the word. "So, why not? Why not condemn Francesco to a lifetime of suffering?"

"Because I love him."

"You've told me that your father loved you, too. He wouldn't want you to live this lifetime of suffering either. Right?"

"Right. But I can't help how I feel."

"Of course, you can. You can change your thoughts and soften your heart, Lorenzo—not easily but you *can*. You believe this or you wouldn't keep coming back." I paused for a few moments. I sensed from his silent contemplation that a crack had opened in a door leading to something new. "A lot of times people have symptoms before a heart attack. Was your father the kind of person who readily talked about symptoms when he was unwell?"

"No. Even when he was ill, he would go to work. He hated going to the doctor. He was stubborn that way."

"So, it's possible that he might have had warning signs of heart disease and didn't tell anyone and minimized them. Right?"

"Yes."

"And it's possible that a heart attack might have been inevitable whether or not he was digging in the garden that day. Right?"

"Yes, but I think it was the physical exertion that must have caused it."

"If you had helped him dig, would he have just sat down and watched you?"

"Certainly not. He would have been digging, too."

"So, if he was going to have a heart attack out there that day, it might have happened whether or not you had helped him." I stopped. I knew that the intellectual discussion, as important as it was, always just coasts on the surface. Logic sets the stage for change but is usually hollow on its own.

I stood up and slowly sat down in the chair beside Lorenzo. My voice became a soft, gentle whisper. "Let's imagine, Lorenzo, that your dad is here with us right now. Can you give yourself permission to speak the words that he might say?"

"Yes."

"He loved you."

"Yes."

"What would he say about your blaming yourself?"

In a whisper, Lorenzo spoke the words. "Lorenzo, you are not to blame."

I repeated the words, also very softly and tenderly.

"You know me, Lorenzo. I would have dug up the soil even if you had been helping me." I echoed the words.

"It was my time. It is not your fault."

"It was my time. It is not your fault." I repeated.

I could see tears streaming down his cheeks.

"I think your dad would probably say—'I love you, Lorenzo. I want you to be happy in your life. Forgive yourself for not helping me that day."

Lorenzo whispered. "He would want me to be happy in my life."

Sometimes small changes in the therapeutic environment can have a profound impact. For Lorenzo, my sitting next to him and echoing his father's words in a whisper enabled a deeper connection between us. This happened because he was ready to change. Had I tried the same intervention in earlier sessions, I am certain that my words would not have touched his heart. It was only now that Lorenzo was ready to care for himself, embrace his father's love, and move toward forgiveness.

There was so much more work for us to do. Decreasing his dependence on alcohol, moving emotionally closer to his wife and children, and transforming his habitual self-destructive thoughts into compassionate thoughts—these would become the focus of his sessions. Here, at last, after many months of work together, we stood at the threshold of his path forward to a better quality of life.

Later that night as I drifted off to sleep, I chose to open my mind for the first time to the gentle and loving voice of my Dad. "I want you to be happy in your life. I love you, Rickey. Forgive yourself for the argument. Forgive yourself for the autopsy."

And so, after fifteen years, that's what I finally chose to do.

9

Always Far from Home

I am remembering Dad's voice now as he speaks about his childhood, taking me far from the pain of his death. He rarely spoke about his early years in his little village in Russia, but when he did, his tone was soft and tender. There was something of his tone in Mukondi's, when she described her village in Kenya. I sigh deeply as I am suddenly caught up in recalling the full horror of her story. I know that as I think about it now, it will once again take my breath away.

"After my mom died, the people in the village took my two sisters and me to my father's house a long way away in a different village. He was recovering from his injuries. He said that I could stay as long as I worked as a maid there. My sisters were sent to another village. I never saw them again.

"One day my father's wife beat me because I broke a glass. After that, he sent me to different people's homes in some other village far away to work as a maid. In those homes, I was often beaten. I begged to go to school. They said that they were paying my father for me to work as a maid, not to go to school. Many times, I went hungry.

"When I was maybe twelve or thirteen, my father sent me to work for an old man. He was in his sixties. My father told me that this time I was not going to be a maid. This time I was going to be this man's wife. My father would be getting more money for that. There was a ceremony. It was really an assault. The man undressed me and himself and laid on top of me. He tried to penetrate but could not do that because I had been circumcised when I was a lot younger. Maybe they did something that made it impossible. He got very mad at me and hit me a lot. I thought that he was going to kill me. He kept saying that he was cheated by my father. He had paid for a wife. He shouted that he would never be able to get his money back.

"This man had other wives and six big sons who often beat me. So many times, the old man tried to penetrate me but he couldn't. After a few weeks, I ran away.

"I was staying by a road at night. A kind driver picked me up and took me to a nearby city. I found a park where I lived for a while. One morning a woman saw me lying on a bench. She took pity on me. I was very thin and had wounds that were not healing. She had someone with a car drive me to a hospital. That woman was my angel. At the hospital, I was grateful to the doctors and nurses. They were kind. They gave me food and water and helped my wounds heal. The doctors did some kind of surgery that made it possible for me to have children. That angel of a woman and the doctors and nurses saved my life."

My heart is breaking again for Mukondi. I am thinking about how lucky I was to have been born into circumstances that allowed me to be sitting across from her rather than in her place. I question whether I would have been able to survive Mukondi's cruel world as she had. Admiration and respect for her well up within me. I feel humble thinking of her.

"What an incredibly strong person you are, Mukondi! Yes, that woman was an angel and the doctors and nurses were helpful, but it all comes down to *you*, Mukondi, *You* saved your life. You never gave up. You lived through horrendous abuse and suffering—and yet here you are. You are using that same strong spirit to help you through this difficult time in your life."

"I don't feel like I have a strong spirit anymore. The pain I have is exhausting. I often wonder why I have survived everything. Does my life have some purpose? I don't know. I married a man who had a job and wanted to come to Canada. I got a job in that warehouse, and then, look what happened to me?! A pile of heavy boxes fell on top of me and gave me all this pain." Mukondi's bitterness and restrained fury filled the room. She rubbed her heavily scarred arm.

"There is no justice in the world. No fairness, Mukondi. You have every right to feel rage and grief."

"Look at me now, Doctor." Mukondi stood facing me, staring directly into my eyes. "I am totally useless. I can't even make a meal for my kids. I can't work."

"I understand this is how you are feeling now. Mukondi, you are not useless. You will always be important to your kids. Look at what an incredible role model you are for them. Despite your darkest moments when you felt like giving up, here you are, Mukondi, wanting to improve your life and believing that you can." I paused. "Mukondi, you remember your loving mother. As long as you live, so do your memories of the person she was. And you can share those memories with your children and friends and, if you wish, with me. You can keep her alive in this precious way."

I learned much about Mukondi's loving mother and the tightly knit community of relatives and friends who had nurtured her during her early years. I understood that this foundation of unconditional acceptance and love had enabled her to choose life over and over again despite the unimaginable storms that had battered her. The love of her mother and community bestowed upon Mukondi the unshakeable belief that she was essentially a good and loveable person whose life was worth saving.

As I think more about our sessions back then, I reflect on how much Mukondi taught me about her culture and traditions. Her description of her childhood village was always filled with wistful feelings. There was a deep longing for home that accompanied Mukondi in every session, a permanent sense of being an outsider in Canada. She never expressed a desire to return to Kenya but, at the same time, yearned to feel back home, the home that she had loved as a child, the home in which she had been loved. Even though she had only known this home for a few years as a very young child, it had left her with indelible pictures, smells, sounds, and emotions that she yearned to recapture. More than that, it was a part of her identity. She was forever a stranger in a foreign land and unable to return home.

I am thinking of another child who felt much the same way—a little boy who was forced to leave his homeland, who would also speak in the same wistful way of his early childhood years in his little village—of his family, friends, the music, the food, the language, the person he had been. Even though Canada became a land that he loved, it could never be the home he had once known. Like Mukondi, he was forever a stranger in a foreign land and unable to return home.

10

Escape from Bobruisk

They burst into the shtetl of Bobruisk without warning. Yechil Aleyahu was eleven years old. It was the summer of 1923.

Yechil Aleyahu was jolted awake by the thunder of horses' hooves, the air-shattering shouts, the cries, and the vacillating glow of yellow, orange, and red lighting his room. He was frozen stiff with fear and too afraid to cry out.

His mother ran into his little room, carrying his two one-year-old brothers, one in each arm, and whispered frantically, "Quickly, Yechil! Put your shirt and pants on—on top of your pajamas." The sight of her contorted face struck him with terror. She ran to the next room and grabbed his two-year-old sister.

The world was collapsing.

Yechil Aleyahu pulled on his clothes and followed his mother as she ran to the front door. She opened it a crack, enough for him to see the horses galloping by. He could see the yellow, orange, and red glow take the shape of flames reaching high into the early morning sky, spewing thick smoke everywhere, obliterating the sun.

"Take your sister's hand and follow me. Run fast!" Yechil Aleyahu ran as fast as he could, pulling his sister behind him. He stopped to pick her up. His mother was running ahead with the twins tucked under each arm and her bag, slung over her shoulder, swinging from side to side. They darted along paths leading to the forest.

The entire shtetl of Bobruisk was covered in a cloud of smoke that grew thicker as they ran. Choking and coughing, they finally made it into the forest where the air was clearer. They continued to run. It seemed as though they had been running for hours when his mother finally collapsed by a tree. Yechil Aleyahu and his sister also collapsed. It was only then that he heard the twins crying as his mother cradled them in her arms. She tried to comfort them and he saw that she was weeping as well. The sight of her tears shook the ground beneath his feet. He had never seen his mother cry.

Yechil Aleyahu stood up and peered through the branches to look back at what had been his world. All he could see was black smoke drifting up towards the sky. He no longer heard the horses, the shouts, the cries. He could no longer see the flames. In his mind's eye he saw his little house burning, and with it his bed, his clothes, his toys, his books, everything he loved. How could this be? He saw the shul burning as well as the little marketplace and the farm and all the animals. He hoped that his friends had escaped into the forest as well. It seemed as though it had all happened in one moment. Uncomprehending and still frozen, he was unable to cry or speak. He grabbed his mother's arm and held on tight. She was his lifeline.

"We have to get to Warsaw and find your father," his mother whispered. His father had left for Warsaw weeks ago. Yechil Aleyahu knew that a cousin in a distant country had sent enough money for his father to make the long journey to that country. His father would be sending money someday so that the rest of the family could follow. Yechil Aleyahu had told his parents that he did not want to leave Bobruisk and all his friends.

Suddenly, that someday was today.

When he was five years old, Yechil Aleyahu watched soldiers marching into the shtetl. They hastily built a long wooden stage with a set of stairs at one end. Two tall posts were mounted at either end of the stage and supported a crossbeam from which hung ten thick ropes with a big loop at the end of each one. Yechil Aleyahu could not make out what these were for. Crowds of people were moving forward, pushing him against his mother's side. He saw the soldiers put the thick ropes around the necks of ten men whom they had brought with them. The soldiers pushed the men off the stage, one by one. Yechil Aleyahu watched them die. His mother explained that these men had killed many Jews. "The soldiers are from the Red Army. They are going to make sure that no one kills Jews again. We will be safe now, Yechil," his mother said with conviction.

Where were the Red Army soldiers now?

Yechil Aleyahu would not remember much about the six-hundred-kilometre journey to Warsaw except the feeling of death surrounding them. He would remember that he had been more hungry, thirsty, and tired than ever before in his life. He would remember the feeling of relief as they entered the big city and the joy of reuniting with his father. But the inner calm he experienced was shattered again when his father departed for the far-off country just a few days later.

Yechil Aleyahu would remember travelling from Warsaw by train and then on a big boat to the new country across a vast ocean. It would seem to him that years had passed instead of only one since his last morning in Bobruisk. His childhood became a distant memory, lost in the fog that greeted the boat as it arrived at the Port of Halifax. He was twelve years old and all grown up.

Through the crowds of people waiting for the passengers to disembark, he caught a glimpse of a man who looked like his father, but was he? His face was worn and he looked much older. Yechil Aleyahu and his mother lined up behind other passengers as two men in uniforms questioned each person. One spoke in a strange language and the other in Yiddish. Yechil Aleyahu heard his mother answer the questions. His gaze remained fixed on the man who looked like his father. The man approached them and showed the men in uniforms some papers. There was no question. It was his father. The men in uniforms waved the family on.

Yechil Aleyahu and his mother and father stopped a short distance away from the line of passengers. Yechil Aleyahu's mother stared at his father and his father stared back at her. No words were spoken for a long time. They did not touch. His father looked down at Yechil Aleyahu with a penetrating, disbelieving stare. Crowds of people were moving in all directions around them. There was much shouting and calling out of names and laughter and crying and thumping of suitcases upon the boardwalk, but for the three of them there was only a deafening deep silence. Looking up at his father, Yechil Aleyahu saw tears welling up in his eyes.

Finally, his mother struggled to form words. "It was typhus, Yitzhak. There was an epidemic in Warsaw. Only Yechil Aleyahu, my special one, my precious one." There were tears in her voice but not in her eyes. She had cried all her tears out long ago.

Yechil Aleyahu buried his memories of his sister and brothers. The guilt he felt to be the lone survivor was too intense to bear. Their names were never spoken again. It was as if they had never been.

"The immigration officer told me that Plotkin is no name for a Canadian. He told me to take Miller instead. So that will be our name from now on," Yizhak's voice trailed off. He was still staring down at Yechil Aleyahu. "Your name, Yechil, is 'Charles' in English. That will be your first name from now on."

Yechil Aleyahu did not like that name at all. It bore no resemblance whatsoever to Yechil.

"Can't I have a name that sounds like my real name?"

"Al sounds like a Canadian name. It is the first part of Aleyahu. You can have Al."

Thus, at the Port of Halifax, Yechil Aleyahu Plotkin became Al Miller, a Canadian boy. Yechil Aleyahu wore this name like a new ill-fitting uniform. As the years passed, it would gradually become more worn and more comfortable, but it would always remain only a uniform.

Walking along the streets to his new Beverly Street apartment, Al was in Toronto, safe from the Cossacks. The strange sounds and sights and sensations that accompanied him did not bring comfort. Rather, they fuelled more anguish in his heart, which burned as furiously as the flames that had consumed Bobruisk and the little boy that he had been.

And Dad's anger about the injustice of life was only beginning.

11

The Domino Effect

Al mastered English easily and retained his facility with Yiddish. Russian brought with it the pain of betrayal and loss. His mother tongue receded to the dark corners of his mind and eventually disappeared completely. His parents spoke Yiddish most of the time and eventually some English. The Russian language was evicted from their hearts as well.

While the sound of Russian triggered painful emotions, the music and dancing touched Al's heart. He had warm memories of the little klezmer bands that had travelled from shtetl to shtetl. Al struggled to recapture feelings of home but the sweet emotions were evanescent, like fragments of dreams that slip away no matter how hard we try to hold onto them.

Al had completed yeshiva in Bobruisk and had memorized many sections of the Torah in preparation for becoming a rabbi. In Toronto, he spent many hours at the library and devoured books on science and religion. He questioned everything he read with his natural talent for critical thinking.

When he was completing high school at age eighteen, Al's life was a wondrous adventure just beginning to take shape. He was certain that communism would save the world. He was inspired by the goals of liberating workers from the bourgeoisie, ending child labour, and achieving income equality for all. What could be more important goals for humanity than those?

Al had two sisters and a brother who were born in Toronto. Throughout the 1920s, they were all hungry most of the time. His mother kept the best food for Al but it was not enough. His father worked as a house painter. Most evenings he was not home. Al often wondered where his father was. The cousin who had paid for them to travel to Canada was running out of money. The smoldering fire in Al's heart about the injustice of life was growing in intensity.

It was 1929. Many of Al's classmates had parents who had lost their jobs. Al heard about Black Tuesday and understood that the stock market had crashed.

One afternoon, Al's mother told him, through her tears, that they could no longer manage on his father's meagre income. He was rarely getting work. "I have to tell you, Al, that your father has been playing dominoes. He has racked up a large debt." Her face was filled with despair and anxiety.

"Dominoes!" Al exploded. He howled and ranted and paced around and around the kitchen like a tiger in a cage, frantic to get out. In his fury, he punched the kitchen table with such force that a glass that had been sitting on it jumped into the air and came crashing onto the floor. It shattered, as did all his hopes and dreams for his future. His mother cried out, begging him to sit down. Screaming, pacing, stomping on the floor, he finally collapsed into a chair and buried his face in his hands. He knew what he had to do. "Dominoes! While we are starving."

Al completed grade twelve in grief, obtained marks in the nineties as usual proclaiming his potential to an indifferent world, a potential that would never be realized. With his teachers' commendations echoing in his mind, he trudged to factory after factory in search of a job every day. He had to save his family. One day in July, Al was hired as a machine operator apprentice by the Molson Bag and Paper Company on 8th Street in New Toronto.

And that was where Dad remained for the rest of his life.

12

The Lesson

I am weeping in my office as I think about the opportunities that had so unfairly been taken from Dad. Then I focus on the wondrous gift of choice that I had concerning my life's path and the daunting responsibility that accompanies that gift: to be true to oneself.

For fourteen years every Saturday morning I took the bus to my piano lesson. I think about one Saturday that seemed no different yet was entirely. A permanent boundary divided that Saturday from all the previous ones. And there was no going back.

I was walking down the snow-covered six blocks on "shanks' ponies," as Lily McKnight, my piano teacher, would always comment. My destination was the Royal Conservatory of Music branch located in a small brick house with a grand piano in the basement. Miss McKnight was walking in from Yonge Street. The cold air was biting.

At age four I had walked down the street with Mom. How different I was at eighteen! Yet the street looked remarkably the same, as did Miss McKnight. She was the same old lady with short, grey frizzy hair. Her wrinkled face had remained the same all these years. The lines on her face expertly concealed her emotions, except when I made a mistake. Most people would not have seen anything. I had no choice but to see her grimace, which was ever so slight and transient, and hear her critical tone, which was ever so soft. At such times, I was shaken, as if she had exploded in rage. I would become very small, sitting on the piano bench, and would quickly formulate a new plan for my daily practice.

Although she always demanded perfection, Miss McKnight was moved, not by my technical accuracy but by the emotion that I naturally poured into the music. After playing the final chords of a piece, I knew by the tiny sparkle in her eye and the momentary smile that flickered around her lips that she had heard my deep feelings giving life to the notes. I was filled with great joy. At times like those, her soul and mine were bound together on a dimension that was beyond words.

Miss McKnight's expectations naturally increased and became more formidable over the years. We never conversed about our families or friends or other activities. Our business together was purely music. Her calm and cold exterior were intimidating. My main mission was always to melt her heart.

This time I had a very different mission.

I cradled my piano books in my arms, protecting them from the harsh cold air and the few snowflakes that were falling. Slowly, I walked down the street. This time I was not fearful of arriving late. I was wishing that the lesson would be short. Miss McKnight often gave me a lesson for over an hour, even though my parents could only afford to pay for one. I was her special student. Although I was proud of achieving this status, it came at a high cost. A tremendous weight was pressing down on me, increasing with each performance and competition.

I listened to the snow crunching under each footstep. A few sparrows chirped from the canopy of the bare branches that framed the street. Their songs were not comforting. The winter scene in front of me looked dismal.

When I turned four, my parents enrolled me in acting lessons at the Medhurst Acting Studio, not because they foresaw that I would become an actress but because they diagnosed me with a condition called shyness.

At the acting school I was able to memorize my lines easily, but just the thought of reciting them in front of my teachers and the other students triggered such intense anxiety that I froze. On many occasions I dissolved in tears on stage. Terrified that I would embarrass myself by making a mistake, I guaranteed embarrassment by crying. My insecurity and shyness grew exponentially until my parents finally concluded that this approach was not the cure for shyness and terminated my acting career.

Mom and Dad could not allow themselves to understand the truth about my shyness and my easily triggered tears. These behaviours were my best defence against Dad's temper, which was extremely frightening and unpredictable. He never touched anyone or broke any objects when he flew into a rage, but his shouting, stomping, and exaggerated gesticulations were terrifying. Each time he saw my tears, he became calmer and his tirade ended sooner. For the longest time I was unaware that my protective strategy had a downside.

Having grown up in a house that was bursting with music every day, music naturally became part of my very soul. At age five I was enrolled in dancing classes. Hearing the music, my feet naturally took flight. I was able to copy the steps that my teacher taught. Without having the same records at home, I was unable to practise. Miss Ross grew weary. She had to reteach the steps that she had taught the week before. My dancing career followed the same footsteps as my acting career. My parents allowed me to hang up my tap shoes and ballet slippers after ten years of hard and frustrating work.

Walking down the street, the cold, biting air coaxed me to hurry and enter the warmth of Miss McKnight's piano studio but my pace remained slow. I tried desperately to freeze my heart as much as the frigid winter air froze my face. I rehearsed the speech again and again, as if the repetition would make me numb to the pain of my torn and broken heart. There was no stopping the storm of emotions that had been stirring in me for years and was now reaching an inevitable climax.

And there was no turning back.

At age four, before I started taking dance and acting lessons, I had sat down on the piano bench in the basement and experienced pure joy when I pressed a key and produced a sound. It was magic. Many times, I sat beside Mom and watched her play Yiddish songs. She could use both hands simultaneously, figuring out the melody with her right hand and the harmony with her left, even though she had never had a lesson.

My piano lessons began with the same teacher as Terry's. A few months later, I was able to play all the pieces in the beginner's book. My passion was ignited. Mom called the Royal Conservatory of Music and was referred to Miss McKnight. The lessons cost significantly more but Mom and Dad did not hesitate and never looked back.

Over the fourteen years of my studies with Miss McKnight, I entered auditions to perform at the Conservatory recitals. Each time I performed for Mr. Ouchterlony, I was anxious, but my grades were always high enough to qualify for the recital.

At each of my performances, I did my best to look confident and composed as I stepped onto the stage and bowed. Sitting in front of the piano, I imagined that the composer's emotions were drifting through time and space into my mind. My focus transformed into a precise laser beam, allowing no distractions of any kind. My fingers, as if possessed by an intelligence of their own, flew across the keys with the ease assured by countless repetitions. My attention was centred on each phrase, the pedalling, the tempi, the dynamics, the rising and falling of sentiment and passion, the miraculous transformation of percussive sound into flowing melody, the music moving forward, always moving forward, like a river moving towards the ocean. After playing the last notes, there would be a few moments of magical silence. My hands rose above the keys and stopped there in a desperate attempt to keep the waves of sound from flying away. The audience waited, holding onto the beauty of the sound after it had disappeared. Those few moments before the applause filled me with elation. The audience and I were bound together by the emotions that I imagined had once filled the composer's heart. What an honour it was to be able to create those precious moments! I kept coming back for more.

Afterwards, many parents and students as well as other piano teachers waited by the door until I came out with Mom and Dad, to say how much they enjoyed my playing. I did not expect to hear any positive comments from Miss McKnight. I often heard other teachers complimenting her as she left the building.

I was alone with the enormous and relentless pressure I felt to maintain the high level of playing that I had established for myself. Each performance added another floor to the tower of expectation that I was constructing. I was the only one who knew that the foundation was shaky. A poor performance at any stage would cause the entire tower to crumble. All the money that my parents had invested, all the effort that my teacher had invested, all the work that I had invested, it was all in that tower, which was getting higher and higher with every lauded performance. The pressure was crushing and inescapable and deadly.

For Miss McKnight, there was never any question about my career path. It was clear in her mind that I would become a concert pianist. She dedicated herself to this mission.

I did not tell Miss McKnight that my first dream was to become a writer.

Sitting back in my chair, I smile. This had always been my dream: To touch other hearts and minds—to paint pictures of the intricate human experience with the rainbow hues of words.

My love affair with our little portable typewriter began when I was six years old. It was sitting on a high shelf in my closet. Curious to see how it worked, I stood up on a chair to retrieve it. I was impressed with how much easier it was to type out a story using two fingers instead of printing out the words.

After finishing a story, I hopped down the stairs to the basement where Mom and Dad stored all their books. There were shelves and shelves of books to peruse. I felt lucky to have such a big library in my own house. When I opened a book that had an interesting title, I pretended to read some of the words. I closed the book and, staring at the cover, dreamed that one day I would be holding a book with my name on the front cover and the title would be of one of my stories.

One day I discovered a book in the basement called *Touch Typing*. It looked very old. I looked carefully at the yellowed and torn pages. This book explained how to type with the fingers of both hands. I was confident that since I could play the piano, I could learn to type with both hands.

I began to make my way through the book. Soon I was typing out story after story much faster than before. Pages filled with one unbroken block of text were soon flowing from the typewriter almost as fast as stories formed in my mind.

Every day I came home from school to the sound of classical and Broadway show records that Mom played. After Dad came home, there were records of the Red Army Choir and Yiddish songs filling the house. The music was a source of inspiration for me to write poems and stories. The dream of becoming a writer continued to grow.

Looking back now, with much affection, I am thinking about my grade five teacher, Miss Ross. She was an older lady, very distinguished in the way she dressed and carried herself. She was tall and had frizzy, short grey hair. One day she asked each of us to make up a story, and we took turns reading our stories in class. I made up a story about being a bubble—floating in the air, so light, playing on the wind, reflecting the rainbow colours of the sunlight, taking in the beauty of the lovely summer day, watching birds fly past as I soared upwards, floating up towards the sun, higher, higher, and still higher, and then POP!

At the end, I felt sad and so did my classmates. The bubble had a very short life. It was delicate, fragile, and, after only a few minutes, was gone.

After that, Miss Ross took an interest in my story writing. I told her that I was writing stories every night. I told her that I wanted to be a writer. She said that it was a wonderful goal.

When my grade six teacher, Mr. Moore, asked each of us what job we wanted to have when we grew up, I told him confidently, "I want to be a writer."

"You can't make a living being a writer," he responded with a mocking tone as if I should have known better. "You have to do something else." Some of the children in the class giggled. I felt embarrassed and dismayed.

Miss Ross had never said anything like that to me.

I went home that night and wrote more stories.

Not long after that, I discovered a posting on the bulletin board at the library inviting young people to submit poems and stories to a new publication called *Young Voices*. I became a regular contributor.

As my thoughts return to the piano lesson with Miss McKnight, I think about how my passion for writing had accompanied me throughout my life, as a dear old friend, even as I dreamed other dreams.

Miss McKnight knew nothing about any of my dreams including the newest one that had become the focus of my thoughts and stirred my passion.

I kept other secrets from Miss McKnight. She did not know that every time I performed, I was unable to sleep for the week before and, when I did sleep, I had nightmares about forgetting the notes. I was unable to eat anything on the day of the performance and was sick to my stomach for hours before. Mom and Dad saw my suffering but did nothing about it. I knew that they loved my playing and were always looking forward to my performances. Perhaps they thought that my anxiety was inevitable. I tried many ways of reducing my fear, but to no avail. My suffering grew more intense as the years progressed and more people attended my recitals and showered me with praise.

As the pressure increased, so did the pleasure I experienced when I played. When I was upset, I found relief by playing. Dad delighted in my playing Yiddish songs while he sang along. Mom loved everything I played. At the same time, almost imperceptibly, the pleasure of playing the piano was being eroded by my performance anxiety.

I drew closer to the house. My heart was pounding. About one year ago as I was preparing for my Associate Diploma exam as a performer, I had made the decision. Another passion had seized me, a curiosity about human nature and an irresistible urge to help others. I had studied books on Freud and Terry's introductory psychology textbook. I was impatient to get started on another path. Even though I was in grade twelve, I had written to the university, asking if I might be accepted into first-year university without completing grade thirteen. I sent a transcript of my high school grades. Mom and Dad did not take issue with my plan. They had always conveyed the message that Terry and I should pursue careers. Neither of them directed us as to which careers we should choose. Nor did they give us any advice.

The letter from the university stated that an exception might be made if I wrote the same entrance exam as the grade thirteen students and scored high enough grades.

I was thrilled when I received the letter announcing my acceptance. There was no turning back.

Arriving at the house, I forced myself to stop thinking and entered the studio. The room was dark. I was surprised that Miss McKnight had not arrived yet. Taking off my coat and boots, I sat on the couch beside the piano. The keys stared at me in silence. Miss McKnight opened the door and came down the stairs.

"Why are you sitting here in the dark?" she asked as she flicked the light switch on.

I took a deep breath. "I wanted to talk with you first." This was a highly unusual remark. Miss McKnight was clearly surprised.

"Okay. What do you want to talk about?"

"I have been accepted by the university. Starting next year, I will be studying psychology as my major. I want to become a psychologist." *There. I had said it. All in one go.* Rather than feeling relief, I felt all the muscles in my body tighten into knots.

"Well, that's fine," she began slowly. "Congratulations. Aren't you in grade twelve though?"

I explained that I had been accepted from grade twelve.

"Why don't you play some of the piece that I suggested last week?" It was clear that she had not heard anything I had said.

"Miss McKnight," I began, breathing more heavily, "I don't think I will have time to continue studying piano next year when I'm at university."

Miss McKnight still retained her usual composure. But her pause felt like a deep chasm that had opened up between us. "Why don't you wait and see?" she said. Then, making it clear that she understood perfectly, she went to the piano bench and began to play the third movement of Beethoven's *Appassionata*, the piece that she had introduced last week. She played for several minutes. It was difficult for me to keep my tears from flowing at the beauty that she was creating and at the farewell that was looming. She was using the most powerful enticement that she could to lure me back.

But there was no turning back.

Miss McKnight abruptly stopped mid-phrase, jarring both of us, reflecting the pain she felt upon hearing my plan. "This is the piece that you should study next to add to your repertoire of Beethoven piano sonatas."

"I have thought about this for a long time, Miss McKnight. I don't think I can do well at both psychology and piano studies." This was the closest I could come to saying that I did not want to become a pianist. I felt that I did not have the temperament to be a solo performer. Miss McKnight could have done nothing to help me reduce my performance anxiety because I kept this problem from her.

Miss McKnight looked at me with sad eyes that I had never seen before. I saw clear through them to the pain of loss that was breaking her heart. She left the piano bench. I wondered if I should stay or leave. My guilt was oppressive.

Seeking the comfort of routine for both of us, Miss McKnight directed me to warm up with my technical exercises. I played them perfectly as usual.

13

Never Give Up

Keeping my promise to Dad, Luke and I wed on May 11, 1975. What a bittersweet day that was! I was in love with Luke and looking forward to beginning our life together. I was also in deep grief. I was preoccupied with concern about Mom. I would be moving away. Terry would be returning to the States. I worried that Mom might become ill and that I might lose her too.

Looking back, it was foolhardy for us to have gone ahead as planned. My smiles and laughter were forced through a tiny opening in a hastily constructed and fragile wall around my broken heart. The frozen, empty expression on Mom's face and her tense, robotic movements reflected her grief-stricken stupor. She could not possibly be present. We felt compelled to fulfill our deathbed promise.

Dad and Mom had saved money to give us the gift of a one-week honeymoon in Barbados. My raw feelings of grief and guilt about Dad and my anxiety about Mom cast dark clouds over my time there. Pretending that a wedding and honeymoon could be joyful only intensified my pain. Celebrating was impossible.

With the advantage of hindsight and greater wisdom, I see clearly that it was no time to be starting a marriage. I was not myself. I was emotionally vulnerable and dependent. Luke was meeting my needs for comfort, solace, and affection. When we met, I was grieving the loss of my uncle and the trauma of witnessing his suffering and watching him die. Now I was grieving the loss of my Dad.

The emotionally vulnerable and dependent person I had become was a beaten down version of me. I would soon rise again and become strong and independent once more. Luke's comfort, solace, and affection would not be enough. Luke could not have known.

A few weeks after our honeymoon, I received the long-awaited letter from the graduate department of the university that Luke attended with an appointment date for an interview. I was overjoyed. I was confident that I would be instantly accepted into the program. My grades had been consistently high. I had graduated with a First Class Honours B.A. I was passionate about studying psychology. *What more could they want?*

There were ten of us who were being interviewed for five spots. Each of the five professors asked for details about my area of research. I had not given this any thought. I had relegated this task to my time in graduate school. I rambled on about various topics that interested me. Leaving the last interview, I was troubled. I had not articulated a research topic.

Another student sat down beside me. "My name is Michelle," she said.

"Hi, I'm Rickey."

"You look upset. Can I help?" she asked warmly.

Michelle's kindness was a comfort. I immediately felt less alone. "I've had a hard time with these interviews, Michelle. My dad died a few weeks ago and I just got married. I don't know if I did well."

"Wow, you've been through a lot. I think it is great that you came. You probably did better than you imagine." Michelle smiled. Her reassurance was sweet and genuine. I was impressed with her support despite the fact that we were competitors.

Back in Toronto, I eagerly awaited my acceptance letter. Every morning I greeted the man delivering the mail. One day he handed me a letter from the university. I ripped open the envelope enthusiastically. My eyes fixated on the second sentence.

"Thank you for attending the interviews on May 20, 1975. Unfortunately, we are not able to offer you admission for next year…"

I collapsed on the floor and cried bitter tears. *How could this be?* I had top grades. I saw myself living with Luke and having nothing to do day after day while he was completing his studies. I could not stop crying. Mom came into the room, read the letter, and wept with me. *I have failed. I have disappointed Dad.*

I was unable to sleep that night, overcome with anguish and grief. At some point, a voice from deep within cried out in defiance, "Never give up. There must be something I can do." All at once, my anguish and grief were transformed into determination.

I contacted our rabbi and asked if he would write a letter of support. He agreed. It occurred to me after a few more days that I needed a strong recommendation from someone who did not attempt to pull heart strings but focused only on my academic strengths.

I made an appointment with Professor Briteman who had taught a course on perception in my last semester. I had achieved an A+ in his course. I told him about my passion to become a psychologist and that the journey had led me to enter university from grade 12.

Dr. Briteman agreed to contact Dr. Cummings, the professor who had signed the rejection letter.

Two weeks after receiving Dr. Cummings' letter, I was sitting with Mom when the phone rang. Always responding to the ring as if it was an emergency alarm, Mom got to it first.

"It's for you, Rickey. It's a man."

"Hi, Rickey. This is Dr. Cummings."

I could scarcely believe that Dr. Cummings had called me. "How would you like to come to our university?"

"Okay," was my rather sad response. *I guess he wants to interview me again.* A moment later. *Oh, my goodness, I think that he is asking if I want to be in the graduate program!*

"Yes! I would love to!! Definitely, Dr. Cummings. Thank you!"

I hugged Mom, my heart bursting with happiness. I imagined Dad smiling.

The echo from the voice within me was reverberating with more intensity than ever: *Never give up.*

14

On My Way

Early in my first year, I learned that each of my four fellow students had a research interest that matched with one of the clinical psychology professors who became their supervisor. I was assigned to Dr. Martin Kramer. Upon learning who my supervisor was, second-year students told me that they felt sorry for me. "He's impossible to work with. He's often angry and condescending and very controlling. He has only one student left, Leon Becker, and he's in his third year." I was told that Dr. Kramer's main research focus was attribution theory. I wondered what that was.

None of the bad press mattered to me. I was indebted to Dr. Kramer for accepting me as his student. *I will impress him. I will make all the professors proud.*

In my first class, Michelle sat opposite from me and smiled warmly. I was happy to see that she had also been accepted. We became instant friends.

Philosophy of Science was taught by Dr. Cummings. After our first lecture, we were given a reading list consisting of fifteen journal articles. I turned to Michelle and commented that the content of the course appeared to be heavy. Michelle whispered, "Rickey, look at the due date for the essay."

The due date was in two weeks. Stupefied, I whispered back, "We have to read and critique fifteen articles and finish the essay on this topic in two weeks while completing all the work required in our other four courses?" She nodded. And so, it began.

Despite the almost impossible workload, I loved Dr. Cummings' course. He touched on topics that I had often discussed with Dad: How can we know what reality is? How do our senses, thoughts, and emotions shape our perceptions? I did not understand yet that these questions were crucial for clinicians as well as for scientists to consider.

One morning when I was visiting Mom, my good morning greeting was suddenly cut short as I glanced into her open bedroom door and saw her face light up with a proud smile as she stared at her reflection in the mirror. She was naked from the top up. I was shocked.

"Rickey, I just got a call from my boss. They have chosen me to be a model for their catalogue for bras. They say I have gorgeous breasts." She turned to show them off to me. They were big, smooth, and plump.

"Yes, Mom. You do have beautiful breasts. You will be a fantastic model. Good for you!"

Driving back to our apartment, I was comforted. Mom was coping better. It was almost one year since Dad died. However, my relief was short-lived.

The next weekend in Toronto, I helped Mom weed her garden. While she was still outside, inspecting each of her perennials that were just beginning to poke up through the soft earth, I went inside for a drink. For some reason I went into her bedroom. One of the folding doors on top of her dresser was open. I walked over to close it when I spotted three bottles of pills and a note lying next to them. "All there is of you is a stone in a cemetery. I have nothing to live for." The bottles were labelled "Valium." I ran outside in panic.

"Mom, your dresser door was open. I saw the bottles of pills. I read your note." I began to cry. Mom's eyes filled with tears. I knew that she was feeling guilty about the pain that she had caused.

Looking back, there is no doubt that a part of her left the dresser door open, hoping that I would see it. Perhaps, this was her way of conveying the agony of her loss. Perhaps, she needed to see my reaction to confirm how much she was loved. Perhaps, she was desperate for more support to help her go on with life. Perhaps, all of these and more.

At the time, the only thought I had was that she was seriously contemplating ending her life. Losing my uncle and father to cancer were tragedies but I felt that Mom's suicide would be an unforgivable crime and an intolerable loss. I felt angry that she was considering ending her life and leaving me. I felt guilty about my anger. I also felt guilty that I was living in a different city and was not calling her every day. I was visiting less often. At precisely the time she needed me most, I was not there for her.

"Mom, I know that going on without Dad is hard. Sometimes the pain is so bad you feel like giving up and ending your life. You won't always feel this way. Please promise me that you won't kill yourself! You must keep going for yourself, for me, for Terry, for her children, and for the children that I might have. Dad would not want you to give up. Your life is precious. *You* are precious." Mom sat down on the chair. I sat on the grass in front of her. We both wept. "I'm sorry I'm not living in the city. I'm not calling you every day. I'm not coming to Toronto often enough."

Mom wiped her tears and responded with a tone of anger. "It's not your fault, Rickey. You need to live your life. I don't expect you to do more than you do. You do more than enough for me." She repeated, "You need to live your life."

"And you need to live yours, Mom. Can you imagine how you would feel if I went through a terrible time of loss and seriously thought about killing myself?" This thought brought a look of horror to Mom's eyes. "I promise you that no matter what happens in my life, no matter how dark things get, I will never kill myself."

It was an easy promise to make. At that point neither of us could imagine that I would ever come close to contemplating suicide. We could not have known that my pledge would be tested by the greatest betrayal of my life.

"I need you to promise that, too." It wasn't a request. It was a demand.

Mom responded to my plea. "I promise. I don't want to cause you so much pain."

"Promise for yourself, too, Mom. Your life can always improve but only if you are here to live it." I stood and held my hand out to her. "Let's go into the house and throw away the pills and your letter. That will be a sign that we have an agreement. I trust you will keep your promise just as you trust that I will keep mine."

As we walked toward the house, I slowed my pace, hesitated for a moment, and then asked Mom, "Would it help you to speak with a professional?" I didn't dare say 'psychologist.'

"No. Absolutely not!" She responded instantly. I knew that my suggestion would be repugnant to her but I felt the need to raise it anyway. Mom rarely discussed her negative feelings with anyone. Pushing them as far away from conscious awareness as she could was her way of coping. Disclosing her agony to me in tears and words in these past few moments was the most open and direct she had ever been about her pain. She could not have been more supportive of my career to become a clinical psychologist nor more rejecting of the possibility of obtaining any type of counselling for herself.

I could not be her psychologist. I was only her loving daughter. I did not have her permission or the right to probe into the shadows and attempt to shine a bright light on dark feelings and thoughts that she needed to hide away. I quickly learned that lesson with friends as well. Psychologists can say things with the best of intentions that, in contexts other than treatment, can be terribly hurtful.

The other lesson I learned was that shining bright lights on the shadows of the mind even in treatment can be destructive. Sometimes the most effective treatment I provided was helping patients seal the vault storing their painful experiences. To probe for an opening would overwhelm their ability to cope. At some level, patients always knew which was best at any moment—opening the vault a crack or keeping it locked. My challenge was to listen for their direction and respect their guidance.

Susan was a young woman in her twenties. She walked into the office stiffly, head held erect, with long, black hair cascading down her back. She brought with her an aura of tension that, judging from the expression on her face, reflected a readiness to fight blended with intense fear. I could see the anxiety in her eyes, which averted gaze and only focused on me momentarily as I spoke. She sat rigidly as I provided my routine introduction. I softened my tone and noticed that her response was to stiffen even more. I had the feeling that at any moment she might jump up and leave. "Let me know if there is any way I can help you feel more comfortable," I added to my usual remarks.

"Okay," she blurted out, as if she was out of breath after just running a race.

"Which would be better for you? If I ask you my usual assessment questions or if you begin and tell me the reasons that you have come and how I can help?"

"Ask your questions." Her tone was a command. It affirmed the structure that she clearly needed.

In that first session, I recall that Susan answered most of my questions with only one or two words—filtering out heavily guarded personal information. I felt like I was walking gingerly on top of a bubble. There was a fragility about Susan.

Susan relaxed somewhat when discussing her primary concern, migraine headaches that she had suffered since childhood. They had become more disabling in her teens. In subsequent sessions, following her lead, we focused on identifying the comfort measures that afforded her some relief from her pain and suffering when her headaches occurred.

Susan woke up each day with an intense fear that a migraine attack might occur at any time and ruin her day. Her anticipatory suffering was even more disabling than her headaches. As we worked together, Susan achieved some insight into the role that her anxious anticipation played in triggering attacks and intensifying and prolonging the pain when a headache began.

Susan began treatment feeling that she was a helpless victim of her headaches. She felt disdain for her body and that it had betrayed her. As she implemented comfort measures, she noticed that the intervals between headaches became longer. By thinking and acting differently when the headaches occurred, she felt more in control. I encouraged her to feel compassion for her body rather than anger. "Naturally, you are frustrated and angry about the headaches. But you need not feel frustrated and angry with your poor body, which is doing its best to cope. Every time you take time to use comfort measures you help your body. You and your body are partners in finding ways to reduce the pain and suffering."

Over time, Susan came to see the intervals between headaches as opportunities to enjoy her life rather than moments filled with dread that the next storm would come crashing down at any moment.

"Why choose to destroy the beautiful sunny moments with thoughts of the storm that has not yet come? Better to think—I will choose to help myself cope with the storm if and when it comes. I will remind myself that the sun will come out again."

When she practised meditation, Susan was surprised to notice the fluctuations in the quality and intensity of her headaches. Prior to treatment, she had experienced each headache as equally disabling and intense, and remaining that way for hours without any change. Noticing these variations allowed her to make better choices as to which activities she could pursue. She no longer stayed in bed all day.

I recall the persistent feeling that I was missing something crucial every time Susan left a session. I continued to feel some anxiety when working with her, fearful that at any moment she might pounce angrily if I said the wrong word. I waited for our connection to be strong enough for me to bring this into focus.

"Every time we meet, Susan, I feel that there is a lot of fear inside. It feels like part of you is ready to defend itself. I find myself feeling some anxiety. Please let me know if I am wrong about this. If I'm right, where is this fear coming from?"

"Well, I'm always afraid a headache will start up."

"I understand that fear. But what about the part of you that seems ready to defend itself—or maybe to fight."

"I don't know. I don't feel ready to fight."

"If it's important for us to figure it out together, we will. It doesn't have to be now." Removing the pressure, I continued to focus on Susan's journey toward better self-care.

I reviewed my notes of Susan's first session to see if I could discern clues about whatever was hiding in the shadows, keeping her guard ever vigilant. I had noted that she delayed in answering a question about her sleep.

In the middle of a session focusing on her migraines, when our conversation was smooth and easy, I took the plunge with a softly spoken enquiry. "How did you sleep last night?"

"Rotten." Her reply was muttered through tense lips, as if it had escaped from tight restraints.

"Sad to hear that. How was it rotten?"

"I have these nightmares." Susan became more rigid. Her eyes narrowed. The tension in the air was mounting.

"How many times in a week?"

"Almost every night."

"What do you do when this happens?" I intentionally did not ask her about the content. *Just ask around the hard part first.*

"I cry a lot. I'm afraid to go back to sleep so I stay up for hours."

"I'm sad to hear you are suffering so much with these bad dreams." I paused to send a warm nonverbal embrace through the air. Susan appeared to relax a little. I allied with her defensive guard. "Without telling me what they are about, unless you wish to, are they about some painful experience?"

"Yes. And I don't want to tell you." Her tone was louder and resolute.

"That's fine. No need. Please don't tell me anything unless most of you wants to. You have helped yourself cope with the migraines better in so many ways. You can also cope better with whatever this is."

Susan became more relaxed as we focused on how she might manage her bad dreams better. Over time she learned to anchor herself in the present after waking from a nightmare. Walking out of her bedroom and drinking herbal tea helped decrease her distress.

"Whatever painful experiences you have lived through, Susan, you coped somehow and survived. Living through whatever happened was much harder than recalling any part of it or dreaming about it. You survived the hardest part. It's history now. Did it happen years ago?"

"Yes. About twenty."

"Think about a history book of your life. It's twenty chapters ago. Long past. Your current chapter is right now."

Susan's past experience remained only an "it" in each session. Without her recounting whatever happened to her, every time we talked about "it," she could not help but recall fragments of her experience and slowly became desensitized to them. In the safe and calm setting of our sessions, Susan was able to put "it" into the past. She was left with a distant memory of an ordeal that she had survived, which lost its power to terrify. Her vigilant guard was relaxing. As Susan felt less anxious, her headaches decreased in intensity and frequency. The feeling of anxiety that I felt in our sessions disappeared. Susan's progress was significant even though she never shared details of "it."

My patients taught me time and time again that there is no one formula, no one way for everyone to move forward. They also taught me that we have the capacity to habituate to even the most horrific traumas.

Thinking about Mom, I reflect on her eagerness to share stories of her childhood with me, much like a journalist, without disclosing the painful emotions that she had experienced. I cannot know for sure how she felt, but as she told me her stories, I could not help but fill in those gaps.

15

Father-Love

Three-year-old Fanny and her four-year-old brother, Louie, woke up to the shouts of their mother and father arguing again. They couldn't understand the words. The shouting crashed like peals of thunder, mounting in intensity. Fanny heard Louie crying and motioned to him to come over to her bed. He ran into her arms. She was shaking in fear as much as he was. Fanny and Louie waited for the usual silence that marked the end of the fight. The screaming reached a frightening climax. The front door slammed shut. It shot terrifying vibrations through the walls and floor and right through Fanny and Louie as they sat huddled together on Fanny's bed. They sat there for a long time, neither daring to move. Louie's cries became more desperate. Fanny held her tears and hugged her big brother. She had to be strong for him. She had to be strong for herself.

Footsteps slowly made their way down the hall to their bedroom. What would Mommy do now?

Fanny and Louie were startled when they saw their father open the door. "You've got to get dressed—right away! Now!" He had never spoken to them in such a harsh way. Fanny and Louie looked at him with fear in their eyes. Where was Mommy?

Their father hastily pulled open the top drawer of their small dresser so hard that it almost fell onto the floor. He threw clothes on Fanny's bed and ordered the children to take off their pajamas. He told Fanny to dress herself and he roughly dressed Louie, ignoring his incessant crying.

"We are going out now," he announced in a stern voice.

"Where are we going? Where is Mommy?" Fanny asked. There was no answer. Their father was already waiting for them by the front door.

Fanny and Louie walked past the kitchen. The table was strewn with papers and cups and plates.

"Come on, both of you!" His impatience and anger seemed to signal some imminent danger. Fanny and Louie rushed out of the apartment. Fanny's thoughts were racing. Where is Mommy? Where are we going? Why is Daddy in such a hurry?

"Where is Mommy?" Fanny asked. Again, her question was met with silence. "Has something happened to Mommy?"

Fanny and Louie walked as fast as they could but their father rushed ahead of them down the sidewalk that was crowded with people coming and going. Fanny held Louie's hand. She tried to keep her eyes fixed on her father through the narrow, shifting spaces forming between the people they passed. It was a very long walk. Fanny became fearful that they might become lost each time she could no longer see her father. He called to them angrily, "Come on, you two! Walk faster!"

Fanny and Louie looked up to examine the faces of each person walking towards them. Maybe one of these people would be Mommy. Fanny and Louie grew more frantic, wondering where she was and where they were going. This part of Quebec City looked strange.

Their father, who was now half a block ahead, pointed to a large brick building. "Come on, you two! See that building? That is where we are going."

When they caught up with him, Fanny and Louie noticed a big sign on the building. Their father motioned to them to go up steep stairs to the two enormous black wooden doors at the top. Fanny and Louie stood in the shadow of the building and waited. What were they waiting for? What was this place? It didn't look anything like their apartment building.

Suddenly, Fanny and Louie became aware that their father had disappeared. They looked up and down the sidewalk and across the street. He was not there. "Daddy? Where are you?" Their plaintive cries dissolved into sobs. Collapsing on the top step in each other's arms, Fanny and Louie cried loudly. They were alone in front of big black wooden doors at the top of steep stairs in front of a strange building far away from home. No Mommy. No Daddy. They were alone and lost in the world.

The doors suddenly parted and a woman looked down at them with surprised eyes. She spoke softly and her voice was sweet.

"Come in. Both of you." Slowly Fanny and Louie rose and walked in. The lady led them into a big room with a desk and a couch and gave them tissues to wipe their tears. She invited them to sit with her on the couch. She touched their hands gently and spoke in a kind, hushed voice.

"What are your names?"

All Fanny could manage was a whisper through tears that were still flowing. "Fanny and my brother is Louie"

"How old are you?"

"I am three. Louie is four."

The lady turned towards Fanny and put her hands around Fanny's in a warm embrace. "How did you get here this morning?"

"Mommy and Daddy were fighting and Daddy brought us here. I don't know where he is. He'll come back, and Mommy too." Fanny looked at the lady through her tears. Louie was still sobbing.

Louie spoke in words broken by his crying, "Find Mommy and Daddy."

"I will help you find them, Louie. Where do you live?"

"A long way down the street," Fanny replied.

"Do you know your last name?"

"Stein."

"My name is Cathy. I will help you. You are safe here." Her voice was comforting.

"Find Mommy and Daddy." Louie pleaded.

"Have you eaten breakfast?"

"No." Fanny said.

"Come into my kitchen and I will give you some breakfast." Fanny and Louie hesitated. "You can eat breakfast while we wait for your Mommy and Daddy."

Fanny and Louie stopped crying when the nice lady gave them glasses of sweet orange juice and bowls of cereal with milk. She sat down at the table with Fanny and Louie after pouring herself a steaming mug of tea.

After waiting in vain all day for their Mommy and Daddy, Fanny and Louie slept upstairs in the nice lady's building. She gave them hugs and tucked them into little beds with soft, clean sheets. Feeling safe and reassured, Fanny and Louie drifted off to sleep. Maybe tomorrow Mommy and Daddy will come back for us.

The next morning Fanny woke up first, and even though she hadn't made a sound, the nice lady somehow knew that she was awake and greeted her warmly. Fanny asked what kind of house this was.

"This is a house of the Lord," she said. "This is a Salvation Army Church." Fanny had never heard of such a building before. She wondered who the 'Lord' was.

The name "Salvation Army" would remain in Mom's mind for the rest of her life conjuring up feelings of love and images of angels. She would never forget the guardian angel who was there for her and Louie when they felt alone in the world.

Three long days passed at the church. The nice lady brought Fanny and Louie some toys, but neither of them wanted to play. They spent hours peering out the window, searching for Mommy and Daddy. As the days went on, they were consumed with anxiety. Where are Mommy and Daddy? Why did they leave us? There were other questions in their hearts, not yet formed into words, that would haunt them for years to come: Why don't they love us? What bad thing did we do?

Early in the morning on the fourth day, there was a loud, desperate knocking on the front door. Fanny and Louie immediately stopped eating breakfast. They heard a familiar voice. Could it be her? Fanny and

Louie jumped up and ran to the front door and into her arms. Their Mommy cried tears of delight and kept saying, "Thank God." And then, "Thank you." to the nice lady who was overjoyed to see the reunion. Fanny and Louie cried tears of relief and clung to their Mommy, fearful that she might disappear again. They would not loosen their grip for hours nor leave her side for many days.

"I didn't know where to look for them," their mother told the nice lady.

"Come, sit on the couch over here." The nice lady motioned to their mother. With Fanny and Louie still gripping each of her arms, she walked over to the couch and sat down.

"I left to find another place to live, and when I came back they were gone. I didn't know where he had taken them." The nice lady offered their mother something to eat and drink, but she said that she needed to leave with the children. She thanked the nice lady over and over again for taking care of Fanny and Louie.

Fanny and Louie loosened their grip on their mother's arms only when it was time to say goodbye to the nice lady. They hugged her. Then they grabbed their mother's hands again and walked out of the building that had been their haven.

"We are going on a train now, Fanny and Louie. We are going to a new city called Toronto. I have found a house for us there." As long as they were with Mommy, Fanny and Louie did not care where they were going.

"Where is Daddy? Is he coming with us on the train?" Fanny asked.

"No. I don't know where he is. We are going to Toronto without him," was all Fanny's mother said.

Fanny's mother did not talk about him again. Fanny's heart was full of anger towards him for leaving her and Louie. It was just as well if he wasn't going to be living with them. She could not allow herself to feel any anger and pain towards her mother for having left her and Louie with him. She could not risk feeling angry with the only lifeline she had.

"I do not believe in father-love," Mom would say for the rest of her life.

16

The Fire

Soon after moving into a small apartment in a house on Bathurst Street south of College, Fanny's mother met Morris Shapiro, who worked as a prompter at the Yiddish Theatre at the Victory. Fanny's home was transformed into a gathering place for everyone who was involved with the theatre.

One day Fanny's mother told her that she had married Morris Shapiro. "Your name will now be 'Fanny Shapiro," she announced, as if this would obliterate her memory of Jack Stein. The name change did nothing to obliterate her strong feelings of disdain that tainted her relationships with Fanny and Louie. They were constant reminders of him.

Fanny was happy to change her last name to "Shapiro." She was relieved to be rid of the connection to her father and grew close to her stepfather who was a warm and affectionate man. She was entranced by his involvement in the theatre and grew to love everything about it.

In the three years that followed, two new brothers arrived, Natie and Billy. Fanny's mother showed her how to care for them when they were infants, and gave her more and more responsibility for their care as they grew older. Fanny was also expected to care for Louie, even though he was older.

After tucking her three brothers into their beds, Fanny would be lulled to sleep by the happy symphony of Yiddish songs filling the house accompanied by multiple overlapping conversations rising and falling with laughter. The continuous opening and closing of the front door were familiar and comforting percussive rhythms. For Fanny, it was a sweet lullaby. She would fall into a deep sleep and dream of becoming an actress, singer or musician and performing on the stage at her stepfather's theatre.

The demands on Fanny's time significantly increased as the Yiddish theatre blossomed and her brothers grew. Her mother and stepfather were away for longer hours in late afternoon and evening. Her mother expected her to supervise her brothers every day after Fanny returned from school. She barely had time to complete her schoolwork. Her brothers got into all kinds of trouble, and her mother was harsh and punished Fanny whenever they did something wrong. Her mother was also especially critical of Louie and beat him often with a broomstick. When Fanny tried to protect him, her mother would hit her as well. Fanny could not understand it. Natie and Billy could do no wrong and she and Louie could do no right. Fanny craved the precious morsels of approval that her mother rarely granted.

Fanny cherished the love and affection that she received from her stepfather. Throughout her life she would remember how often he would sneak upstairs into her bedroom late at night with freshly fried latkes that were being devoured by the theatre gang. Her mother was a good cook and the latkes were always crispy on the outside, and deliciously soft and flavourful on the inside. Her stepfather would even bring up a plate of sour cream for dipping.

At the same time, another memory would be permanently imprinted in her mind. She would never forget how, one night, her stepfather came into her room without latkes, and told her that he had forgotten to wish her sweet dreams. He bent over to hug her, and then slipped his hands under the sheets and touched her bottom over and over again. From that moment on, an undercurrent of insecurity poisoned their relationship. Fanny's mother was the only anchor in her life, despite the fact that her approval and love were always just out of reach.

Fanny found solace at school. Her creative writing talent and love for reading were praised by her teachers. She had a special relationship with the school librarian, who put books aside for her. Books were her best friends.

Fanny's days at school became painful. A group of children in her class teased her about her name. Pointing to their rear ends, they would call out loudly, "My ass is a fanny. Fanny is an ass."

She hated her name. She began a campaign to convince her mother to allow her to change her name to Faye. Finally, tired of the nagging, her mother relented. Fanny became Faye and the teasing stopped.

One day when she was ten years old, Faye was washing the kitchen floor. Every few minutes she darted out of the kitchen and then rushed back in again. She had to make sure that her brothers were still playing in the next room.

Suddenly, Faye was seized by a sharp pain in her right side. It took her breath away. She was immobilized. There was no question that she had to be silent. To complain about pain invited more pain from her mother. Noticing that she had stopped washing the floor, her mother spoke sharply, "Faye, keep washing. It needs to be clean before supper."

Faye was waiting for the pain to subside. She did her best to continue to wash the floor. Despite her best efforts to push it aside, the pain kept reasserting itself and grew more and more intense. Finally, she told her mother.

"Mommy, I have this terrible pain in my side. It's getting worse all the time."

"Don't complain, Faye. It will go away. I don't want to hear another word about it." Her mother put a baking pan loaded with cookies into the oven and left the kitchen.

As the hours passed, Faye became incapacitated by the pain. Seeing her in this condition, her mother called for an ambulance. Faye was taken to a hospital alone. She was diagnosed with acute appendicitis. She would have to undergo emergency surgery.

Faye had never been in a hospital before. She found herself lying on a large hard table with a very bright light above her. All the people around her were wearing masks. Only their eyes peeked out. No pairs of eyes were looking at her. The pain felt as if it was cutting her from inside. She was terrified.

From inside a mask, she heard a man's voice saying that they would be giving her a needle in her arm and stomach and that it would stop all the pain. He said that they would be removing her appendix.

Faye heard two men speaking clearly. "Cut here. Just like this. Like I showed you. Good. That's right. Make the incision this way. And now the clamps. Good. Clean the bleeding area. Go ahead. Good job. Yes." Then there was a pause and a gasp from one of them. "Look at that. Good thing we got to her quickly or that could have burst. And then what would have happened?"

"She would have gone septic," the other voice replied. "She could have died."

"That's right. She's lucky that didn't happen. Take a good look at that so you know how one looks before it goes. Don't know why people wait so long before coming to the hospital. Her mother should never have waited so long. Be careful. Slowly. Good. You removed it very nicely. Good work. Tie off the blood vessels. Very nice. Now, for the sutures."

Faye was just a body being cut and sewn like a garment, a convenient opportunity for teaching. The terrified little girl inside was invisible and totally alone.

Faye's mother required her to make a speedy recovery so that she could mind her brothers, do the housework, and attend to her homework as usual.

And Mom did exactly that.

One weekend day, her brothers ran off towards the Kensington market and went directly to the garbage pile behind one of the stands. Faye raced after them, calling out that they should come back home. They ignored her. The garbage-pile adventure was too much fun to resist. Who knows what treasures they might find in there?

The little girl in her immediately joined her brothers when she saw the huge pile looming in front of her, the air electrified by their excitement. They all jumped in and plowed through the rubbish with eager hands. The smell of rotting food and the thick swarms of fruit flies descending on them from all directions were of no importance. Natie shouted, "I found bananas. Whole bunches!"

The other children ran around the pile to his location. There were bunches and bunches of overripe bananas peeking out from the pile, like bars of gold sparkling in the sun. The children tossed the bananas onto the ground. They had never seen so much food in one place, and it was all theirs to eat and bring home. Mom will be so happy. This is free food. And it will be enough for all of us to have for days and days, Fanny thought.

When they could find no more bananas, the children sat down by their treasure and feasted. It had been a long time since Fanny felt full. Her brothers were always fed first and given more than she was. This time there was enough for all of them. After filling themselves up to capacity, they tucked as many bananas as they could into their pockets and under their arms, and held as many as they could squeeze into their little hands. They could hardly contain their excitement.

Their mother was waiting at the door. Her face was contorted. Her eyes were flaming with rage. "Where did you take them?" She shouted at Faye, "and where did you get those filthy bananas?"

"We found them behind the market. They were going to be thrown out," Faye said anxiously, not wanting to admit that they had found them in a garbage pile. The weight of her mother's anger was crushing. The boys ran into the kitchen and piled the bunches of bananas on the table.

Her mother continued to scream at her. "Look at your brothers. They are covered in filth. What a stench! You will need to bathe them and yourself and wash all the clothes. You need to wash each of those bananas and then wash the table thoroughly. How can I use the table now with all that filth on it! You should know better, Fanny."

Faye felt guilty that her mother was so upset. She should have known better. The little girl inside was hidden away again as she washed each banana, cleaned the kitchen table, washed each brother in turn, dressed each in clean clothes, washed their clothes and her own, and hung the clothes on the clothesline.

Exhausted, Faye turned to her beloved dolly, her one toy that her mother had bought her long ago, and hugged her close. Then she dressed her dolly in one of the luxurious outfits that her mother had sewn for her. Her mother was an excellent seamstress and had made everything that Faye wore. When sewing for Faye, she would often take leftover scraps and sew another addition to the dolly's wardrobe. The dolly and her growing wardrobe warmed Faye's heart. Each outfit her mother made was a gift of love that softened all her mother's painful blows.

"Faye, you did a terrible job washing the boys' clothes! They are still dirty and smelly!"

Before she could offer to rewash the clothes, her mother grabbed the dolly out of Faye's hands and the large bag of her dolly's clothes. She left the room in a rage. Faye ran after her.

"What are you doing with my dolly?" Faye cried. "I will rewash the clothes. I am sorry about the bananas, Mommy."

Fanny looked on in horror from the top of the basement stairs. Her mother threw her beloved dolly and all her clothes into the fire burning in the furnace. Her mother marched upstairs, past her. Fanny was frozen in grief listening to the crackling sounds of the flames as they burned through her heart and reduced her mother's love for her to ashes.

17

My Bobby

'Bobby' was the name we gave to my Mother's mom. When I was ten years old, Bobby moved into our house. She was sixty-five years old. Bobby had been living alone in an apartment since Mom's stepfather, Morris Shapiro, collapsed and died from a heart attack on the stage of the Victory Theatre during a performance in 1954.

Mom and Dad bought a bed and put it in the basement opposite the piano where I spent many hours practising every day.

Bobby was a big, warm, loving grandmother. I loved snuggling up to her in the back seat whenever Dad drove us anywhere. Every evening she sat on her bed listening to my practising. Whenever I turned my head to look at her, she would be smiling. She clapped enthusiastically after the last note of anything I played, even scales. She told me that my playing was beautiful. I would rush into her arms for lots of hugs.

After one year, Mom told me that Bobby would be moving into an apartment in a house not far from us.

"Why is Bobby moving out?" I asked sadly, anticipating the loss of my adoring fan and her warm cuddles.

"Bobby has bought a variety store. She wants to earn some money." Mom paused and looked down as if contemplating whether she wanted to say anything more. Looking up, she continued. "Bobby wants to live on her own. It's hard for her to live in the same house as us."

This surprised me. Bobby always looked happy to me. I was aware of some arguments that Mom and Dad had about her but I did not know what they were about. There was sadness and anxiety in Mom's face as she walked away.

I was too young to have known that Bobby's moving in had disrupted my parent's lives and had increased their workload and expenses. I now understand that Bobby must have felt the resentment that Mom and Dad tried hard to conceal.

While I was sad about Bobby moving out, I was excited to think about her variety store. I imagined that the shelves would be bursting with candies. I imagined devouring my favourite treats: marshmallow ice cream cones, little wax bottles filled with syrup, bubble-gum cigarettes, candy necklaces, Pez candies, jawbreakers with gum centres, sweet tart candies, striped gum and, best of all, Aero chocolate bars.

For the next three years, every Saturday and Sunday, and sometimes in the evenings after school, Mom packed some of our supper meal and asked me to take the bus to Bobby's store. Bobby welcomed me with warm hugs and treated me to a free candy. I could have my pick from the whole store. Mom explained that Bobby was paying for all the candy herself. I always came with five cents and left it by the cash register while she was eating in the back room. I did not want her to have to pay for my treat. Sometimes Bobby found the nickel before I left. Those times she would give me an extra candy and tell me that it was her way of thanking me for delivering the meal.

Bobby had a bed and a television at the back of the store. While she the enjoyed the food that Mom prepared, I sat in the front pretending that it was my store. Whenever a customer came in, I called her and she would return to the front.

When I was twelve, I overheard Mom and Dad discussing problems that Bobby was having managing the store.

"Your mom is losing a lot of money, Faye."

"Why is this happening, Al?" Mom asked.

"People come into the store and take things without paying. Children rush in, steal candy, and run out."

A short time later, Mom told me that Bobby's store was closed forever.

One afternoon, when I came home from school, I found Mom sitting on the couch in the living room.

"What's wrong, Mom?"

"Bobby is in the hospital." Mom's voice was weak and unsteady. "She has a brain tumour called a meningioma. She passed out in the bank and someone called an ambulance. I got the call a few minutes ago. She must have come to and told someone our phone number." Tears were streaming down Mom's face. I hugged her.

"Bobby will be all right, Mom. She has to be." I could not imagine any other outcome.

Dad came home from work early and drove us to the hospital. Mom told me that Bobby would have to undergo brain surgery. I was frightened.

I saw Bobby for a short time that day. I held her hand, hugged and kissed her. She did not talk to me and looked very scared. That made me even more frightened.

Mom came into my bedroom that night and cried. She said, "Bobby was so sad when they came to shave her head. She always took pride in her golden blond hair. It was so sad." I cried with her. I thought that it would be awful if all of my hair were shaved off.

Bobby survived the surgery. We were told that the operation went well. Even so, Bobby never opened her eyes. We visited every day. I spoke to her, hugged her, kissed her, and asked her how she was feeling. Bobby did not answer.

I waited for Bobby to wake up.

The following Sunday, December 17, 1967, Dad drove me home from religious school as usual. When I walked into the house, Mom was sitting on the couch in the living room, frozen in grief.

"The hospital called. Bobby died." I cried in Mom's arms. She held me tightly. Soon after, our relatives arrived. The whole house was weeping.

God wasn't there for Bobby.

After the funeral, Mom came into my room and said, "It is very hard to put your mother into the ground."

I could only say to her, "Yes, it is. But it is only her body." When I watched the coffin being lowered into the cold ground, I wondered, is that the end of Bobby? Or is Bobby's spirit alive somehow?

"What happens after we die, Mom?" I asked as we drove home from the cemetery.

"We don't know, Rickey. No one has ever come back to tell us."

Dad offered a clearer answer. "There is nothing left of us after we die. Only memories of us in those who loved us and, if we are lucky to have children, they are a form of immortality."

I didn't like either answer. Dad paused and then continued, "Funerals are for the living. Life is for the living. The person who is gone, is gone."

Every time I practised piano, I was convinced that I could hear Bobby applauding. I would imagine feeling her warm arms hugging me again in a loving embrace.

Years later when Mom told me stories of her childhood, I found it impossible to reconcile her description of her abusive and cruel mother with my Bobby. They could not possibly be the same person. Her stories tainted the memory of my loving Bobby and complicated the simple affection I felt for her.

My struggle to accept both sides of Bobby have never reached a satisfying conclusion.

18

Some Things Are Worth Fighting For

I often overheard Mom telling Dad that she felt guilty for not having done more for her mother. I could not understand that. Mom had done more for her mother than any of her brothers. She was the only one who prepared dinners for her. Mom and Dad were the only ones who had invited Bobby to live with us for one year. There was no reason for Mom to feel guilty.

Dad told her, "We never feel that we have done enough for our parents." It was more than empathy for her. It was an admission that he felt the same.

Mom must have felt rage toward her mother for all the pain that she had caused her and, at the same time, guilty for feeling that way. Her mother had come back for her in Quebec City and had provided her with a home during her childhood. Mom must have felt that she was a bad person to feel rage toward a mother who had done so much good for her.

Dad felt disgust toward his dad for gambling and for failing to support his family, forcing Dad to assume that role. He must have felt guilty for feeling that way because his father had saved him and his mother by arranging for them to travel to Canada.

My parents never spoke directly about their anger toward their parents. I wonder if they ever shared their feelings with each other.

Patients often felt guilty for the angry feelings that naturally exist alongside loving feelings for parents and children. I reflect on the powerful and destructive message we internalize as children, that we should only have loving feelings for our parents, and later on, for our children, as if love is simply devotion, affection, and caring. Genuine love is always complicated by vacillating and conflicting emotions.

Many of my patients felt too guilty to disclose the pain that their parents had inflicted on them let alone their angry feelings. I helped patients see guilt as useful only when it motivates an apology for causing another person pain and is accompanied by a commitment not to repeat the act. Otherwise, guilt is toxic. I taught patients that their angry feelings were a superficial layer, riding on the surface of hurt feelings, like waves riding across the surface of the deep ocean.

I smile reflecting on how difficult it was for me to implement concepts that were so easy to teach.

With Terry married and living in the United States, Dad working, and my attending university, Mom, who was fifty-five years old, was becoming more and more agitated. Every day she completed the household chores and read novel after novel. She spent hours reading her notes from lectures on philosophy and religion that she attended with Dad at synagogue. She spoke to her friends on the phone. Throughout the afternoon, she gobbled up Licorice Allsorts and Laura Secord chocolates. Having been deprived as a child, Mom delighted in the abundance of treats that were now available. Even so, this abundance was never satisfying. Nothing that she did dispelled the gnawing emptiness within.

When Dad returned home each day, he told Mom about the events that had occurred at the factory. He spoke of his hopes for advancement. Then he embarked on a discussion with me about current events, science, or religion. He excluded Mom from these conversations, destroying any pleasure that I might experience. Every time Mom contributed, Dad ignored her. His disrespect was intolerable. I repeated and emphasized every comment Mom made, provoking Dad's anger.

"Dad, listen to Mom. Her question is a really good one." Each time Dad got up and left the table, pursing his lips, which reflected his anger. He looked like a fish when he did that.

Dad's refusal to include Mom undermined her already shaky self-confidence and intensified her chronic shame about having only a grade eight education. It also fuelled a fire inside her that could not be snuffed out.

Over time, I grew more and more angry with Dad to the point that I refused to engage in intellectual discussions with him. Dad and I had many arguments about his rude behaviour. His refrain was a rhetorical question that he blasted at me. "Do you think it is right for children to judge their parents?" I dared not answer. However, I was thinking 'Absolutely. I am eighteen years old, and I have a keen awareness of right and wrong. What you are doing is wrong.'

I wish that I had had the courage to say this to him.

During reading week when my university classes were cancelled, I picked up the newspaper and searched the want ads for part-time jobs. I spotted an ad for telephone sales operators for a department store. I cut the ad out and showed it to Mom.

"Mom, it is not good for you to sit at home and just clean, cook, and read. It would do you a world of good if you got a part-time job. Here is one that I found that I'm sure you could learn how to do. It is taking orders from the catalogue over the phone. What do you think?"

Mom studied the ad. "I only have a grade eight education. They won't hire me."

"There is nothing in the ad about a minimum educational level," I pointed out. "Mom, you should try. Wouldn't you be happier working part time rather than just sitting at home every day?" We both knew the answer.

We also both knew that Dad would be furious if Mom obtained any kind of job. For him, his ability to support his family financially was proof of his success and was a major component of his self-esteem. He had worked continuously and had saved enough money to buy a home for his family, to pay for his daughters' dancing and music lessons, to pay for both to attend university, and to pay for my sister's wedding while, at the same time, supporting his wife. Having a wife who worked, even part time, would be an intolerable insult.

I spent the weekend coaching Mom so that she could respond appropriately to interview questions, especially any that targeted her education. We practised until she became proficient and confident in her responses. With each roleplay we did, Mom's enthusiasm and motivation grew, as did my respect and admiration for her courage.

I wished Mom good luck as I drove to university on the day of her interview. I could hardly concentrate on the lectures. When I came home after classes and opened the front door, I was greeted by Mom's ecstatic announcement. "They hired me on the spot! I start training next week!"

"Congratulations!" I threw myself into her arms and we hugged for a long time. Then she began to speak slowly and softly.

"Rickey, your Dad is not going to like this one bit."

"I know, Mom. This is essential for you, isn't it?" We both knew that it was. "Dad will just have to get used to it, that's all. And he will— somehow."

As anticipated, as soon as Mom told Dad that she had been hired, he exploded. His shouting and stomping around the house were of an intensity that I had not seen before. He said terrible things to her, telling her that she was not smart enough to work, that she would not be able to learn how to do it. Why wasn't she satisfied with the money that he was making? Why didn't she appreciate him? Wasn't it true that he had bought her everything that she wanted and that he even earned enough money for vacations in Florida? All of these questions were fired at her at the loudest possible volume, machine-gun style. Her news was catastrophic for him and his response was catastrophic for us.

Mom told him that she felt as if she was dying sitting at home every day and needed a job to survive. He correctly understood that my silence expressed strong support for her. Mom yelled at him that he did not love her. He yelled at her that she did not love him. The conflict rose in intensity until Mom could not tolerate it anymore and left the house.

I left the house and ran after her. Mom was almost running down the street, as if escaping from a house on fire. When I caught up to her, I saw that she was crying. We walked together silently for over an hour. I found myself feeling hatred for Dad's cruel words and his unreasonable, incomprehensible behaviour.

Only then did I become aware of the enormous reservoir of anger that I felt towards him for his frequent and often unpredictable explosive rages that intimidated and scared me all the years of my life. This latest explosion tipped the reservoir over and I lost sight of all that I loved about him. I told Mom that I wished that Dad was dead. Mom recoiled in shock. "Don't say that! He's my life." Her response was unfathomable and triggered more guilt. I felt terrible that I had caused Mom more pain. I felt like I was a very bad person and tried to forget what I had wished for.

The fight lasted for days. It was their longest, most intense period of strife. Mom held her ground despite Dad's ongoing rages, which alternated with long periods of frigid silence. He slept on the couch and refused to eat any of the food that she prepared. He grimaced in pain whenever I dared to look at him. He pursed his lips so tightly and for so long that I thought that they would become a permanent feature.

Mom did not speak to him. Each evening she tossed the food left on his plate into the backyard for the birds. It was her habit to toss any food that wasn't eaten or that didn't meet her standards into the backyard for the birds. I never told her that it wasn't just birds who ate the meat and pasta and whatever other food ended up in our backyard.

I delayed returning home after my classes every day. The tension at home was intolerable. I hated Dad for creating it. I could not understand his obvious double standard. He expected his two daughters to complete university and pursue careers but he was adamant that his wife not work. It made no sense to me.

This wasn't the first time I was confronted with his double standard. After Mom obtained her driver's licence, she drove me to the library one afternoon. Driving toward the front door, she became aware that she was on the wrong driveway. It was too late. We heard loud, grating, gut-wrenching noises on both sides of the car as it became wedged between two trees. Mom backed up and drove quickly home. When Dad saw the damage, he erupted in rage. His hurtful words and screaming effectively destroyed Mom's desire to drive. She never drove a car again.

When I was a new driver, I was fearful to tell Dad about a fender bender that I had caused while attempting to park. I anticipated that he would scream at me. "Oh, don't worry, Rickey," he began calmly, "these things happen to all new drivers."

I can imagine how hurt Mom must have felt hearing his calm reaction to my mishap.

On the fifth day of the most bitter conflict they had, Dad came to the realization that he had lost. He had no choice but to accept Mom's decision, indeed, to accept her for the person she was. He began to interact with her respectfully again and she reciprocated. Although their battle ended, it took me a long time to forgive him, and even longer to forgive myself. My relationship with Dad had become a lot more complicated.

Mom learned how to do the job much more quickly than she anticipated. Shortly after starting the job, Mom was praised by her supervisor for being an excellent telephone sales operator. She was especially skilled when dealing with angry customers. *No wonder!* Living with Dad had provided her with more than enough practice.

Mom transformed herself by working. Every day when I came home from university, I was met with her animated and excited account of her day at work. On days that she worked, she would rush home to prepare dinner. Dad was angry whenever he had to wait for his meal. As her confidence grew, she became more assertive and was less intimidated by his temper outbursts. I became more and more proud of her.

About six months after she started to work, I did some research into options for mature students at York University. "You've always said that you feel bad that you only had a grade eight education. Here are university level courses that anyone over fifty can take for a low fee. You have the money since you've been working. Why don't you take one course and see how you like it? If you don't like it, you can always withdraw."

The course that interested her most was English literature. She had already read most of the classics that were the focus of this year-long course. I told her that I would help by editing any essays that she was required to write. Buoyed up by her success at work, she registered at York University and enrolled in a first-year English literature course.

During her year at university, it was obvious that Dad was treating Mom with a lot more respect. His outbursts became less frequent. He did not say much about her becoming a university student. Perhaps, he felt that there was no point in trying to hold her back. Perhaps, for now, he had no more fight left in him. I think that, despite himself, he felt proud of her. Although no words were spoken, I felt that his unusually quieter mood also spoke of his envy for the opportunity she had. He had advanced in the factory to become the production manager. But he never achieved his dream of studying at university. My anger towards him slowly melted into heartfelt compassion.

Growing up and watching their stormy love affair, I often wondered how it was that they had chosen to marry. I think back to the stories they told me about their first encounters. Even now, I am left with more questions than answers.

It is often powerful feelings that propel us forward when we choose a partner, emotions that cannot be adequately explained and analyzed, and that often fly in the face of reason.

19

Not at First Sight

Al started to work at the Molson's Bag and Paper Company in 1929, when he was 17 years old. As the years passed, his hatred toward his father grew.

Al's mother, Rose, worshipped him. Rose cooked his favourite food and served him the biggest helping. Al expected no less for his sacrifice.

"Al, you will always be my special one, my precious one," his mother would tell him each night before he went to bed.

Al's work ethic was impeccable. He was at the factory at seven o'clock every morning even though his shift started at eight. During that hour, he examined the machines and carefully explored how each one worked. He mixed various inks to learn how to create different colours, saturations, and textures. He experimented with the stamps to note how the colours of the letters contrasted with background shades. Al's goal was to advance to the position of mechanic.

Each time a machine broke down, and his boss, Mr. Molson, hired a mechanic, Al studied every move that the mechanic made like a medical intern observes a surgeon performing an operation. It didn't take long before Mr. Molson took note of his skills and called upon Al before hiring a mechanic.

At the conclusion of his tenth year at the factory, Al was promoted to the position of mechanic and machine operator and received a raise. His mother and siblings were ecstatic. Al had enabled his sisters and brother to attend school with full stomachs. They would never have to leave school to get jobs. Al was proud of his achievement but also consumed with envy and grief for his sacrifice.

Al was a voracious reader and made frequent trips to the library. His views about communism were reinforced. He dreamed of a world with social ownership of all production and distribution, 'from each according to his ability; to each according to his needs.'

Al had witnessed the suffering of workers during the Great Depression. He had been moved by the 1935 dockers' strike at the Ballantyne Pier in Vancouver and had been repulsed when he learned about Bloody Sunday in 1938. Workers who had been on strike at the Vancouver Post Office had been beaten by the police. Al felt fortunate to have a job and to be paid a decent wage. He knew that many other workers were suffering terrible injustices. In his mind, unbridled capitalism was monstrous. He believed that communism would bring fairness, equality, and security to all.

One day when Al was on his way home from the factory, he overheard a co-worker talking about the United Jewish People's Order, a group that supported Marxism. He attended his first meeting in 1939 and quickly became a vocal participant. He invited his sister, Sylvia, to sing in the choir that some members had formed.

One evening, five years later, Hilda, Faye's closest friend, told her that she had heard about this group. "It has something to do with politics. Fritzi is interested. Let's all go to the next meeting."

In the main room, the meeting began and a tall, slim, dark-haired man stood up and spoke in a commanding voice. "I want to welcome you all here. It is wonderful to see some new faces. We stand with all the workers in the world who are oppressed. All that we work for will one day be shared fairly." Everyone applauded. "My name is Al Miller." Al provided an eloquent lecture about the principles of Marxism.

Faye turned to Hilda. "He's brilliant, isn't he?"

"Yes, and quite good looking, too."

The meeting progressed with discussions about ways of providing support to Joseph Baruch Salsberg who had been elected as an alderman on Toronto's city council. There was an announcement that he might run in the provincial election in 1943.

At the conclusion of the meeting, Al invited questions.

All the political talk bored Hilda and Fritzi. They left early. Faye remained to the end. She had a question but was too anxious to raise it in front of everyone.

Faye had just completed grade eight when the Great Depression exploded in her world. Faye had to get a job.

When she attended the meeting, Faye was twenty-eight years old. She had been working for ten years at the Silk Knit factory where she operated a sewing machine to make lace.

As she moved closer to Al, she was struck by his handsome face, which, together with his intelligence and eloquence, conspired to make him irresistibly attractive. "I know that your group supports Joe Salsberg. If he gets elected, what would he do for us?"

"You obviously haven't been listening to anything I said," Al's tone was patronizing. "I explained how he wants to form better unions to represent the interests of workers, including those in the garment industry. I also explained how he wants to stop racist policies that ban Blacks and Jews from using certain swimming pools in Toronto." Then his tone became scolding, "If you had been listening, you would have heard all that." He abruptly turned and walked away.

"I was listening!" Faye retorted loudly. "Thank you for taking the time to explain!" She said with biting sarcasm. She did not know whether or not Al had heard her but she did not care. What a rude, arrogant man, she thought.

The next time she met Hilda and Fritzi, Faye told them about her encounter with Al. "He is horrible! What a nerve, talking to me like that, after saying that he welcomed newcomers! I hope I never see that man again."

Al's handsome face, slim build, dark wavy hair, and brilliant mind guaranteed him popularity with women. He was proud that women adored him. No matter which woman he dated, for some strange reason he kept remembering the face and voice of that woman who had asked him the question at the meeting a month ago, and her feisty retort. There was something attractive about her that he could not identify. It was more than her lovely face, which, with each passing day, he remembered as more and more beautiful. He looked for her at each meeting, but, alas, she was never there.

One of Al's friends knew Hilda. Al called her and found out where Faye lived. After supper he showered. He was fastidious about his personal hygiene since working at the factory was a dirty job. He combed his thick, dark hair until every hair was in place.

As Al approached Faye's home he saw an almost constant stream of people entering and exiting. He wondered if there was a party going on. As he drew closer, a chorus of familiar Yiddish songs spilled out of an open window along with the delectable scent of fresh latkes. The front door was open as he approached. He felt welcomed by the joyful commotion and walked inside. Looking into the kitchen, he saw an older woman frying latkes and singing along with a group who were in another room. People in the hallway continued to carry on their conversations in Yiddish. No one noticed his presence.

How strange! At his home, the front door was always locked and no one ever came to visit. His house was quiet. This house was alive with conversation, laughter, and music, and with people coming and going.

Even though his back was turned, he sensed that someone was staring at him from the end of the hallway. He spun around. His eyes met Faye's. Her shocked expression melted as he smiled. Despite her best efforts to conjure up her negative feelings, a smile of delight lit up her face. Slowly she walked down the hall, oblivious to the people she brushed by who were still involved in their conversations. Al made his way outside. He knew that Faye would follow.

Faye was flattered that Al remembered her and had made a point to find her home. She was curious about him. Their conversation flowed effortlessly. They told each other about their jobs, their families, and their friends. They discussed their sympathy for the poor and jobless. They shared thoughts about the books that they had read. They discovered that they had often visited the library on the same day.

When they discussed religion, Al told her that he was Orthodox and kept strictly kosher. Faye said that her family was not religious. Neither of them felt that this difference was important. After all, Al thought, if the relationship works out, Faye will meet my needs and keep a strictly kosher home.

After they parted, Al walked home, smiling all the way. Faye's smile did not fade until she was fast asleep.

As the weeks flew by and his relationship with Faye grew closer, Al felt increasing pressure to invite her to his house to meet his family. He was filled with anxiety about this. His father was never at home. The mood in the house was as downcast as his mother's mood. He worried that Faye might think less of him after the visit. One fall evening, Al finally summoned the courage to invite Faye to meet his family.

Faye was greeted politely by his mother who invited her to sit in their small living room with Al's sisters Sylvia and Susan, and brother, Solly. Faye was immediately struck by the stillness in the house. There was a heavy sadness in the air that hung like thick fog. The house was sparsely furnished. There were no pictures on the walls. Looking down, Faye saw a layer of dust that had accumulated on the area rug.

"It is good to meet all of you," Faye began in her most cheerful voice, attempting to dispel the sadness. "Have you been living here long?"

"Pretty long," Rose responded quietly. A long awkward silence followed.

"Sylvia, Al told me that you sing in the choir at his group's meetings. Do you like singing there?"

"Yes. I do." Sylvia's curt response was followed by the same uncomfortable silence.

"It's too bad I don't have a chance to meet Mr. Miller. Please let him know that I wish he could have been here."

Rose winced at the mention of her husband's name. "He's out tonight," was all that she said.

Faye was desperate to end her futile attempts at conversation. She was irritated that the task had fallen on her. Al did not help at all. No one asked her anything about her life and her family. There was no offer of food or drink. She did not see the lack of hospitality as unfriendliness. It was sadness; intense grief, as if someone had just died.

Faye looked at Al with eyes pleading to leave. Fourteen-year-old Susan was squirming in her chair and suddenly jumped up. "Let me give you a tour of our house." Everyone relaxed as Faye and Susan left the room.

Faye followed Susan up the narrow staircase into the hallway adjoining several tiny bedrooms. "I look up to my brother, Faye. We all do," she whispered. "He's more like a father to us than our father. We would not have survived if it wasn't for my brother. But, Faye, he has a really bad temper. You are an absolute angel to be in love with him. He is not easy to live with. I love him but I'm afraid of him."

The warning came as a most unwelcome shock.

"Don't worry, Susan. Al has never been angry with me and we have been dating for almost one year now."

As they walked back to her home, Faye and Al had nothing to say. The required formality had been completed. Faye could not wait to return to her boisterous home, which seemed more alive than ever. The chatter and singing drowned out Susan's warning, which moved to the very back of Faye's mind.

Faye's mother began to sew her wedding dress in the fall as her wedding date of December 22, 1944, drew near. Faye's friends took up a collection to buy her white canna lilies for her wedding bouquet.

Al was glowing as he watched his beautiful bride walk down the aisle, arm in arm with her mother and stepfather. Al was wearing a black rented suit. He had bought a simple gold wedding band to match the engagement ring he had given Faye a few months earlier. Under the plain canopy, Faye walked around Al seven times. The devotion and love they exchanged in their glances each time Faye faced Al was so strong that they barely heard the rabbi's words. When Al smashed the glass, there was a deafening chorus of mazel tovs.

A small band from the Yiddish Theatre played one of Faye's favourite pieces, by Iosif Ivanovici, the Waves of the Danube waltz, also called

The Anniversary Song. Faye and Al rose and danced as husband and wife. Then everyone danced the horah to klezmer music.

For dinner there were little sandwiches prepared by the Yiddish Theatre group and for dessert, cookies and cakes that Faye's mom had baked. There were short speeches and a toast with glasses of soda and juice. A theatre friend who had a camera took a few photos.

Al had rented a small apartment, which became their first home. Shortly after the wedding, Faye was promoted to forelady at the Silk Knit factory. Al looked forward to the day when his wife could become a proper housewife and not have to work. Faye shared his goal. She was looking forward to becoming a mother.

From the outset, Faye had a struggle on her hands trying to please Al with her cooking. She had no problem agreeing to keep strictly kosher. However, no matter how much effort she put into the meals, most of the time Al would push his plate away with disgust, and angrily leave the table.

On their first anniversary, Faye decided to surprise Al by making a brisket. This was a delicacy that took a full day to prepare. She was certain that Al would love this meal.

Faye set the table and placed a candle in the middle. She created an anniversary card for Al and placed it on the table in front of his chair.

When Al came home, he looked worn. The aroma in the air caught his attention. "What have you cooked?"

"It's a surprise, sweetheart," Faye began. "Happy anniversary!" Faye hugged him.

"Happy anniversary," Al responded in a tired voice. He proceeded with his usual ritual to shower and clean away all evidence of the factory. When he entered the kitchen, they exchanged anniversary cards, proclaiming their love for each other. They hugged and kissed.

"Look what I made for us! It's brisket!" Faye announced exuberantly. She served Al and then herself and lit the candle and waited.

Al's downcast expression after he swallowed his first bite of meat cut through her heart. "Is something wrong?" she asked.

"This meat is dry like sawdust!" Al pushed the plate away.

"It is not dry like sawdust at all!" Faye responded angrily. "The meat couldn't be any juicier. It soaked in the braising juices before you arrived."

"No. It has been ruined. I'm not eating that!" Al got up from the table leaving Faye in tears. She felt as rejected as the meat on his plate. Al returned to the kitchen a short time later and began to open cupboards, removing cans of beans and corn. "There must be something decent in this house to eat!" he shouted, ignoring Faye's weeping.

The next day Faye poured the contents of the roasting pan into one of the many large plastic Molson bags that Al had brought home, tied up the top, and dumped it into the garbage can outside.

Faye never stopped trying to please Al with her cooking. For years she served up her self-esteem to him with every plate of food. Every time his temper flared, Faye recalled Susan's warning. Despite the pain he inflicted, Faye's love for Al and her commitment to stay with him did not waver.

20

The Breaking Point

In 1945 Solly Miller was eighteen years old. He had just graduated from high school and was searching for a job to help support the family. He knew that Al could not send money to the family indefinitely now that he was married.

One evening Solly was walking home with a friend. Looking up at a stop sign, his friend challenged Solly to jump up and touch the sign. Solly's friend tried first and hit the sign with his right hand. Solly jumped up. The top of his head bumped into the sign. He touched his head and was relieved to see that it was not bleeding. "I'm okay," he said as they continued their walk. When he got home Solly casually mentioned to his mother that he had banged his head on the stop sign while playing with his friend. Rose ran her fingers through his hair and detected a small bump. "It's nothing, Mom." Solly said good night and went to bed.

In the morning, Rose prepared breakfast as usual and waited for Solly to come downstairs to join Sylvia and Susan. She went upstairs and called out behind his closed door, "Solly, wake up. Breakfast is ready." There was no answer. Rose trembled with fear as she opened the door to see Solly's lifeless body lying face up on his bed, his gaze permanently fixed on the ceiling. She was paralyzed by the horror of the scene. She could not utter a word for a long time. Then she collapsed on the floor, wailing loudly, and crying out, "How can this be? He is eighteen years old."

Susan and Sylvia ran upstairs. The three of them clung to each other, their weeping and cries of disbelief swirled around them like a hurricane sweeping through the house.

Even when Rose stood up again, her spirit was still lying on the floor in a pool of tears, and that is where it remained for the rest of her life.

Rose called Al and could barely get the words out. He called an ambulance and then ran to the house. He hugged his mother but there was no consoling her.

Weeks after the shiva, Al opened a letter that his mother had received from the hospital. The description of the deceased read like an excerpt from an anatomy text. Al made himself read every word. The letter ended with the probable cause of death: a cerebral hemorrhage due to an aneurysm that was likely congenital and could have occurred at any time.

Unbeknownst to the family, Solly's friend, who heard the dreadful news, was consumed with guilt. He felt certain that the game had led to Solly's death. Every February 9 for many years, a letter with no return address and no note inside was sent to the Miller's home with a one-dollar bill. Al believed that it came from Solly's friend.

Somehow, Rose found the strength to continue to care for Sylvia and Susan despite her deep grief and depression. It's hard to imagine how she carried on after losing three children in Russia and then Solly and having a husband who was not there for her.

Each of the many degrees of resilience requires a choice. In the face of calamity, do we choose self-care or self-destruction? Do we choose to love others or withdraw?

I have never fully understood what accounts for the choices so many of my patients made to climb up from their pit of despair and embrace life again. Hearing their stories, I inevitably asked myself if I were faced with such calamities, would I make that choice?

21

The One with No Name

It was 1952. Earlier that year Dad had learned that his father was at the end of his life with lung cancer. Dad visited him in the hospital during his last weeks and was filled with ambivalent storms of emotion. There was no peace in his heart as his father's coffin was lowered into the ground.

Shortly after the funeral, Mom told six-year-old Terry that she was going to have a baby brother or sister. The pregnancy was uneventful. Labour lasted only for a few hours. Mom was ecstatic when the physician presented her with a beautiful baby boy. Dad's heart sang. He planned the bris. It would help lift his mother's spirits for sure. It certainly lifted his. Mom and Dad began thinking of names.

Two days after giving birth, Mom was sitting up in bed, her breasts filled with milk, in anticipation of the nurse bringing her baby to her as usual.

As she waited, Mom could hear the tiny gurgling and burping sounds coming from inside the drawn curtains around the beds of the other three women in the ward as their babies suckled. The beautiful sounds triggered her let down reflex and milk dribbled from her swollen breasts. She waited.

And waited.

And waited.

Finally, a physician and nurse walked solemnly up to her bed and drew the curtain quickly. The nurse was holding some kind of equipment with a rubber funnel.

"I'm sorry to tell you this, but your baby has died." The words, spoken without a pause, without any warning, exploded in the air. Mom could not breathe.

You must have the wrong mother. My baby looked fine. He had all his fingers and toes. The expressions on the faces of the nurse and physician made it clear that there had been no mistake.

A long silence followed. Finally, tears were falling down Mom's face, a seemingly endless stream of agony. She felt heartbroken for herself and for Al. How could he possibly cope with yet another loss?

The nurse showed her the breast milk pump and told her how to use it. Mom wanted to throw it at the physician and nurse as they walked out of the room. Instead, she forced herself to press the funnel against her swollen breasts and pump out the milk while she watched the other nurses tenderly carry the newborns across the room and down the hall to the nursery. She knew that the nurses would be bringing the babies back a few hours later. She hated her swollen breasts and the milk they exuded. She hated her body for failing her and her baby. It was the ultimate betrayal.

Mom was forced to endure the torture of watching the other three mothers lovingly receiving their babies again and again and listening to the sounds of the mother's tender words and the babies suckling, sounds that ripped Mom's broken heart into shreds. It seemed like an eternity before she was allowed to go home.

There was no funeral for the dead baby boy. It was as if he had never been.

Soon after this loss Dad was rushed to the hospital. He was moved into intensive care with ulcerative colitis. Every day Mom visited with Terry and heard the physician's dismal prognosis.

"He might not survive. There has been a lot of internal bleeding. His gut is completely inflamed."

Each evening Mom and Terry lingered by Al's bedside for hours, wondering if this would be the last time they would see him alive. He darted in and out of consciousness, death making its strong appeal to his wish for an end to the pain. The bleeding ulcers in his gut were burning him from the inside out as much as his grief. Death tempted him with the promise of peace and escape from this unjust world.

Dad resisted. He could not allow himself to succumb. To do so would be the ultimate self-betrayal. What of his mother? What of his wife and daughter? And so, slowly, he climbed back towards the light. It took weeks before he was well enough to be discharged home where Mom took care of him.

After Dad recovered, Mom told him that she could not go on unless she had another baby. Not long after, she became pregnant again.

When Mom was in her last trimester, Rose was diagnosed with tuberculosis and hospitalized in a sanatorium. Al knew that she would not survive long. Ever since Solly's death, he felt that his mother was holding onto life by a thread.

I was born on April 1, 1953, a few months after Rose died. My parents celebrated my birth as the dawn of a new era and held their breath for the first few days, praying that I would survive.

Mom's choice was to repress her pain about the loss of her baby and push it as far away from conscious awareness as possible. She could not allow herself the luxury of feeling compassion for herself as this would bring with it the danger of releasing a flood of pain and risk emotional collapse. She treated others in the same way. 'Pull your socks up. Stop feeling sorry for yourself. You've got to go on.' These were mantras for herself and for me during hard times. For this reason, despite her loving and soft heart, she often came across as cold and unfeeling.

The thought that comes to mind now is the irony that Mom, with her tough exterior, often referred to Terry as a cold and unfeeling person, without every acknowledging that she often came across that way, too.

22

Never the Same

Even though we know that each child in a family is unique, we still often react with surprise. "They are so different even though they were raised by the same parents."

The parents are the same in name only. The relationships between the mother and father and each child can never be the same. The parents' circumstances and their life experiences vary over time. The way they interact with each child is unique. And each child is a unique human being and interacts with each parent differently.

The circumstances of Terry's birth and childhood and mine could not have been more different.

Mom was thrilled when she became pregnant with Terry in 1946. She continued to work at the Silk Knit factory until late into her ninth month.

Mom and Dad celebrated the arrival of their first born. For the first few years, child care went smoothly and came naturally to Mom. She was happy to give up her job to be at home with Terry. Dad earned enough for his wife and baby girl. He was proud that his wife did not have to work and that she was a real housewife.

According to Mom, all this abruptly changed when Terry was three. Terry started to vomit just about everything she ate. Mom tried to give her different foods but the outcome was the same. Concerned because Terry was losing weight, Faye took her to Dr. Snelling, her paediatrician.

After completing a thorough examination, including chest fluoroscopy, Dr. Snelling reassured Mom. "She is fine. I see nothing wrong. This is probably only a phase and will pass."

In the days that followed, Terry continued to vomit after every meal. She continued to lose weight.

After supper one night, as soon as Terry swallowed her last mouthful of food, Dad unleashed threatening, furious words. Hunched over, facing Terry directly, his body struck a terrifying pose as he screamed. "Don't you dare throw up!" His shouting escalated in intensity and he stomped his foot to emphasize his words. Dad's shouting carried with it a threat that something terrible was going to happen if Terry vomited again.

"Al, stop shouting at her! They can hear you in Hamilton! Sit down! Look at how you have terrified her!" Mom shouted back.

Dad sat down, his body tense, ready to explode again if he saw any sign of another vomit eruption. He stared at Terry, daring her to call his bluff. Mom told me that Terry cried for a long time afterwards and could not be comforted.

Dad's terrifying fury did its work. Terry was cured. She never threw up again after a meal.

My parents did not know that they had fanned a smouldering fire, ensuring that it would continue to burn. It never occurred to Mom and Dad that Terry's problem might have a psychological origin, that perhaps it was her way of communicating that her emotional needs were not being met. It never occurred to them that Dad's furious and terrifying behaviour had damaged their relationship with Terry and caused her great pain.

After their baby boy died, Mom and Dad were too preoccupied with their grief to consider the impact this loss had on Terry. Neither did they consider the impact Dad's hospitalization and coming close to death had on her. The way that they related to her was also influenced by Terry's unique temperament and personality. As a child, they described her as extraverted, bold, defiant at times, and very intelligent.

My arrival after the loss of their baby boy was greeted as a blessing. The easy and affectionate temperament of their new baby girl was a welcome focus for my parents, carrying them away from their almost intolerable pain of loss.

It would have been natural for Terry to resent the love and affection Mom and Dad bestowed upon the new baby, thus, fuelling the fire burning within her.

Mom and Dad related differently to each of us as we did with them. As the years unfolded, the chasm that separated Terry and me became much greater than the seven years between our births.

I admired Terry's verbal fighting skills except when she turned them on me at which times I was utterly defenseless. Whenever Terry teased and hurt me, I was left with more anger towards myself than towards her. As time went on, I became more and more fearful of Terry. She became primarily a source of pain to be avoided.

Terry never backed down from Dad no matter how loud he shouted. Whereas my defense was to cower and cry, Terry would shout back and jab Dad with unexpected and logical responses. Clouded by anger, he was unable to refute logically and could only shout and fire back insults. Terry would continue to slice through his rage with razor-sharp retorts. I hated the arguments that she provoked and fuelled. They left a suffocating tension in the house that often lasted for days. Coping with the frequent arguments between Mom and Dad was hard enough.

I resorted to biting my nails without conscious awareness of the reasons and, very often, without conscious awareness that I was doing it. Later, I understood that as Dad, in particular, hated the way my nails looked, this habit served the dual purpose of reducing some of my tension and getting back at him. When he shouted at me to stop biting my nails, I felt more anxiety and anger and I automatically bit them more. It was a cycle that repeated itself for years.

Terry seemed to take pleasure in provoking Mom and Dad, especially shocking them. One weekend day, a very strong, smoky odour was seeping out of her bedroom. When Mom opened the door to investigate, Terry walked out, her chin held high, proudly displaying a pipe held between her teeth. It had the desired effect.

"This is a terrible thing that you are doing, Terry! What kind of a girl smokes a pipe!"

Dad jumped out of his La-Z-Boy chair and screamed louder, "No girl should ever smoke a pipe! What's the matter with you?"

Of course, their reaction ensured that Terry kept smoking her pipe. Looking back, I see how we were both motivated to provoke Mom and Dad, albeit in different ways.

Terry and I took piano lessons. There was one piece that Terry liked to play a lot. It was 'Jesu, Joy of Man's Desiring' by Bach. To this day, every time I hear that piece on the piano, my heart warms as I recall Terry playing it in the basement on our little apartment-sized piano.

I was nine years old when sixteen-year-old Terry began her university studies, having completed high school in three years rather than four. One late spring day in her first year, Terry told me that one of her professors had invited her to spend the day at his house and that he had a swimming pool in his backyard. She asked me if I wanted to join her. I was thrilled. She had never asked me to go anywhere with her.

While I was swimming, the professor greeted Terry warmly and asked for my name. He motioned for Terry to go inside with him. I was pleased when Terry told him that she wanted to watch me swim instead.

The professor's wife was lying on her stomach on her lounge chair, tanning herself. As I was swimming lengths of the pool, she turned over so that she was lying on her back. I couldn't believe my eyes. Her big, ballooning breasts were in full view, pointing skywards. I had never seen a woman topless before. I stopped swimming and didn't know where to look. Terry saw my discomfort and chuckled. She came over to me and said, "It's her home. She can do what she wants." It seemed to me that she was doing something bad.

A radio sat on a little table by her side. The joyful tones of Ronald Binge's *Elizabethan Serenade* drifted through the air. Terry was in the pool swimming with me. I felt the embrace of the gentle breeze and the warmth of the sun shining down on us. The water sparkled and shimmered as did the delight in my heart.

For a brief moment in time, my sister and I were friends.

23

Eyes Wide Open

By the time I was studying psychology at graduate school, I had spent years observing and trying to analyze the patterns of interactions that took place between Terry, Mom, Dad, and me. I understood that getting what I wanted depended more on the nature of my relationship with the other person at the time than on the specific words that I used.

How is it that I discounted the importance of my relationship with my patient when I attempted hypnosis for the first time? I naively thought that I only had to use the right words.

Dr. Cummings taught us a straightforward relaxation procedure to induce a trance. We watched as he hypnotized a patient behind a one-way mirror. Each of us would do the same with a different patient while the others watched.

When it was my turn, I was terrified. I focused on saying all the right words and in the most hypnotic tone I could muster. Carolyn was a young woman with short blond hair and lovely blue eyes. Her posture was relaxed in contrast to mine. After I introduced myself, and told her a little about hypnosis and how it might help her reduce her anxiety, she responded softly. "Yes, I'm ready to try."

Struggling to focus on the patient rather than on the one-way mirror, I began. "When you are ready, you can close your eyes and begin to feel yourself going down deeper, towards a comforting feeling of relaxation…"

Carolyn sat in front of me, stiffly, with her eyes wide open. I continued with the induction just as I had been instructed, using my most soothing tone.

"Just let your eyes close, easily, and naturally…" Her eyes remained open.

"You can loosen the muscles all around your face, your forehead, your eyes, your cheeks, your mouth, your jaw… just as much as you would like. Let the tension dissipate. Feel your eyes gently and easily closing…" Her eyes were still open.

I tried to hide my frustration with Carolyn. Refusing to give up, I continued to give her suggestion after suggestion that her eyes would close to the point that I began to hypnotize myself.

The session was interrupted by a soft knocking on the door. I excused myself, opened the door, and was embarrassed to see Dr. Cummings smiling at me. He ushered me into the hall.

"Rickey, you can go on while her eyes are open. She doesn't need to close them." That idea had never occurred to me.

During the discussion with the class afterwards, Dr. Cummings turned to me. "I knew what you were saying in your head, Rickey. 'Close your eyes, God damn it!'" Everyone laughed. So did I.

Dr. Cummings went on. "When we use the patients' behaviour as grist for the mill, they cannot fail. In your case you could have said, 'Let your eyes close or keep them open. Do whatever you choose as you let the tension go.' Psychological treatment is evidence-based and also an art requiring creativity and flexibility. Be wary of manuals or cookbook approaches. They may be useful guides but there is no one approach that helps everyone. Each psychologist establishes a unique relationship with each patient. It is this relationship, not technique or approach, that accounts for outcomes more than anything else."

Carolyn must have seen my frustration and likely felt frustrated herself. I looked forward to our next session when I would focus, first and foremost, on building a compassionate working relationship with her, whether she chose to open or close her eyes.

24

The Emerging Scientist

In many of our supervisory sessions, Dr. Kramer discussed his research about attribution theory. He explained. "The way people attribute outcomes determines how they act. Some mostly attribute outcomes to others or to chance while some mostly attribute outcomes to themselves." I did not have sufficient interest to consider the significance of my own attributions. Now I know that attributing most outcomes to my own efforts is a strength when it inspires me to work towards goals but a weakness when I blame myself for outcomes that are out of my control. Achieving a balance between the two, that is the goal.

I was pressed to find a research topic for my Master's thesis. Journeying from lonely times in my childhood to basking in my love for Luke, the importance of social intimacy jumped out as the focus. Having a close relationship appeared to be crucial for emotional and physical health. I dove into the research literature. There was an important gap. I could not find a measure of social intimacy that could be applied to any kind of human interaction.

I was anxious when I pitched my Master's thesis proposal to Dr. Kramer. I expected that he would want me to engage in his research. His authoritarian manner was as intimidating as his height and his booming voice. He was a tall, slim man with a very commanding presence.

Looking back, I can see that in many ways, he reminded me of Dad. No doubt, my experience dealing with Dad helped me cope with Dr. Kramer.

I summoned the courage to speak assertively. "My goal is to construct a measure that assesses the level of closeness that one person has with another. There is evidence in the literature that supports the hypothesis that intimacy moderates stress and plays a protective role in health."

It was an easier sell than I had anticipated. Dr. Kramer immediately began to work with me, posing questions that I should consider in order to reach my goal. He could not have been more encouraging. I was greatly relieved.

In a class about cognitive-behavioural approaches, Dr. Thompson asked us to guess the modal number of publications of all the psychology students who had graduated from the university to date. "What number occurs most often in this set of data?" No one guessed. "It's zero!" He said angrily. "That means most of our students have published nothing! Your class has shown great promise with your research backgrounds. I am certain that the modal number won't be zero for you."

I was not at all motivated to publish papers to build my curriculum vitae or to bring honour to the university. However, I could not have been more motivated to publish a paper that furthered our understanding of human behaviour.

Working on my first draft of the social intimacy scale, I spent hours every day for weeks keypunching cards in the basement of the mathematics building. It was often difficult to concentrate due to the deafening noise made by the enormous computers that stretched from one wall to the other, taking up most of the basement. I fed the cards into the computer again and again to obtain various statistical analyses. After that, I stood in line to wait for the printer to produce endless perforated sheets of data.

My analyses provided support for the scale's reliability and construct validity. I was intrigued by the possibility that social intimacy might predict physical health and recovery from illness and injuries, as well as help people cope with stress. Thus began my life-long journey into the fascinating realm of health psychology, focusing on the intricate interplay of mind and body.

After I completed and defended my Master's thesis, Dr. Kramer encouraged me to write a paper to introduce the intimacy scale to the world. It was thrilling to think that if my scale was published, it might help other scientists discover more about the important role of close relationships.

Dr. Kramer and I were delighted when *The Journal of Personality Assessment* accepted my paper without revisions. Almost immediately, other researchers contacted me to ask permission to use the Miller Social Intimacy Scale in their investigations.

Each time a researcher employs the scale, I feel tremendous satisfaction that I have contributed a little to our understanding of human interaction. Each enquiry also leaves me with a deep feeling of gratitude that I had the opportunity to study at university. I never take this privilege for granted.

When I was in my fourth year, Luke graduated. He wanted to establish his business in Toronto. I looked forward to moving back to Toronto so that I could be closer to Mom. I rented a room near the university and drove in on Mondays, returning to Toronto on Thursdays each week. I was highly motivated to complete my graduate training as soon as possible so that Luke and I could be together all week.

Dr. Kramer asked me to help him with his research that involved using his video recorder. On one occasion, he stormed into my office and accused me of leaving his camera on the day before. "I told you that you have to shut it off and cover the lens with the cap! Otherwise, the whole thing can burn out." His roar was extremely embarrassing. Not only did Leon witness this attack as he was in the office at the time but I was certain that all the students and professors down the hall had heard it as well.

"Dr. Kramer, I am certain that I turned it off." I was shrinking before him and began to doubt myself. *Had I turned it off and covered the lens?*

Dr. Kramer paused and looked up as if something had just occurred to him. I made myself even smaller, prepared for more shouting. Then he began in his usual loud tone. "I just wanted to see your reaction. I know you turned it off. I scared you, didn't I?" Turning to Leon, he said, "Did you see her face when I shouted at her and she thought that she had ruined my camera?" Dr. Kramer snickered. Leon's sympathetic look only intensified my embarrassment.

Dr. Kramer's behaviour was impossible to understand. A short time after this incident, he invited me to join him for dinner at his home. He and his wife were hospitable, warm hosts, and I enjoyed spending the evening with them. It was clear that Dr. Kramer liked me. There was something that I liked about him.

I studied almost every day for a full year before passing 'Specials.' These were comprehensive written examinations that covered the universe of psychology and required creative thinking more than just regurgitating facts. They took two full days to write. I was relieved when Dr. Thompson came to my office a few weeks later and simply said, "You can go on now." This indicated that I had passed. There was no celebration of this major achievement.

However, there was a very memorable celebration that took place after the five of us successfully completed our first year. This was validation for our professors that they had made the correct admission choices and that each of us would achieve our Ph.D. degrees.

Dr. Collin, who co-led our hypnosis course, announced that he would like to celebrate with us at a restaurant close to campus. He was serious, emotionally controlled, and never joked with us. I hoped that he might loosen up during this event.

When we sat down to order, I was surprised when Dr. Collin ordered three bottles of wine. Dr. Collin filled our glasses generously and immediately refilled them when they were empty. As the evening progressed, we all loosened up.

After a delightful meal, Dr. Collin told us that he was taking us to a show. I wondered what kind of movie he had in mind. Turning to Michelle, I said, "I don't know whether I will be able to understand any movie in my intoxicated state."

We piled into Dr. Collin's station wagon.

"How strange!" I say loudly, the words echoing in my empty office. *Who knows how much he had to drink?* At the time, it did not occur to me that Dr. Collin may have been impaired and should not have driven us anywhere even though it was a short drive to the theatre. My only thought at the time was that he was generous and kind to buy us dinner and tickets to a show.

Inside the theatre, I was surprised to see the stage moving up and down after I took my seat. In fact, the entire theatre appeared to be moving up and down.

"Where is the movie screen?" I asked Michelle.

Michelle mumbled her answer. "I don't see it, Rickey. I've never had so much alcohol in my whole life."

After several minutes, loud pop music with a heavy bass sound and a lot of percussion filled the theatre. Women and men began to dance on the stage. "I guess this is a dancing show," I said to Michelle. All at once, the men left the stage and the women began to undress. I had never seen a dancing show like this before. The women did not stop undressing until they were nude, although it took them a long time before all their clothes were off. Then they left the stage and the men came back. I wondered if the dance required the men to do the same thing. I had heard about women taking off their clothes in certain shows, but not men. This dancing show was different. The men began to take off their shirts, their pants, even their underwear. They were quite pleasant to look at, although every part of them was bobbing up and down as was the stage. I thought to myself, well, at least this show is egalitarian.

After the show, I called Luke and asked him to pick me up. The next morning, I woke up with a massive headache.

I was proud to hold the record at that time for graduating from the combined Master's and Doctoral program in five years. The average was ten. My efficiency was a direct reflection of my motivation to live with Luke full-time and to obtain a position in a general hospital.

The day that I left the university after defending my dissertation, Dr. Kramer met me in the stairwell. I spoke warmly to him. "I want to thank you for all your help and support. Goodbye for now."

"I don't know how you can say goodbye," was all Dr. Kramer said. He had sad eyes as he looked at me and then continued to walk upstairs to his office.

25

Waking Up in Detroit

I was thrilled when I was accepted by a psychiatric clinic in Detroit, Michigan, for my required one-year internship. I had been granted interviews at three internship settings, all of them in the United States.

In August, Luke and I drove across the border and rented an apartment on Sixth Avenue. Luke's cousins who lived in Detroit contributed a bridge table and chairs for our kitchen. We bought a bed and a few inexpensive folding chairs for our living room. Detroit newspapers became blinds for our windows.

Luke commuted to Toronto on Tuesdays and returned to Detroit on Saturdays. Every Saturday evening, I drove to Windsor and waited impatiently for his train to arrive. We rushed into each other's arms for a long embrace before driving across the border to enjoy dinner at one of our favourite restaurants. Even though we spoke on the phone every day, it was difficult for us to part for five days each week.

The first day of my internship, I drove to the clinic using the route that I had practised a few times in the previous week. Anxious and excited, I pulled into the parking lot. A security guard came up to my car.

"Good morning," I said cheerfully.

"Ma'am, why are you pulling into the parking lot?"

"I'm one of the new psychology interns," I said proudly.

"You can't park here," was his response.

"Where are we supposed to park?"

"On the street. Wherever you can find a space."

Surely, he must not have heard me. "You don't understand, sir. I am one of four psychology interns starting to work today." There was no question in my mind that this afforded me sufficient status to park in the clinic's lot.

"I understood perfectly," he said in a snarling tone. "Go find a place on the street. Only staff park here. Now back out!!"

How insulting!

The search for parking on one of the local streets in downtown Detroit was frustrating and time consuming. It was an aggravating treasure hunt that I had to engage in every morning of the year.

My internship hours were brutal. My day at the clinic began at seven thirty in the morning and continued into the evening. I worked fifty to sixty hours every week. On weekends I woke up, ate breakfast, and went back to bed, where I slept for much of the day.

I was assigned two rotations of six months each. One was with outpatient children and adults and the other was with inpatient adolescents.

The clinic drew patients from inner-city Detroit. I was working with people whose problems were more serious than those whom I had treated in Toronto. Many nights I was kept awake by questions about the decisions I had made and the words that I had spoken.

During my outpatient rotation with children, I was surprised to learn that the clinic did not have a playroom. Dr. Peroni, my supervising psychologist, allowed me to borrow the toys, games, and puzzles that he kept in his office.

My first patient was Paul, a seven-year-old boy. He was depressed and hardly spoke. He meandered around my office, exploring the toys and games. He was silent while he played with them.

During our third session, Paul began to work on a jigsaw puzzle and invited me to help him. Slowly he began to tell me bits and pieces about his family. He told me that his father often hit his mother and that he was afraid of him. With Dr. Peroni's expert supervision, I made a point in every session to fully accept Paul's feelings, stress that he was not to blame for his parents' conflicts, discuss ways in which he could keep himself safe, and affirm his self-worth. Like many children in similar situations, he felt that his parents were fighting because he was a bad boy; that it was his fault.

After one of our sessions, I accompanied Paul to the waiting room as usual to meet his mother who always drove him home. The receptionist turned to me and said that Paul's father would take him home as his mother was not available. Seeing his father, Paul froze. His father stood up and staggered towards us. He almost tripped over his feet. As he drew near, the strong smell of rum was thick in the air.

"Let's go," he said loudly, and putting his hand on Paul's back, shoved him forward, hard. Paul almost fell.

Without thinking it through, I began. "Wait a minute, sir. I think Paul left something in my office. Can you wait a minute?"

They stopped. I ran to Dr. Peroni's office and knocked. There was no answer. I went to my office and called the receptionist at the front. I said that there was an emergency with a child and could she please ask Dr. Peroni to call my office from his home. A few minutes later he was on the phone with me.

After describing the situation to him, I said, "His father is drunk. Should we call the police? Should we call Children's Protective Services?"

"This is a judgment call, Rickey, but I think it would not be helpful to call the police or Children's Protective Services now. I think we should assume that his Dad will get him home safely. He doesn't live too far from the clinic, just a few streets away. Let's confirm that they get home safely," he said. "Then, yes, we need to call Children's Protective Services. They will send a social worker to Paul's home and tell the parents that under no circumstances should they drive under the influence. They will also assess Paul's home environment. This is risky, too, Rickey. Paul's parents will probably assume that the call to Protective Services came from our clinic and they may pull Paul out of treatment. But given that there appears to be violence between the parents and the father is driving while under the influence, I don't think we have a choice."

I ran back to the front lobby and told Paul and his father that nothing had been left behind. "Sorry for the delay."

I watched as Paul followed his father out the door, trying to dispel the image of a car crash that etched itself vividly in my mind.

I anxiously waited. One hour later I called Paul's home, ostensibly to confirm his next appointment and was greatly relieved when his mother answered and confirmed that Paul was home. The next day I contacted Protective Services. I was up nights worrying about the possible negative consequences of their intervention over which I had no control. I had to accept the fact that there was no guarantee that Paul would, in fact, be protected or that he would return for more treatment.

All Dr. Peroni could say was that "Our best clinical judgement rests on a foundation of many unknowns. All we can do is try our best to protect and help the child." I was humbled by his admission that he did not know whether contacting Protective Services would lead to a positive outcome.

During my adolescent inpatient rotation, one of my assignments was to co-lead a group psychotherapy program with a psychiatry resident. The group was composed of ten teenage boys, none of whom wanted to participate. All of them had been hospitalized against their will.

Every time I entered the unit, I could feel hostility emanating from the teenagers. Some had been admitted for intense anxiety or obsessive-compulsive disorders, others for depression, and some for antisocial behaviour. They were like caged animals, filled with anger toward their keepers and I was one of them.

The idea of implementing group psychotherapy with such patients was preposterous. *How could we persuade these obviously angry teenagers to participate at all let alone in a way that would be therapeutic?* Dr. Warner, our supervising psychiatrist, said that the established ground rule was time out for any boy who refused to speak. The boy would then have to sit in a separate room by himself for thirty minutes. This was even more preposterous. I immediately understood that this would likely be a rewarding rather than a punitive consequence. *Wasn't it obvious that psychological treatment cannot be forced on anyone?*

The first session resulted in eight of the boys refusing to say a single word. They did not appear to be bothered at all when my co-leader,

Catherine, gave them time out. I envied them. I wish that Catherine had given me a permanent time out from this destructive group.

There were many moments when Catherine implored me to say something to the group. Most of the time I said nothing, just like the depressed and angry boys. I could think of nothing to say having been thrust into a situation that ran counter to everything that I had been taught and believed about psychological treatment.

After our third session, I reflected on how we all felt trapped in this group. I was not free to leave nor could I put an end to this group program. There must be a way to make this better. I decided to change our totally unproductive agenda and introduced our fourth meeting by stating the obvious.

"The way we are running this group is *crazy*." I said. The boys and Catherine both looked shocked. "It's not at all helpful for any of you. Do you agree?" I had not trusted Catherine enough to discuss this with her first. I was worried that she might not agree to go against the rules and that she might report me to Dr. Warner. I went on. "It doesn't make any sense to give you time out if you choose not to speak. Do you agree?"

After this question, all the boys nodded.

"I propose that no one be required to say anything. Catherine and I, as your leaders, will be happy to listen if there's anything you want to tell us. A ground rule that I suggest is that no one hurts anyone by what we say or do. Can we agree with that, too?"

Again, there was unanimous nodding.

"You can tell us how you feel and what you think about your experiences here with us or with others on the unit. You can say how frustrated you've been with us as we've tried to run this group program. I bet you have found this *very* frustrating." A few boys nodded. "But if you decide it's best to be silent, that's fine, too. And unless we are worried that you might harm yourself or others, we will keep what you say confidential. Can we all agree to keep whatever is discussed here, confidential?"

More unanimous nodding.

There was a long period of silence after my introduction. I sat comfortably waiting. Catherine was silent but began to look more relaxed. We both felt less pressure to make the group work. Now, it was up to the boys. Beginning with respect and the freedom to choose to speak or not, I was hopeful that rapport would follow.

After a while, one of the boys expressed his angry feelings about being pressured to attend the group. Other boys joined the discussion. Catherine and I listened and validated their feelings. Over the next few weeks, most of the boys actively participated. The boys who chose to be silent observers were equally respected. Gradually, the program became therapeutic.

While co-leading the group, I was also assigned to take on an individual adolescent inpatient. Mark was a thirteen-year-old who was diagnosed with oppositional defiant and attention deficit disorders. His parents had recently separated.

In our first session, Mark immediately began shouting loudly, telling me how furious he was with his mother. "She told me that we were going to visit my cousin downtown!" he yelled. "Instead she drove me here! I did not know what kind of building this was, so I got out of the car and went in. When I found out, I said that I would kill her! Good thing for her that she's not here now or I would!"

Mark's threat and rage upon his arrival had guaranteed his admission.

"No wonder you are so angry with her, Mark. I get it."

"You don't understand a thing!" Mark got up from his chair and rushed out of my office and into his room on the unit. I followed him. Before I could say anything further, a nurse entered his room with a pill to sedate him.

"He has thrown chairs at people and has punched the walls so hard that his knuckles have bled. We can't let him get out of control. It's not safe." Her explanation had a defensive tone in reaction to my critical expression. Then I thought, perhaps she was right to sedate him.

Developing rapport with Mark was a slow process. Sitting in an office together, we were both stiff and tense. He rarely spoke. I suggested that we go for walks. We walked up and down the halls near my office. Perhaps because no words were spoken while we walked, trust was building. Perhaps the walking was also helping him to blow off some steam. It certainly helped me relax.

After several silent sessions, Mark pointed to an area at the back of the clinic where there were two chairs. There were no people nearby. He sat down and turned to me. "I will never forgive my mom. She told my dad to get out of the house. I can't forgive her for sending him away. I can't forgive her for tricking me into coming here. She sent me away just like him." Mark looked towards the sky and began to weep. Then he bent over and held his head in his hands.

"You feel so deeply hurt, Mark," I said as I worked hard to dispel the strong urge to wrap my arms around him.

Mark was silent for a long time. He stopped crying and began to tremble. His entire body was shaking. I asked him gently, "What is the shaking about, Mark?" The sad expression on his face turned to one of fear. "Are you feeling afraid?"

"Yes."

"Afraid of …?"

"Hurting…" his voice trailed off.

"Afraid of hurting?"

"I could *really* kill her. I have thrown chairs at her. I have punched walls. I smashed her dishes. At those times, I'm so angry, I have no control."

"Have you injured her?"

"No. Not yet."

"Feeling really, really angry, like there is a fire inside burning so hot you feel you cannot control yourself—that *is* very scary." Mark looked directly into my eyes. He had heard my genuine understanding of the terror that often accompanies a rage so intense it feels like all control is lost. "Mark, you *do* have control. You have *chosen* not to hurt her. You *don't want* to hurt her." I paused. There was silence for a few minutes. Then I asked, "What could happen if you chose to hurt her?"

"She might call the cops. I might go to jail."

"What other bad things could happen? Do you think that you might lose your relationship with her in some ways? You've told me that sometimes she helps you, right?"

"Yeah—when Dad yells at me, she tells him to stop. It doesn't work."

"But at least she tries. You feel at those times that she cares about you. Maybe you are afraid you would lose her help and her love? Maybe you would feel guilty if you hurt her?" I paused. "It's natural that you have mixed feelings about your mom—sometimes you feel really mad at her and other times you appreciate that she tries to protect you and loves you."

"No. She hates me. I've broken dishes. I smashed her favourite vase. I punched holes in the walls. She keeps saying I'm like my dad and she hates him."

"If she hated you, Mark, what would she have done after you smashed things and punched holes in the walls?"

"She would have called the cops. She called them once on dad."

"But she didn't call the cops on you. She took you to a hospital. I know that you are very mad and hurt about the way that she did that. But taking her son to a hospital, is that something a mom does if she hates him?"

"No. I guess not."

"I don't know your mom at all so I'm just guessing here. Maybe your mom didn't know what to do. She didn't want to get you in trouble with the police. She wanted someone to help you. That's something you do when you love someone. You are here because you were punching holes in walls and breaking things and yelling and screaming and running away from home. You didn't know what else to do with all your angry and hurt feelings. And your mom didn't know what to do either. I am hoping that we can help both of you." Mark stood up and walked slowly around the chair, as if in deep thought. Another long period of silence followed before I began again. "There's nothing wrong with feeling angry, Mark. It's what we do with that feeling that's important. Look at your poor knuckles." I said softly, with compassion as Mark turned his hands over to reveal the bruises, fresh bloody scratches, and scars. "Poor knuckles." I repeated even more softly. "They don't deserve to be bashed and hurt like that, do they?"

"No, they don't." Mark was looking at them closely as if for the first time. It seemed that he had never considered the extent of the damage that he had done to them. "It's so hard not to punch the walls. She makes me so mad."

"It would be a lot better if you got away from your mom when your angry feelings are getting hot and go to your bedroom. You could punch the bed or your pillow and say angry words out loud. Your angry feelings could come out safely that way. You wouldn't hurt yourself. You wouldn't hurt your mom. Your angry feelings would be less scary. You could then take some time to breathe more slowly to help yourself cool down. You could do the same thing here when you feel angry."

We practised deep, slow breathing before our session ended that day.

What stays with me when I picture Mark is the dramatic change that occurred in his appearance as he let go of most of the tension in his body. More than anger and pain, his eyes had always conveyed great fear. I watched as the fear faded. As he relaxed, the soft features of his face emerged and for the first time I noticed how handsome he was. He had an adorable face with large brown eyes, encircled by long eyelashes, a small nose, plump cheeks with dimples, and thick lips.

I understood the fear that crept back into Mark's face when our session ended. *Did either parent want him? Did either of them feel that he was a loveable, worthwhile person? Was he destined to be like his father who often lost control of his anger? In the heat of the moment, would he be able to prevent himself from killing?*

There was a time long ago when I knew something of that fear.

26

Discovering the Killer

*P*aradell Farms was located a half-hour bike ride from my home. Every July I joined Mom and Dad as we drove to the farm to buy raspberries. When I was nine, I asked the owner if she needed more pickers. I was thrilled when she said that she did.

My friends, Cynthia and Helen, were excited to pick raspberries too. It was our first real job.

Cynthia and Helen lived close to my house. We played together almost every day. Cynthia's mother baked delicious Ukrainian pastries, which she shared with my family, and Mom baked the best strudel in the world, which she shared with Cynthia's. I saw Cynthia's mother a lot but seldom saw her father.

One day, Cynthia was riding her bike towards my house. I was watching from my front lawn. Her front bike wheel ran over a large rock on the road. The bike swerved. Cynthia tried frantically to get her balance back, but the bike kept going down on an angle and all at once she was lying on the road crying. I could see that both her legs were cut and bleeding. Before I could move, her father came running out of the house. I was relieved. *He will take care of her.*

To my horror, Cynthia's father was enraged and began to scream at her. "You broke the bike! Do you know how much it cost? Do you expect us to pay for another one? Why didn't you watch where you were going?" He went on and on yelling at her while she was lying on the road crying and bleeding. I could not believe his behaviour. Dad often yelled so loud that I was fearful. The house would tremble with his fury. All the same, there was no question that if I was injured, he would help me. I felt very sad for Cynthia.

After a few minutes, Cynthia picked herself up and limped towards her house. Her father had taken the broken bike into the garage and disappeared. I was too afraid of him to offer to help her. *How could her father be so cruel?* I wondered where her mother was.

My friend Helen had her own challenges. When she was very young, she had polio. It left her with a permanent limp. At school, kids made fun of her. I decided to be a good friend to her and invited her to play with Cynthia and me whenever I could. She appreciated my including her. When we played with the skipping rope, she would hold one end all the time because she could not skip. She didn't seem to mind.

We biked to Paradell Farm every day for three weeks. We earned five cents for each pint of raspberries that we picked and felt grown up because we were making money.

More than the money, for me the most wonderful thing about this job was eating raspberries. I treated myself to a handful of berries every time I finished a pint. That made me a very fast picker. The raspberries were big, juicy, and the perfect blend of tart and sweet. I delighted in the subtle difference of flavours that each individual raspberry had.

One beautiful summer day we were picking raspberries under an endless deep-blue sky. We chatted and sang songs as we picked.

Helen stopped singing abruptly and shouted angrily at me. "Rickey, you stole one of my pints! I had ten and now I have nine."

I was shocked by her accusation. We weren't even picking on the same side. "I didn't touch your pints, Helen. You must have miscounted. We are picking on opposite sides and you know that I didn't cross over to your side." I thought that this would be the end of it.

"You are lying! I had ten. And now I have nine. Give me back my pint!" She demanded, screaming louder.

Cynthia and Helen were now facing me on my side of the row. "Give her back her berries!" Cynthia yelled.

"But I didn't take them," I repeated. I felt frightened and angry. They had never ganged up on me like this before. An ominous tension filled the air. We were good friends. I could not comprehend what was unfolding.

"You are a dirty, lying Jew!" Cynthia shouted. She lunged at me, throwing me over onto the ground. Her body was on top of mine, pinning me down. She held both my hands against the ground so hard that I could feel stones cutting through my skin. She glared at me with eyes aflame with rage. She thrust a knee into my stomach and held it there so that I was unable to breathe.

A sudden, terrifying surge of energy took control of my body. I was possessed by rage that I had never experienced before. In an instant my arms were propelled by an unimaginable power. I could only watch as Cynthia was flung through the air. She landed some distance away. Her body broke through the bushes and hit the ground with a loud thump.

Was she dead?

Helen gasped loudly. Cynthia wasn't moving. I only breathed again when I saw that she was alive. She opened her eyes, which were staring at me in fear and disbelief.

The power that had commandeered my body slowly dissipated. I looked at my arms, which were still tingling from the counterattack they had launched. I began to feel that they were mine again.

I stood up, trembling with a horrifying insight. I knew that the power that had surged to the surface was more than self-defence. It was intense anger at having been unjustly accused and viciously attacked; at having been cruelly betrayed by my friends.

Lurking within me was the power to kill.

Cynthia slowly rose to her feet. I was relieved that she did not appear to be injured. In a frightened voice, she managed to hurl more insults at me. I was too shaken to react to her words. My silence and stillness gave her strength. Her insults grew louder and more confident. I paid no attention to her. As she yelled, she kept her distance. She was afraid of me.

I was afraid of me, too.

No one had ever called me a dirty, lying Jew before. I was stunned. The idea that I had been accused of being dirty and dishonest by my friend caused great pain but nothing compared to the agony of these insults being connected with my being Jewish—that was an attack on the very person I was. To think that these words had been spoken by my friend was shocking.

Helen just stood there, silently.

All this paled in comparison with the realization that I could have seriously injured or even killed Cynthia. I felt committed to controlling this raging force within me. I did not want to hurt. I did not want to kill. Discovering that potential shattered the belief that I was essentially a good person.

I quickly cashed in my pints, got on my bike, rode home, quickly ran into my room, and wept.

After that, my friendships with Cynthia and Helen were never the same. And neither was I.

The potential to harm and kill another person that had been dormant within me could no longer hide in the shadows.

27

Black Day in July

Early in the morning on a summer day in 1967 we were driving into Detroit after a vacation in Florida. I was fourteen years old. Mom was sitting in the front, helping Dad with directions, and I was riding in the back. Terry had not joined us for this trip.

The first thing I noticed was smoke in the distance. Dad said that it was either coming from a factory or a fire.

All three of us became increasingly anxious as we approached the city. There were no other cars on the highway.

Dad took the exit to the tunnel but after he left the highway he noticed a sign indicating that the tunnel was closed.

"Don't worry," he told us calmly, "there's a bridge to Canada." The only problem was that he did not know how to get to the bridge. He asked Mom to study the map as he drove on city streets searching for a sign.

Suddenly we found ourselves on a very strange city street. There were no other cars driving on the street even though there were four lanes altogether. Large groups of people were running down the sidewalk in both directions, rushing into and out of stores, carrying bags filled with heavy things, weighing them down. People were spilling onto the street. I heard shouting and yelling, although I could not make out what they were saying. Dad stopped the car by the side of the road while Mom continued to study the map, trying to figure out where we were and how to get to the bridge. Dad shouted at her, "Come on, Faye! How do we get to the bridge?"

"I don't know," she said, her voice trembling. "I don't know the name of this street. Can you see a sign?"

Dad grabbed the map. I knew that he wouldn't be able to figure it out either. We were lost. People were crowding around our car.

Then I saw flames. There were fires leaping from the doors and windows of nearby buildings and houses. More people were rushing into the streets, screaming. Thick smoke was pouring out into the street. *Where were the fire trucks?*

I could not believe the scene that was unfolding in front of us.

Dad threw the map down in frustration. He began to drive very slowly forward. The people who had been standing in front of our car moved away. After driving a short distance, we came to a much larger crowd of people who were standing in the middle of the street, completely blocking the way. I looked up into a glaring wall of eyes. More people gathered until we were surrounded. I felt intense anger closing in around us. Through the closed windows I could hear shouting and swearing. Somehow, it did not seem that we were the only targets. Many were screaming into space, looking up, and pouring out their rage to the smoke-filled sky. The sounds they were making were deafening. Their eyes were burning with anger. Some were throwing rocks at stores, smashing the glass. It was only a matter of time until they pounded our car with rocks or worse.

They were one writhing creature tormented by an indescribable pain, screaming out to the universe.

The tension building in the car approached the intensity of the rage around us. We were frozen in fear.

Dad slowly rolled down his window. A young man rushed over. His eyes met Dad's. The man's face was dripping with sweat. His clothes were torn. He was holding a large rock in one hand. He thrust his face into the opening and shot a terrifying glance at Mom and at me. His face moved closer towards Dad's. Dad did not move back. Neither did the man. I saw him move his hand back, winding up to smash Dad with the rock. I held my breath.

"Excuse me, sir, but we are trying to get back to Canada," Dad started softly. "We are lost. Can you please point us towards the Ambassador Bridge?"

At this, the young man's facial expression instantly relaxed. It was as if the flaming anger in his eyes had been snuffed out by a sudden gust of wind. I was surprised to see how handsome he appeared. The rock in his hand moved slowly down until it was hanging limply by his side. There was a gentleness about him as he answered and kindness in his voice. It was as if he had become another person.

"You go down dis road," he said softly, pointing, "and then you hang a left, pass a few lights. Go right at the sign. There's less ruckus on those streets but, man, you'all in a real hot mess." Mom was writing his directions on the map. While the rock was still sitting firmly in his hand, ready to kill, he expressed genuine concern for our safety. It was impossible for me to understand the contradiction.

"Thank you, sir," Dad said, and the young man replied, "Uh-uh" as if there was nothing unusual going on.

Swept up by the fury of the crowd, the man could have easily swung the rock at Dad. The crowd around him was all too ready to be mobilized and swarm our car. Hearing my Dad's polite and respectful tone and words seemed to have inspired the angry man to make a different choice, one that must have been extremely difficult for him to do. Despite the fire burning within him and around him, he chose to return Dad's respect and gentle tone. He chose to help rather than harm.

Perhaps, taking their cue from the man's backing away from our car, the crowd parted as Dad started to drive slowly forward. As we drove away, I turned to look through the rear window. The street became engulfed in flames. The young man who had helped us disappeared from view. Everything was on fire behind us and around us. I heard my parents breathing quickly and felt the car accelerate. There was panic in the air. Dad followed the young man's directions, which Mom read out loud. Exactly as the man had told us, there were fewer people and fires on the streets that he told us to take. At the entrance to the bridge, there were police everywhere. One of them waved us onto the bridge. I saw fear in his eyes. Ours was the sole vehicle driving toward Canada.

After we cleared customs, I turned around to look out the back window. Across the river the entire city was throwing up great balls of fire. The buildings were billowing black smoke that formed thick clouds moving towards us. As Dad had left his window open, I could hear a deep groan as if the city across the river was in its death throes.

Dad was not worried about getting a speeding ticket as he accelerated onto the highway that would take us safely home.

In the days afterwards, Dad explained what had happened. "Forty-three people died and three hundred and forty-two were injured and almost one thousand four hundred buildings were burned. Most of those killed were blacks shot by the Detroit police and National Guard. They reacted with unnecessary violence with their guns. Many lives were lost. Many were hurt."

"Why did this happen?'

"There is a part of Detroit called Virginia Park. Sixty thousand people, mostly black, live there. They are very poor and live in small apartments. Many have no jobs. The white people go to Virginia Park during the day to work. After work, they go back to their nice, big homes in other parts of Detroit. The black people in Virginia Park could not see any way out of their poverty. Rickey, whenever there is a huge gap between the rich and the poor, there will be big problems sooner or later. The poor people were so angry and felt so hopeless that they lit fires, stole things, and fought with the police."

I felt compassion for the poor people of Detroit.

Permanently etched in my mind was the image of the man who approached us as an angry beast, ready to pounce, but who had, in a matter of seconds, chosen to transform himself into a respectful, helpful soul.

Some of my patients made a similar transformation over a period of years. I picture Arit sitting across from me now. He was in his forties but appeared much older. He was a tall, muscular man. Thick curls of his wavy black hair fell across his deeply wrinkled forehead. He had a stern expression and dark eyes that gazed directly into mine, never wandering away during each of our sessions. Sitting at the edge of his chair, he appeared ready to launch out of it. In every session Arit brought high levels of tension with him into the room.

The physician's referral note indicated that Arit had taken a sick leave from work a few months earlier due to depression. He was prescribed antidepressants but remained significantly disabled. Arit worked as a superintendent of an apartment building where he lived alone.

Eight years ago, the Children's Aid Society had found that Arit had repeatedly physically abused his son, then age eight, and daughter, then age ten. During the investigation Arit was forced to move out of his home and was only allowed to have supervised contact with his children. His wife filed for divorce. His children refused to see him shortly after the marital separation. He had not had any contact with his son and daughter for the past seven years.

Arit disclosed that he was deeply troubled by his broken relationships with his son, Krish, and daughter, Akshi, who lived with their mother. He was overwhelmed with guilt for the harm that he had caused his children. Unwilling to forgive himself, he felt that it would be impossible for his children to consider forgiving him. He was living a life of relentless self-criticism. His internal flames were consuming him from the inside out. "I am a monster," he began. "I treated them worse than my father treated me. I should have learned from that, Doctor."

Arit described the beatings that he had endured at the hands of his father who he said was an alcoholic. "He and my mom came from Pakistan with nothing. His furniture business failed and he turned to drink. That's when he started hitting my mom and me. I was six years old. That went on until I was ten. Then he left us."

"You suffered terribly, Arit. You were an innocent child."

"I have so much anger toward my dad."

"Naturally and it must be hard for you to manage that anger. How do you do it?"

"I have decided I do not want to be like him. Now when I get angry with someone, I take a break. I tell them I'll get back to them later. I go somewhere to calm down. I don't want to be like he was. And I won't touch alcohol. That stuff is poison. To be honest, I am not always successful."

"That's very impressive, Arit. You're working hard to control your anger."

"Yes, but nothing can change what I did to my son and daughter. There's no excuse for that. I should have done better." Arit went on to disclose, with tears streaming down his face, details of incidents when he had hit his son and daughter. Even though I was witnessing Arit's sincere remorse, I had to work hard to look beyond the negative judgements that these scenes triggered within me. I struggled to find my capacity for forgiveness, which was essential since the goal was to help Arit forgive himself.

"Does it help you to review those times when you lost control of your anger?"

"I feel I need to be honest with myself about the harm I did."

"How will you know when you've done enough of that?"

Arit paused a long time before he answered. "I don't know."

"Do you think, maybe you have replayed those scenes in your mind enough times? Perhaps it's time for you to change your focus from the past that you regret to the present. The past is the past but now there are choices you can make."

Arit nodded in agreement.

"Replaying those scenes is punitive and keeps you depressed and unable to improve your life now." I paused, inviting Arit to lift himself out of the past. "I understand from Dr. Morris that you stopped working a few months ago because you felt so depressed. What happened a few months ago?"

"I called Anaya for the first time and asked to speak to Krish and Akshi. She shouted at me. 'You're a bastard! You have no right to ask to speak to them after what you did to them. And they don't want anything to do with you.' Then she hung up. It sounds hopeless for me. It was wrong for me to expect anything better from my kids, but from Anaya? She didn't have to yell at me like that!"

Arit went on to speak angrily about his wife who he said had been verbally abusive and condescending during their marriage. He said that she complained that he was never there for her. "She was right about that in the end but not at the beginning, before the kids. After the kids, all she did was take care of them. It was like I wasn't there at all. We got into a lot of arguments. She said all I was good for was making money. She made me so mad. The kids made me mad, too. They'd make a lot of noise no matter how many times I told them to be quiet. I should never have taken it out on them." Arit dissolved into tears. "Krish and Akshi don't want anything to do with me. I don't blame them. I miss them terribly. They were a part of my life which I have lost forever."

"Perhaps, not forever. You feel some hope, Arit, or you wouldn't be sitting here with me now."

Many sessions passed before Arit felt courageous enough to reach out to Krish and Akshi for the first time by sending each of them letters. He knew that they might not respond but he felt the need to communicate his feelings to them. Arit wrote the letters over the course of six weekly sessions. He drew from memories of good times that he had enjoyed with each of them. He filled each letter with his deep regret for the pain that he had caused. He wrote that he could understand if they did not want to have anything to do with him but hoped that they might change their minds in the future. Although he wrote that he had been physically abused by his father, he did not use that as an excuse for his behaviour. Arit cried in each session as he wrote the letters, read what he had written out loud, and revised them.

As he worked on the letters, Arit became more motivated to take better care of himself. He was eating more regularly, sleeping better, and started to take daily showers again. Eventually he resumed work. By reaching out to his children with humility, honesty, and compassion for them, Arit moved toward forgiving himself and feeling compassion for himself. He also allowed himself to feel hope that they might reach out to him.

A few months after he sent the letters, Arit received a response from Akshi. In her letter, she expressed her hurt and angry feelings but also referred to some of the positive memories that he had included in his letter. Arit and Akshi continued to correspond with each other over time, and their letters began to include tiny bits of their day-to-day lives.

Arit felt encouraged and sent Krish a greeting card with a brief message of love and hope that they might see each other at some point. Arit left his last session saying that he would not give up. "It might take years," he said. "As long as I am alive and they are alive, there is hope."

As challenging as it was to help patients who disclosed that they had been violent in the past, nothing was more difficult for me than helping patients who contemplated violence in the future.

I cringe as Ken's face comes into view. Ken's expression was always intense, eyes aflame with anger, a piercing gaze that shot right through me in a threatening way. He was tall and sat back in his chair with his long legs stretched out and moved his arms and hands quickly and wildly as he spoke. Whenever I responded, his hands fidgeted, as if possessed with energy that they could barely contain.

In every session, Ken's stories floated through the air quietly at first but rose to a crescendo of fury, resentment, and desolation, culminating in his saying that he would kill himself at some point in the future.

Ken told me that he had seen other psychologists who had not been helpful. "What was not helpful? I want to make sure that I come through for you, Ken."

"They weren't with me."

"What did they say or do that gave you that feeling?"

"I just knew they weren't with me. That's all." He said angrily.

"Ken, if at any point you feel that I am not with you, please let me know."

"Yes, I will."

Ken disclosed his history of tragedy and pain quickly, as if it was too painful for him to dwell on any part for more than a moment. "My uncle sexually abused me many times when I was under the age of ten. I married Marion and we were happy for twenty years. We had two daughters, Paulina and Cathy. Marion had a heart attack two years ago. When she died she was only forty. I met Barbara not long after and fell in love with her. We lived together for one and a half years. I trusted her." Ken paused, gritted his teeth and drew his arms and legs in tightly.

"We had a joint bank account. One day, a few months ago, she was gone. Just like that. And the next thing I knew, my money was all gone. All my money.

"The bank and the police told me there was nothing they could do because it was a joint account. A lawyer told me that we were not even common-law because we had been living together for less than three years. He said there was nothing he could do for me. I was robbed, conned."

"Betrayed. Deeply, deeply hurt."

"But that's not even the worst of it! A week after she left, when I was at work, I got a call from the emergency department that Cathy was in intensive care. I rushed to her bedside but I was too late. She was already dead. The doctor told me that it was fentanyl. I knew Cathy was using weed but I didn't know she would take fentanyl. Paulina told me that Barbara was into drugs. I never knew that! Barbara must have given Cathy fentanyl. Where else would she have got that? Barbara killed my baby!" Ken pounded his fists on the arms of the chair. Tears welled up in his flaming eyes. He breathed heavily, ready to attack.

I leaned forward and waited for Ken's breathing to slow. We sat in silence for a long time.

"What's the point? May as well be dead.," he shouted.

"What has kept you going, Ken?"

"My eighteen-year old daughter, Paulina. I am all she has."

"Have you tried to kill yourself?"

"No. But I think about it all the time, every day, since Marion died."

My rapport with Ken was tenuous. In every session, I felt as if our relationship hung by a thin thread. I struggled to understand the nature of that thread and how to strengthen it. Most of the time when I offered support, Ken responded angrily and repeated his wish to end his life. When I challenged him in any way, no matter how gently, he responded angrily as well. When I listened and paused as I struggled to search for a response that might help, he stared at me, waiting, ready to pounce. I invited Ken to focus on our relationship. "No matter what I say or how I respond, I seem to be on the wrong track. How can I be more helpful?"

"You should know. You are the professional! Don't ask me!" Ken shouted.

"You feel a lot of anger and pain, Ken. I want to help. I am a professional, yes, but you are the expert when it comes to knowing what you need. Please help me come through better for you."

Despite his chronic suicidal thoughts and frequent angry outbursts, Ken kept coming back. My colleagues with whom I consulted on a regular basis said, "You must be doing something right. Otherwise, he would terminate." I did not find this particularly helpful.

No doubt our working relationship was fragile. I was anxious that any word or nuance might trigger his anger. I also feared for his life even though in each session I checked whether Ken had any imminent intentions of killing himself. I was only somewhat relieved each time when he confirmed that this was not the case.

Six months into his treatment, Ken told me that Paulina had been seriously injured in a car accident. She had been hospitalized for a few weeks and was recovering at home. Ken's intense anger and pain about all the hardships that he had experienced poured out of him in a torrent of fury. He shouted angrily, swore, pounded the arm rests, stomped his feet, all the while focusing on Barbara's betrayal. "There's so much injustice that you've had to cope with, Ken. You're angry that Paulina was hurt in this accident and worried about her. You are furious with Barbara."

"I feel like I need to kill myself. Not right now because Paulina needs me. But what's the point? All my life I've been a good person and look what I get for it?! Someday I am going to kill Barbara's sons. She killed Cathy! She robbed me! I don't have enough money to care for Paulina! I want Barbara to suffer."

"It's so much more than a betrayal, Ken. You believe she caused Cathy's death. No wonder you feel rage and want her to suffer. She has caused you terrible pain."

"No! It's not about the terrible pain that she has caused me. It's the death of Cathy! It's Paulina's suffering now. I don't think you believe me when I say that someday I am going to kill Barbara's sons. I mean it!" Ken glared at me.

"I hear you, Ken. You are grieving the loss of Cathy. What a terrible shock it must have been for you! And what a terrible loss! I can see that it is very hard for you to be gentle with yourself as you grieve. Your rage is understandable. You feel like killing Barbara's sons."

"No. I don't *feel* like killing. I *plan* to kill them someday."

"If you kill her children, what would happen to you?"

"I would end up in prison or I would kill myself."

"Either way, you will be unable to care for Paulina. That would be very sad for both of you. It won't change what Barbara did. It would only make things worse for you and Paulina."

"I will wait until Paulina is older and doesn't need my care."

"How would it affect Paulina if you killed them? If you ended up in prison? If you killed yourself?"

"She would manage. She won't always need me."

"You have told me that you love her and she loves you, Ken. Killing Barbara's children would hurt you and Paulina. How would you feel about yourself, Ken? Despite all the pain you've experienced in your life, you have told me that you have chosen never to be violent; that you are a good person at heart."

"That's true. Everything is different now. You don't get it. I mean to do it in the future." Ken shouted.

"I hear how serious you are. I fully accept your pain and anger but not your plan to kill Barbara's children."

Ken looked at me with a piercing gaze. Looking into his eyes, I could see his rage building. He was sitting perfectly still. "Now I am *really* angry," he shouted. He stood up and stomped loudly as he walked to the door. "You didn't hear me at all! You people don't get it! I won't be coming back. Thank you for trying to help me! You are all the same! None of you get it! None of you!" Ken disappeared down the hall in a flash.

I stood in my office for a long time, reviewing Ken's words and my words. I was filled with self-doubt, questions as to what to do next, and afraid for Ken's life and Barbara's sons.

Later that day I called Ken and left him a voice mail. "I'm sad about the way our session ended, Ken. I apologize for whatever I said or did that upset you. You said that I don't get it. You may be right, Ken. I am trying my best to understand but maybe I don't get it all. I know that you have suffered so much. I know that there is no justice or fairness in the terrible things that have happened to you. I sincerely care about you and want to help. I am here for you in any way that I can."

My colleagues with whom I consulted reassured me that there was nothing further I could do. I contacted the College of Psychologists to consult with the expert who provided advice regarding tricky clinical issues.

"There is no imminent threat that he will act on his suicidal or homicidal thoughts, right?"

"That's right," I said. "He is motivated to take care of his daughter who was seriously injured in a motor vehicle accident."

"Then there's nothing for you to do. You would call an ambulance for him if he was imminently suicidal. You indicate that this is not the case. You would call the police if you judged him to be of imminent risk to this woman or her children. You indicate that this is not the case. It sounds likely that his need to take care of his daughter means that it is unlikely he will act on his suicidal and homicidal thoughts."

A major question remained unanswered: how could I have been more helpful?

Ken called me one month later to say that he was so upset about his daughter's condition that he was unable to work. He was crying. "I don't feel like life is worth living but I'm staying around because Paulina needs me." Then before I could say anything, he said, "I do not want to see you again," and he hung up.

Two months later, Ken called again. He said that his daughter was seeing a neuropsychologist because there was evidence that she had suffered brain damage in the accident. "The insurance company knows that I saw you but because I have problems with you, I need to see someone else. That's what I want." I was greatly relieved to hear that Ken was still alive and was planning to work with another therapist. I told Ken that I hoped that he would receive the help that he needed and that Paulina would improve. Our working relationship ended softly, but ended nonetheless.

I continue to feel responsible for the breakdown in my work with Ken. I understood that I had crossed the line when I said that I could not accept his homicidal plan. Perhaps, he did not believe that I truly understood how angry and hurt he was. Perhaps, he was enraged because I pointed out that carrying out his homicidal plan would hurt him and Paulina. I understood that my anxiety that he might kill himself and Barbara's sons upset the power balance between us.

Sitting here now, many questions still swirl around in my mind concerning Ken's sessions. One thing is clear: helping Ken more effectively at that time was beyond my ability. I did the best I could at that time.

Accepting one's limitations is humbling.

I think about how easy it was to teach anger-management strategies to my patients, encouraging them to pause and breathe more slowly early on as anger was building before it reached a climax and excusing themselves from others politely by saying that they needed a break to regain self-control. Many sessions focused on safe ways to discharge angry feelings.

It is easy for us to be self-destructive; to act out of anger and justify our behaviour afterwards; to be oblivious to the harm we cause ourselves by harming others. We know that our anger becomes a tsunami only when we build the wave. We know that no matter how provoked and hurt we feel, we can always choose to let the wave dissipate without causing harm. It is a very difficult choice to make in the moment.

There are many unanswered questions. How is it that the furious man surrounded by a raging mob chose to put down the rock and help us that day in Detroit? How is it that Arit chose to control his anger better and accept responsibility for his abuse of his children? How is it that Ken chose to keep going and help his daughter in a loving way despite his rage? How is it that I choose to control my angry feelings in one situation and not in another?

28

Grand Dilemmas

During my internship, consulting with my supervisors and fellow interns was invaluable. Grand rounds provided a very different type of education. They taught me how damaging it is when teaching becomes divorced from respect and care for patients.

One morning, Dr. Warner asked me to present Mark's case at grand rounds later that week. "Ask both parents to attend," he said.

Being chosen to present at grand rounds was supposed to be an honour. It meant that the chief of staff believed that the therapist was doing excellent work and had a lot to teach others. Grand rounds were attended by the psychiatry residents, psychology interns, chiefs of the departments, and many of the nurses and social workers.

I was not honoured. I was troubled. How could I protect Mark from the distress of being put on display and feeling pressured to answer questions in front of such an audience? I feared that our fragile therapeutic relationship would be demolished.

The format of ground rounds involved the primary therapist describing the case and the patient's progress in treatment. This would be followed by the therapist's leading the patient into the room. Both would sit at the front. The therapist would then ask the patient highly personal questions. I was always embarrassed for the patient. Every time I sat at the back of the room, cringing with each probing question that was asked. Therapists aimed to impress the audience with their expertise. It felt to me as if they were tearing their patients' clothes off in public, laying bare their vulnerability for all to see. It was so painful for me to watch that I often left early.

How is it that my supervisors approved of this clearly unethical and obviously counter-therapeutic process? How could I persuade Dr. Warner to make an exception for my patient?

"Dr. Warner, interviewing Mark at grand rounds would be counter-therapeutic. He is just beginning to cope more effectively with his anger. As you know, he has been violent at times. I am worried that he may act out during or after rounds. Let me discuss his progress in treatment without requiring him to be present."

Dr. Warner thought for a few minutes about my proposal and then agreed. "Okay, Rickey," he said, "but make sure his parents are there."

"No problem, Dr. Warner." I was too relieved to think through this requirement.

"What are you talking about?!" Mark's mother shouted at me. Her eyes welled up with tears. "I have not had any contact with his father since he left for that other woman! We've been communicating with each other through lawyers. I can't tolerate being in the same room with him. I can't do that." I was surprised to see panic in her eyes when I had expected only anger.

"Ms. Jamison, you would not be required to talk to him at all. Mark will be our focus. At any time, you will be able to leave the room if you felt the need." I don't think that Ms. Jamison heard any of my words. She was sobbing uncontrollably. I felt guilty for causing her pain and bewildered at the same time. I understood that she felt angry and hurt by her ex-husband, but why was she feeling such dread and panic at the thought of being in the same room with him?

I sigh heavily. Many years later I would finally understand her reaction.

Ms. Jamison left our meeting after reluctantly agreeing to attend.

Looking back, I deeply regret my abuse of power in this situation. Ms. Jamison must have felt that her son would not receive the best care from the staff if she did not comply. I gave her no option. She knew that if she left the meeting early, Mr. Jamison could use this as evidence against her in their legal battle, advising the court that she did not care enough to attend the entire meeting. She felt trapped.

Having asked Dr. Warner to make an exception to exclude Mark, I did not have the courage to ask him to exclude her as well. I was worried that if I did so, he might become angry, change his mind, and insist that Mark attend. The format of grand rounds had not been altered in any way throughout my internship year. I would be pushing my luck to ask him to make two changes.

Mr. Jamison instantly agreed to attend.

At grand rounds, I provided details about Mark's progress in treatment that I had reviewed with him beforehand. There was much discussion about treatment recommendations in view of the high-conflict situation between his parents but no consensus was reached. I did not feel that anything useful came out of this meeting.

Ms. Jamison sat stiffly throughout and stared out the window much of the time. She breathed heavily, clearly struggling to contain her emotions. She stayed until the end, as did Mr. Jamison. Neither parent said anything. I wondered whether either had heard anything.

Afterwards, Dr. Warner congratulated me. "That was an excellent grand rounds presentation. You have obviously done great work with Mark." I thanked him politely. His praise left me feeling empty. I could only think about Ms. Jamison's obvious suffering and how she had avoided looking at me throughout the meeting.

Mark was discharged a few weeks later. I stood beside Mark in the lobby when his mother arrived. She walked up to me. I greeted her while looking away. I was still feeling guilty. "I want to thank you for all you did to help Mark. You are going to become an excellent psychologist." Given the pain that I had caused her, I felt that I did not deserve her compliment.

Recalling her words now, I feel humbled by her kindness.

During my internship year, my closest relationship was with my fellow intern, Riva. Our friendship was a life raft keeping us both afloat through the emotional tumult of working with our patients and dealing with the staff.

Riva's rotation was on the in-patient children's unit. She was treating

Leila, an eight-year-old. Both her parents had died. Leila was living with her only remaining relative, an aunt who had been emotionally and physically abusive. Riva told me that Leila's worst fear was that her aunt might suffer a heart attack and die while beating her, leaving her with no one to take care of her.

Leila's aunt had brought her to the hospital after Leila stopped talking, eating, and drinking. Children's Protective Services became involved. Riva's supervisor told her that when Leila improved, Protective Services' plan was to return her to her aunt and to monitor her closely. Riva looked at me sadly. "For some reason, they believe that her aunt will stop being abusive. Protective Services will place Leila in foster care if her aunt abuses her again. What would be wrong if I adopted her? My husband and I would be happy to take care of her. She would never be abused again."

Indeed, I thought, why not?

Now that I view this with the benefit of experience over the years, I question if this would have been in Leila's best interests. Riva would be taking Leila away from the only family she had. Perhaps her aunt was receiving some kind of counselling while Leila was in the hospital. Riva was desperate to rescue Leila. Our strong desire to rescue can easily propel us to act without stepping back with humility and more objectivity, to assess whether our intervention would actually be in the best interests of the other person.

Riva continued. "Am I really doing anything good for Leila? When she leaves here, what reassurance do we have that she will not be returning to the same horrific environment? I can't change her aunt's behaviour."

"We should be treating the parents or caregivers." I began. "They are the only ones who can change their child's environment. They have much more power than we do because they are with their children on a daily basis. If they learn how to improve their caregiving, they will be more capable of dealing with problems that arise now and later on. The children and their caregivers will both benefit from having closer, more loving relationships. When we treat the children, we pathologize them;

we hurt their self-esteem by giving them the message that they are the problem or worse, that they are crazy while neglecting to help their parents and caregivers."

My discussions with Riva had a major impact on the direction that I took in my practice later on when parents asked me to treat their young children. Rather than automatically agreeing to assess and treat their child, I began by discussing the possible benefits of working with them instead. Sometimes it was most effective when both approaches were combined. More often parents chose to enter treatment without my ever meeting their child. When parents understood their children better and the interaction they were shaping, they often changed their responses and observed improvements in their children's behaviour. I was always impressed that such changes occurred in a much shorter time than I could ever have achieved in weekly sessions with their child, if at all. Parents left treatment feeling empowered and closer to their children.

Navigating the challenging waters of my internship and struggling with many grand dilemmas was stressful and exhausting but also essential for my development as a psychologist.

29

Racism Unveiled

The area of Detroit in which the clinic was located was very different from the part of Toronto where I had grown up. This became most apparent to me the day when I stopped at a grocery store close to the clinic. As I was shopping, I felt uneasy. People were staring at me. Then I noticed that all the customers and employees were black. I was the only white person. I felt very uncomfortable. I felt that I was an unwelcomed outsider. I completed my shopping, quickly, pretending to be unaffected.

As I went to my car, I thought about how the issue of race had never come up in my supervision sessions nor in my mind. I deeply regretted that I had neglected to ask the boys in our inpatient group program, most of whom were black, how they felt about working with a white psychologist. Did they question my ability to understand and help them? How had they dealt with discrimination? Did they experience discrimination while at the clinic? I had treated them all with a colour-blind attitude because it didn't matter to me whether they were black or white. *How naïve of me to assume that it didn't matter to them!*

Years later I was treating Salim. He was a short overweight man with little tufts of curly hair atop a deep ebony face. He was dressed in a grey suit and appeared sad as he slumped into the chair.

Salim was trained as an engineer but had been unsuccessful in finding a job in his area. He had settled for a job working as an assistant to the president of a small technology firm. This position was far below his skills as an engineer. He was angry with himself for failing to succeed in his career and criticized himself harshly for taking his current job.

Salim shared his condo with Wayne, a nurse, who worked night shifts at a hospital. He denigrated himself for never having established a close relationship with a woman. Now that he was approaching the age of fifty, he felt that the chances of marriage were low as were his chances of having a family. He was grieving these losses.

Salim's anger toward himself for failing to succeed in his career and remaining single culminated in his disdain for certain parts of his body. He was highly critical of his balding which he felt made him look a lot older. He coped with his pain by overeating and denigrated himself for his weight gain.

Salim was born in Toronto but his parents came from Senegal.

"As you grew up, went to school, and began to work as an engineer, what experiences have you had with discrimination?"

"A lot. Not so much in my school years and at university, but when looking for jobs. That's when I felt it was a handicap to be black. My fellow engineering friends who were white were getting hired by big firms. I was cast aside. Now I'm a lot older. You know it's a white man's world. I have to support myself so I need my job but I hate it." Salim shed some tears but quickly wiped his eyes. He looked at me with a sullen expression as if there was nothing that could remedy his situation in any way, daring me to come up with a contrary view.

"There is so much pain that you feel about the injustices you face, about the many hurdles you're up against, Salim. It is taking a lot out of you to keep working at this job."

"I have no choice. I need the money."

"You said that you felt discriminated against when you were competing for jobs as an engineer. That must have been very hurtful. How do you feel about working with me? I could understand if you doubt my ability to understand."

"No. Not at all. So far, I have the feeling that you do understand."

"Well, please tell me if you feel that I don't at any point. In what other situations have you encountered discrimination? Is this happening in your day-to-day life and at your current job?"

"Sometimes in restaurants white people are served before me even though I was clearly there ahead of them. I've walked out of those places. There was an incident last week when I waited at a counter in a store for service. A white woman came later, and the clerk served her. I told the clerk that I was there first. The clerk accused me of being rude and told me to wait my turn. The white lady said nothing. I don't think I have ever heard a clerk accuse a white person of being rude when not served in the right order. At work, there are some people who listen to my ideas but others who do not. I don't know if those who ignore me do that because I'm black or for some other reason."

"I share your anger and hurt feelings about this discrimination. How do you handle those situations?"

"I repeat my comment, always politely, but it still goes nowhere, and I am left burning, like I'm not worth anything."

"Can you feel compassion for yourself?"

"Not so much. I have made a lot of bad decisions in my life especially where jobs are concerned."

"You could not have done otherwise at the time. It's easy to judge yourself with hindsight, Salim. We all regret decisions we have made once we see how things turned out. Regret is understandable. Self-denigration is punitive and is not justified. We cannot know the future."

"I should have known better back then. There was a job I was offered that I did not take."

"What was the reason at the time?"

"It was with a small firm, and I did not see any room for advancement. It was a huge mistake."

"It's easy to say that now. Salim. The truth is you do not know if it would have been a good thing if you had taken that job. All you know is that, at the time, it did not look like a job you should take. You made the best decision for yourself at that time."

In one of his later sessions, Salim disclosed that reading the Bible was often a comfort. He said that he did not attend Church but that he often prayed.

"Your faith is important to you."

"Yes, it is."

"Do you see any inconsistency between your strong Christian faith and your self-condemnation?"

Salim looked surprised. "What do you mean?"

"Well, you see Jesus as forgiving, kind, and loving, right?"

"Yes."

"Well, doesn't Jesus want you to be forgiving, kind, and loving to yourself?"

Salim thought about this for some time. "I am forgiving, kind, and loving."

"To others but not to yourself, not yet. But you could be. You could forgive yourself for mistakes you have made and stop blaming yourself for not taking paths that you now feel would have been better for you. You believe that Jesus still loves you despite your mistakes and despite your regrets."

"Yes, I believe that." He said solemnly.

It took many months of intensive work before Salim chose to feel some compassion for himself. Focusing on his belief that Jesus would want him to forgive himself and be loving and kind led him to change his eating habits. At one point Salim began to walk for exercise. Slowly, he chose to be courageous and disclose some of his painful experiences to friends, deepening his superficial relationships. He moved toward accepting his body and appreciating his good health.

Salim's sessions were peppered with stories of moments in his day-to-day life when he saw white people favoured in a myriad of ways, many of which were new to me. These incidents reinforced Salim's deeply ingrained feeling that he was inherently less worthy of respect and love, complicating his progress.

I am thinking how racism can so easily become unconscious and invisible to those who send it out into the air, like a poisonous gas that is toxic to all who breathe it in.

What comes to mind now is a brief encounter with a salesperson that Amani and I had when we were setting up our office in 1990. We were at the department store investigating telephone sets.

After examining various sets, Amani asked the saleslady, "Please tell us the pros and cons of each of these."

Looking only at me, the saleslady answered in detail. As she spoke, I grew increasingly uncomfortable. I looked at Amani, hoping that the saleslady would pick up my cue to look at Amani.

Amani continued as if there was no issue. "We have two offices and a reception area. We need three lines. Which one would be best for us to buy for that area?"

The saleslady responded and continued to look only at me even though I had not said a word to her. It was as if Amani was not there. I interrupted her.

"Ma'am, my friend has asked you questions but each time you answer, you look only at me. Why is that?"

The saleslady immediately looked embarrassed. "I'm sorry," she said. For the first time, she answered while looking at Amani.

After purchasing the phone sets, Amani told me that this often happened when she was with a white friend even when the salesperson was not white. She added, "You have told me that you have experienced discrimination as a Jew, but your skin colour does not announce your difference to others. My skin colour immediately says that I am from India or Pakistan."

"I hope that you don't mind my correcting the saleslady."

"No. I don't mind. But I doubt that it will change anything."

"Remaining silent certainly won't. Perhaps, that lady wasn't even aware of what she was doing, Amani. Maybe now she will be."

After we left that encounter, I turned my attention to examine myself more closely than I had ever done before. I had always believed that I was free of prejudice. But now, for the first time, I considered whether some insidious racism had infiltrated me without my conscious awareness. *Do I give preferential eye contact or special attention to people who look like me or who I know are Jewish? Do I avert my gaze or withdraw even slightly when I speak to someone who looks different or who speaks with an accent indicating that they might come from a different country?* This was the beginning of an important kind of self-examination that continues to this day.

I recall Mom telling me that she had to change her last name on a job application from "Shapiro" to "Star" before she could obtain a job at a hot dog stand in 1943 at the Canadian National Exhibition. "Shapiro is a Jewish name," she told me. "If they knew I was Jewish, I would never have been hired."

When I was sixteen, I was placed as a typist by a temporary employment agency in the editorial department of a major Toronto newspaper. In a small lunchroom with about fifteen other employees, almost every day I heard 'jokes' about Jews. Some people said that some of their best friends were Jewish, as if that justified their clearly anti-Semitic remarks. I still feel ashamed that I laughed at their jokes. I was a Jew in hiding despite feeling proud of my heritage. I wanted to belong, to be accepted. My fear of being ostracized by the group was far stronger than my pride.

Looking back, I soften my critical thoughts about my sixteen-year-old self. She was young and inexperienced.

If I was in the same situation today, would I act differently?

Once, when I was ten years old, my father chose to confront racism directly. *Would I have the courage to do as he did back then?*

Was he courageous or foolhardy?

30

A Water Fountain in Georgia

Mom, Dad, and I were on our way to Florida for one of our frequent summer holidays. I was ten years old. My gaze was fixated on the passing scenery, trying to catch my first glimpse of a palm tree. The first palm tree confirmed our arrival in a different country and time, a place of summer sun, an ocean to splash in, a beach for building sandcastles, a place and time far away from school.

Mom told Dad that she needed him to stop somewhere soon so that she could go to the washroom.

Driving along with the windows open, I hadn't realized how hot it was outside until the thick, oppressive air rushed into the stopped car. I was curious about this place called Georgia, so I opened the back door and got out, ready to explore.

Mom took off, practically running to the washroom, while Dad took my hand and led me towards a playground. He told me that he was thirsty and was looking for a water fountain.

A lot of children were swinging and going up and down slides. I asked if I could join in but Dad said there wasn't enough time. He was leading me to a water fountain that was at the side of the washroom building, next to the playground. There was a large sign attached to the wall above the water fountain. Dad stopped walking abruptly. He looked at the sign and turned to me, and spit out the words, "That is absolutely disgusting!"

Dad gripped my hand harder and I could feel his whole body become tense. The sign said 'Coloured.' Then I noticed that there was another fountain at the other end of the building. It had another sign that read 'Whites Only.' I thought that these were very strange signs.

Both water fountains looked the same to me. Neither one was coloured or white. They were both a dingy grey.

It was only then that I noticed that all the children playing nearby were black. At the other end of the building there were swings and slides and all the children playing there were white.

Dad tightened his grip and walked with me towards the 'Coloured' water fountain. As we approached, a lot of people turned to look at us. I felt as though a million eyes were upon us. With each step forward, I felt tension building in the air. It quickly became as thick as the sweltering heat. I didn't dare look at anyone. Everything was quiet. I felt that we were in danger.

Mom was already back in the car. I saw her staring at us. She waved to us, frantically, beckoning us to get back into the car. She appeared to be frightened and angry at the same time. Dad must have seen her, too. He bent over and drank the water from the fountain. Then he offered me a turn. He held me up so that I could drink. It was hard to swallow even though the cool water was refreshing. I felt something bad was about to happen.

Dad put me down and turned to go back to the car. I was looking up at a sea of people who were standing around us, blocking our path. They all looked angry. Some were black. Some were white, although they did not stand all mixed up in front of us. The black people were on one side. The white on another. Some of the white people stood on our path, blocking our way to the car. Both groups were united in one silent, oppressive, threatening stare. It was penetrating. All the eyes were menacing.

Dad was now breathing heavily. That made me even more scared because I knew that he was frightened. He was silent as he led me straight forward until he almost collided with the people who were standing in our way. They slowly parted as we walked forward. I feared that the tension would boil over as we continued to walk between the two columns of staring eyes. From both sides I heard grunting and angry words that I did not understand.

Why was there such a commotion about taking a drink from a water fountain? It did not make any sense to me. *What bad thing had we done?*

I was relieved when we reached the car. Dad accelerated fast. Mom was shouting at him. "How could you have done such a thing, Al? And with Rickey beside you? What on earth were you trying to achieve? You aren't going to change anything by risking everything!" Mom was relieved and furious at the same time. Dad was unusually silent as he found his way onto the highway once more. I think he needed time to recover. He must have been terrified.

The silence in the car continued for a long time. Then Mom began in a softer voice, turning to me. "It is wrong to judge anyone by the colour of their skin or by their religion or by anything other than what kind of person they are. Do you understand? The kind of person someone chooses to be is all that matters." I told her that I already knew this. "In Georgia and in some other places, black people are not allowed to sit wherever they want on a bus, are not served at certain restaurants, cannot swim in certain pools, cannot play in certain playgrounds, cannot drink from certain water fountains, and cannot even use certain bathrooms— all because they are black."

All I thought was that I never wanted to go back to Georgia. *That's a dangerous place.*

31

A New Beginning

My internship experiences were transformative. I think about the many skills I learned, my increased awareness of the ethical issues that arise during treatment, my sensitivity to cultural influences, and my increasing respect for the courage and resilience of my patients.

My passion for health psychology did not diminish even though my internship experience was limited to helping psychiatric patients. As soon as Luke and I moved back to Toronto, I began searching the newspapers for a position in a general hospital. At the same time, we decided that the time was right to have a child.

Luke and I both wanted to have children. There was no question and no discussion about this life-changing decision. Luke and I, like our parents, simply understood that marriage necessarily led to children. *How foolhardy it was for us to plunge into parenthood without any consideration of the positives and negatives!* We had carefully weighed the pros and cons before every other decision we had made. We did not consider for a moment the enormous changes in our lifestyle and in our relationship that would accompany the birth of a child.

Nine months after we moved back to Toronto, Angela made her presence known. Luke and I were overjoyed.

Soon after this momentous event, I obtained a position as staff psychologist at a major teaching hospital in Toronto.

32

Merging Body and Mind

D r. Wilson, my new boss, welcomed me warmly. He was an older man, somewhat overweight, with a long face framed by a thick, black beard. He spoke softly and slowly and looked at me with kind eyes.

"Dr. Wilson, I am fascinated by the emerging field of health psychology. Do you think that we could extend psychological treatment beyond psychiatry to medical patients to help them cope better with pain and stressful medical procedures, and to make recommended lifestyle changes?"

Dr. Wilson's face lit up. "Yes. That would be an exciting development."

In those first few months, I visited the university's medical library every day. Climbing the steep, narrow metal stairs up to the stacks, I studied articles that investigated the effectiveness of psychological treatments for pain.

Steven, my first patient, was in his twenties, and struggling with hemophilia. He suffered disabling pain in his ankles due to arthritis that was caused by frequent bleeds. I treated him as an outpatient with a variety of pain management interventions.

While working with Steven, I created an outpatient pain management program. Treating eight patients at a time, my goal was to provide general information that could be useful for everyone while, at the same time, spending some time attending to each patient's unique emotional needs. At the conclusion of each session, I led the group through meditation or progressive relaxation, educating them about the different applications of each and encouraging them to practise on their own.

My job required that I assess psychiatry inpatients. I had been trained to write reports that combined information that the patient provided in a structured interview with my observations and psychological test data culminating in a formulation of the origin and nature of their problems. Treatment recommendations were included after the diagnosis. When I presented at rounds, the psychiatrist rushed me through my presentation to hear my diagnosis. A decision was made as to which medications to administer based on this label.

Even though psychiatric outpatients were routinely referred for psychological treatment, the inpatients received none. Their treatment was receiving medication and participating in groups led by the nurses and social workers. I asked Dr. Wilson, "Why don't we start providing treatment to the psychiatric inpatients? They need treatment even more than the outpatients who are referred to us."

"The nurses and social workers do that. Our role on the inpatient unit is to provide psychological assessments."

I concluded that the psychiatric inpatient unit was an entrenched, closed system that I could not change.

While the psychiatrists limited my role to that of diagnostician, the physicians and nurses on the medical departments readily welcomed me as a treating psychologist. I was soon providing treatment to groups of cardiology and neurology patients. In these weekly sessions, I invited patients to discuss the emotional impact of their health problems, their coping strategies, the impact that their health problems had on their relationships, and the lifestyle changes that they anticipated making. As with my outpatient group, I included meditation or progressive relaxation at the conclusion. As they left the session, many patients said that they appreciated the opportunity to disclose their emotions and to improve their coping skills. The physicians and nurses noted that many of the patients who participated recovered more smoothly and were easier to treat. I was soon leading regular inpatient groups on five different medical units.

Disease and injuries affect us emotionally and physically as well as our relationships with others. It followed that inpatients who had the opportunity to disclose their emotions in a supportive environment and learned more effective ways to cope would do better emotionally and physically.

Physicians on the medical units began to refer individual inpatients. One of the first was Janet who suffered multiple injuries in a motor vehicle accident as a pedestrian. She was in her twenties and recently married. The first time I met her I was shocked to see the extent of her injuries. Her terribly disfigured body screamed out in pain to me. Arriving at her room for her first treatment session, I observed the nurse changing her dressings. I felt sickened to see the burns to her arms and mutilations to her lower limbs. As the nurse left her room, I heard Janet thank her for completing the painful procedure.

As I introduced myself to Janet, I saw her shining eyes looking up at me. With difficulty, she sat up a little. She thanked me warmly after accepting my offer to reposition her pillow. Her blond hair was long and curly and danced about her shoulders as she moved. She held out her hand, which was connected to several intravenous bags hanging by her bedside, to shake mine.

"Have a seat, Doctor." She said warmly, as if I was a guest in her home.

"Thank you, Janet."

Janet spoke freely. She recounted her fear when she first regained consciousness in the hospital hours after the accident. She spoke about her anxiety about dying and her anger toward the truck driver who had veered into her while she was crossing the street on a green light. She expressed gratitude for her husband and two children who visited her often. "I am so lucky to be alive."

I guided Janet through a progressive relaxation procedure in that first session, adding suggestions that she commend herself for all she was doing to help herself. Later we discussed different strategies for coping better when the pain level was high and employing distraction techniques when the pain level was lower. Over the month that we met, Janet practised the strategies I shared with her. She made steady progress in her recovery both emotionally and physically.

I worked with John at the same time. He was in his twenties and married. He lay stiffly in bed the first time we met and averted his gaze as I introduced myself. The nurses had initiated the referral, reporting in his chart that he was rude and angry.

John had also been hit when crossing a street and had suffered similar injuries as Janet. Despite these similarities with Janet, his suffering was far more intense. His muscles tightened throughout his body whenever he was awake and especially when the nurse entered his room to change his dressings. Even before she touched him, he would shout out in pain and tell her to stay away. He was terrified.

Why was John suffering so much? Then, I thought, perhaps the more important question was why was Janet suffering so much less?

In one of our early bedside sessions, John said, "I should have known that the truck was going too fast. I was an idiot! I kept walking! It's been two weeks since I was hit, why do I still have so much pain? I should be better by now. What's wrong with my body that it isn't healing? These nurses and doctors don't know what they are doing! They aren't helping me at all!"

John's anger turned in an endless self-destructive cycle, from blaming himself to blaming the medical staff. Underneath his intense rage was great fear. I could see that he was fearful that he might not be able to tolerate the pain, that he might not recover, that he might die. The greater his distress, the more stress hormones he was pumping into his body, increasing his pain and suffering.

I met with John every day for a short time with my goal of building trust by accepting his emotions with compassion. Later in that week, I asked John if it would help him cope better with the change of dressings if he had some control during the process. He readily agreed.

I discussed this with his nurse. "He's such an angry man, always rude! Yes, I would be willing to take longer to change his dressings if he calmed down," she said.

I was with John the next time his dressings were changed. I coached him to relax his muscles as much as he could and to tell the nurse when he was ready for her to begin. I reminded him to tell her to stop if he needed a break and to breathe more slowly while she completed the procedure. All through the ten minutes, he was quiet. I spoke very softly near his ear. "You can be so proud of yourself, John. Your nurse is helping your body to heal. You are helping your body to heal by relaxing and breathing more slowly. You can choose to ask her to stop any time you need a break. You have control."

As she left his room, the nurse turned and said, "John, you did so well." For the first time since his admission, the nurse responded with a compliment and for the first time John said thank you.

As John felt more in control, I encouraged him to embrace himself with compassion rather than self-blame and to accept that he could not have foreseen the accident.

Many of my outpatients who were suffering with chronic pain had also experienced some kind of emotional trauma in the past, which appeared to heighten their sensitivity to pain. They appeared to have fewer emotional resources to cope with their chronic pain. Having coped with a previous trauma was emotionally and physically taxing, leaving them with fewer resources to cope with another source of stress.

I am thinking about Cathy, an outpatient who I saw in my office. She was referred by her orthopaedic surgeon. She had debilitating back pain for which she had undergone a spinal fusion. However, her back pain continued, unabated.

Cathy was a petite slim woman, with long black hair framing her beautiful face. She was forty years old, married, and had three children. She told me that she was born in Hong Kong and that her parents still lived there. Cathy told me that she was unable to continue to work as a lab technician due to her chronic back pain, which was the result of a lifting injury at home. It was easy to establish rapport with her. She was receptive to implementing constructive thoughts and self-statements to decrease her pain and benefited from learning meditation. She freely disclosed her feelings and thoughts about her back pain, and her frustration and disappointment that the surgery had not cured her.

Although Cathy was articulate, there was a strange hesitancy that occurred seemingly at random intervals in every session. "Cathy, I've noticed that from time to time, you start to complete a thought but stop just for an instant before continuing. Did you notice that this happened a moment ago?"

"Yes, it happens like that sometimes when I talk about my brother, Bob. It's nothing."

"Perhaps. But then again, the hesitation may be trying to tell us something."

Cathy was sitting rigidly upright in the chair. Then she sighed deeply, hunched over, and looked down. "I know what it is. It's difficult to say."

"No need to say what it is right now unless most of you feels it would be helpful. Trust your own judgment." Cathy folded her arms across her chest as if she was hugging herself. "When you think about it, what emotions do you feel?"

"Afraid."

"Afraid of?"

"I don't know."

"Maybe afraid of the feelings coming up? It takes a lot of courage to let them be."

"The pain is too much." The words slipped out quickly, softly, like drops of water escaping through a tiny hole in a high dam.

"Whatever happened, you already lived through it. That is much harder than thinking and talking about it now. It is history. Look up, Cathy. Where are you now?"

"In your office."

"What year is it?"

"2010."

"Right. You are safe here and now." Cathy looked up and scanned the office. "We can talk about something else if this isn't the right time. I will follow your lead. You know what's best."

Cathy's gaze settled on the view out my window. "No, I need to go on with this. I was maybe seven or eight. It was late at night. I woke up to find my oldest brother, Bob, naked on top of me. He was sixteen years old. He was pulling my panties down. Seeing my eyes open, he pressed his hand hard against my mouth and whispered 'Don't make a sound or I'll hurt you.' I didn't know what he was doing but I knew it was something very bad. He was hurting me a lot. Doctor, I felt like I wasn't in my body anymore. I was watching Bob hurt me from somewhere else. I was hanging in the air like a ghost. I watched myself trying not to scream. It was only when he left my bed that I returned to my body. I know it sounds crazy."

"No. It isn't crazy at all, Cathy. It's called dissociation. Your brain tried to protect you by allowing you to feel some distance away from what was happening. It's an automatic survival response." I paused. "Did Bob say anything more to you?"

"He whispered 'Don't you tell anyone. If you do, no one will believe you. They will think you are a very bad girl for making up such a story. And then I'll come back and hurt you again.'" Cathy's tears were flowing as she continued to look out the window.

"What a terribly scary, confusing, and painful trauma to have lived through as a young child! Did this happen more than once?"

Cathy reached for a tissue and dried her face. She turned to look back at me. "No. Maybe because I did not tell my parents. This is the first time I have told anyone."

No matter how many times I heard patients disclose that they had been sexually abused, I felt immediately furious with the perpetrator and heartbroken for the innocent child. It was always tempting to coast intellectually on the surface and say all the most compassionate words without feeling pain. It was all too easy to become jaded and protect myself.

I remember inviting Cathy to feel proud of herself for having the courage to disclose the assault. "Can you feel compassion for the little girl that you were? She was not in any way responsible for her brother's actions, was she?"

"No, she was not responsible. I know that now, Doctor. But after it happened, I felt ashamed. I felt that I did something bad."

"Naturally, as a little girl, you felt ashamed and that you did something bad. Now as an adult, you know better. It is only your brother who should feel ashamed. You deserve only compassion."

"Doctor, trusting men has been hard for me."

"It's easy to understand. You are scared about being hurt again by a man. Despite that fear, you should be proud of yourself, Cathy. You chose to marry David. You chose to trust another man."

As Cathy stood up to leave the session that day, I knew that this was only the beginning of a long journey for her. We went on to explore whether it would help her to disclose the assault to others, including her husband. We explored strategies for decreasing the anxiety that had interfered with her enjoyment of physical affection and sexual encounters with him. Many sessions focused on how she wished to cope at family events that her brother attended. We also discussed the possible connections between her emotional pain and her chronic back pain.

While there was no question that Cathy's chronic back pain arose from a lifting injury, it diminished in intensity as she coped better with her emotional pain. Helping patients cope better with emotional pain led to a decrease in physical pain and vice versa. Working with my pain patients taught me that emotional and physical pain have much in common. It has become clear to me that our bodies are changed by our physical and emotional experiences and that these changes are intertwined in complicated ways.

As an adult, Cathy was still experiencing her trauma through the eyes of an eight-year-old. Her thoughts, feelings, and perceptions had been frozen in time, powerfully influencing her behaviour behind the curtain of her conscious mind. Now she was finally able to look at the events through more rational and compassionate adult eyes and free herself from decades of guilt, shame, and fear.

The wave of sadness swirling inside me now as I think about Cathy as an innocent child of eight triggers tears in me for the hurt little girl I was. Like Cathy, I experienced the same survival response.

33

Dirty at the Cleaners

Mom was an excellent seamstress and made most of my clothes. One day she told me that she didn't have time to hem a skirt that she had made for me. She told me to go to the cleaners at the shopping plaza a few blocks from our house.

I was twelve years old and grown up enough to go to the plaza by myself. This was my first trip there without Mom.

When I arrived, the man at the front desk ushered me into a dressing room down the hall. I overheard him speaking with the woman at the front. Something about their conversation left me with the impression that she was his wife. The man directed me to put the skirt on so that he could pin it. He pulled the curtain.

I folded up my jeans and put them on the bench. After I put the skirt on, I opened the curtain and the man came in. He knelt down on the floor and started to pin the hem. "Turn around so that I can pin the back. The skirt is very well made. Your mom did a good job," he said.

When I saw that he was finished pinning, I expected him to get up and leave the dressing room so that I could get dressed again.

He did not get up.

I felt his hands creeping slowly upwards along my legs. I didn't know what was going on. *What is he doing?* I didn't know where to look or what to do. His hands found themselves on my stomach. They kept snaking upwards, feeling my sides, and then the centre of my chest, and then, very slowly, his fingers were on each of my small breasts, touching them from all sides over and over. I wanted to run away but was too scared to move or speak. I was struck silent by a storm of disgust, confusion, fear, and shame, emotions that I had never experienced before.

All I knew was that something terrible was happening to me. *Something shameful.*

Suddenly, I was looking down from the ceiling. I was a horrified spectator watching the man's hands rippling under the little girl's T-shirt down below. I was gripped with terror as I watched. I did not know how to rescue her. I felt utterly helpless. All I could do was watch and wait until the nightmare scene ended. It seemed forever before his hands left the little girl's breasts. I watched him stand up abruptly and heard his shout expressed in a whisper, "Get dressed! Then leave quickly!" He was clearly angry with her.

As if commanded by his alarming tone, I returned to the trembling body of the little girl. I felt searing shame. *I had done something terribly wrong.* My little breasts that had only recently started to grow were now soiled and repulsive. *I hated them.*

I took off the skirt and pulled on my jeans as quickly as I could. I raced down the hall and out the door. The woman at the counter ran after me to give me the ticket for the skirt. I grabbed the ticket without looking at her. She could not see the panic in my eyes, commanding me to run away as fast as I could from that man and, even more urgently, from the memory of what had just happened.

I was close to Mom and shared most things with her. But not this. I was too ashamed, disgusted, confused, and scared. The swirling storm of emotions was too intense to feel, let alone share.

My little breasts, which had been budding in their innocence, were now guilty of betraying me. They were dirty and needed to be hidden away. I could not bear to look at them and wished they would stop growing. In the months that followed, my breasts grew larger and I was terrified that they would betray me again. I was relieved to hide them in the first bra that Mom bought me.

Whenever Mom sent me to the cleaners for a pickup, I rushed in and out. Each time my heart would pound with uncontrollable anxiety.

I put all my energy into pretending that nothing had happened. Most of the time I managed to forget. But when I went to the store or even saw it from afar, panic and shame would overtake me. The sensation of his hands on my breasts and my guilt and shame haunted me for years.

In my twenties, I finally chose to challenge the irrational thoughts that I had carried with me for so many years. I began to appreciate the beauty of my body and let go of the feelings of guilt for the actions of that man. I finally chose to feel angry with him. I finally chose to see myself as an innocent twelve-year-old girl and to see the man as being totally responsible for assaulting me.

As I made progress toward coping better, I began to feel another pain, the pain of regret that I had not told Mom, which would have allowed her to take action that might have saved other little girls from being assaulted by that man. I spent years struggling to accept that I could not have acted differently at twelve or even in my teen years. By the time I was able to cope better, the cleaning store had long since closed.

My regret lingers still.

34

The End of the World

Although I was shaken by the assault by the cleaner and fearful every time I saw the store, the fear did not generalize. My fear left when the cleaning store closed.

My response was altogether different in 1962 when I was faced with the threat of losing all I knew, all I loved, and my own life. I was nine years old.

In the middle of an arithmetic drill, Ms. Dunsel, my grade four teacher, announced, "There it is again, class." She was annoyed at the interruption. The muted sound of the siren was wailing from the intercom. The drill was familiar. Ms. Dunsel reminded us to get under our desks even though most of us were already there.

The siren stopped. Over the intercom Mr. Roberts, our principal, said, "This is only a drill, boys and girls. If it had been a real emergency, I would be telling your teachers exactly what to do. Continue with your lessons now." A few minutes later we were chanting the eight times tables again. *Too bad it wasn't a fire drill. Those ones lasted longer and we got to go outside.*

It had been an ordinary morning. Mom woke me up with her usual way-too-happy songs, which she trumpeted into my bedroom as usual. "It's time to get up. It's time to get up. It's time to get up in the morning," followed by, "It's a great day for the Irish." I never knew where she got that one from as we didn't know anyone who was Irish. Terry and I were jolted awake by her cheerful singing. Neither of us was ever cheerful about getting up to Mom's exuberant, sunny songs.

As I walked to school, I was hoping that Mom would not make roast beef again for supper. It was one of Dad's favourites. I hated it.

Every time she made roast beef, Mom would insist that I finish the portion on my plate. The meat staring up at me from my plate looked more disgusting each time it was presented. Long after my parents finished their meal and Mom had washed, dried, and put away the dishes, I was still sitting at the kitchen table with that horrible slice of roast beef staring up at me. Patiently, I waited until Mom went to the washroom.

Quickly, I silently opened the bottom drawer under the counter and grabbed one of the many bright orange plastic sandwich bags that Dad had brought home from the factory. I withdrew one twist tie. Gleefully, I stuffed the roast beef inside, secured the bag, and then slowly, and quietly, opened the back door. Tiptoeing onto the wooden deck, I threw the bag underneath it. I was fast and silent, making my way back to the table and my empty plate before Mom returned.

"Good for you. It took you long enough," she commented. I left the kitchen, triumphant.

One afternoon I returned from school to see Mom in a panicked state.

"What's wrong, Mom?"

"Puddles is stuck under the back porch."

"Let me help." I joined her and we both lay down on the grass. Puddles, our German Shepherd, Collie, and Husky mix, was crying, struggling to get out. His back legs poked through under the porch. The more he wriggled, the further forward he went. It seemed that he could not go into reverse.

Mom and I grabbed Puddles' legs and pulled gently. We were relieved to see that he was uninjured. "I wonder what possessed him to crawl under the porch," Mom said. I did not know either.

Shortly after this event, Mom and Dad decided that the old wooden porch needed to be replaced. The concrete replacement would leave no space underneath. Puddles would never be trapped again. When the renovation was underway, the workers called for Mom to look at something. They pointed to an ocean of bright orange plastic sandwich bags lying in mounds on top of the soil where the wooden porch had been.

"What on earth are those?" Mom asked the construction workers.

"We thought that you would know."

Mom called me to have a look. She bent down and retrieved one of the bags. She opened it slowly and we both immediately recoiled from the overwhelming foul odour. She threw the bag onto the ground. Peering inside, I saw the liquefied, decomposed, brown remains of a slice of roast beef.

It was shocking to see how many roast beef dinners Mom had made over the years. At the same time, I was impressed to see how well the plastic bags had held up. Molson Bag and Paper Company makes very good plastic bags, I thought. I had expected them to disintegrate over time.

The confession came slowly to my lips. "Well, Mom, to tell you the truth, they contain roast beef—or what was roast beef." Mom's horror transformed instantly into hysterical laughter. The workers joined her.

"You mean, these are all those roast beef dinners you refused to eat—all the ones you pretended you had eaten?" I nodded sheepishly. "No wonder Puddles had wedged himself under the porch! He must have smelled the meat. This is disgusting. Get rid of them!"

I happily gathered up the bags and threw them into the trash can. After that, Mom never insisted that I eat roast beef again. I ate the vegetables she served, which she was kind enough to keep separate from the meat.

My thoughts return to that day in grade four. After the arithmetic lesson it was time for social studies. Ms. Dunsel began to describe the different provinces and natural regions of Canada. She stopped in midsentence and darted to the window. She looked frightened. *What had she seen?* Then we heard the soft but familiar wail of the air-raid siren. I knew that it wasn't another drill. The sound was coming from outside.

Ms. Dunsel cranked open the window. The sound of the siren burst into the classroom, starting at a low pitch and steadily rising until it hit a terrifying peak and then wound down, only to rise again and again. When I looked back at the classroom, I saw that most of the seats were empty. My friends had disappeared. Children and teachers were stampeding down the hall towards the doors to the yard. There was shouting and crying and the thunder of many feet running.

I entered the hall and was suddenly caught up in the chaotic, panicked mass as it surged towards the doors. Some children tripped and fell. The mass of feet jumped over them and on top of some of them. I was afraid that I might fall and be crushed. The wailing siren grew louder as I was shoved outside by the crowd. I fell onto the grass and saw feet running everywhere. The teachers were driving their cars out of the parking lot, almost colliding with each other, barely missing children who ran right in front of them. The panicked teachers fuelled the panicked mob of children, who spilled onto the main street, oblivious of the cars that skidded to a stop, their tires screeching. The cries, shouts, screams, honking of horns, screeching of tires, all accompanied the incessant rising and falling tones of the air-raid siren, proclaiming the end of the world. I knew that bombs would soon be falling from the sky and destroy everything. I had seen it on television.

I ran across the field to the small opening under the fence that led to my street. I used this opening only to enter and exit the school yard when I was late, as it was hard to get through without hurting myself. I ducked down under the fence, squeezed through the opening, and ran home as fast as I could.

Then, the siren stopped.

I finally arrived at home and threw open the front door. I collapsed into Mom's arms, weeping hysterically. I was inconsolable.

"It was a false alarm," she said. "I heard on the radio that there was a problem and the air-raid siren went off by accident. It was a false alarm. Everything is okay, Rickey. We are all safe."

I did not feel safe. The scene of children and teachers running for their lives was already a deeply and permanently engraved image in my mind. Her words could not be true even though I so longed for them to be. *She is only trying to comfort me, trying to protect me from the terrible reality that the bombs will soon fall. She loves me. What else could she possibly say at a time like this?*

Mom turned the radio on in the kitchen and sat me down on a chair in front of it.

"Listen to the announcement," she said as she handed me tissue after tissue.

It took me a long time before I stopped crying enough to hear the announcement. "There has been a false alarm." I needed to hear it over and over again before my eyes were dry and my breathing slowed.

A week earlier Mom and Dad had explained that Russia had built bombs on an island called Cuba and that this island was near the United States and Canada. They had shown me where Cuba was on the globe. Dad told me that if Russia launched their bombs, they would come from Cuba. *Why would Russia do that? If Russia does that, wouldn't the United States and Canada send bombs to destroy their country?*

"Many people in Russia and many in the United States and Canada would die if either country bombs the other."

"Aren't the leaders of both countries smart enough to figure that out?"

"We hope so," was all Mom and Dad said.

I thought you had to be smart to become the leader of a country.

Mom and Dad told me that they hoped that President Kennedy was smart enough to lead America out of this crisis and that this would keep us safe as well.

For many months afterwards, the sound of any kind of siren shattered my sleep and left me panic-stricken during the day.

I was already fearful of thunderstorms. That fear had taken root when I was three or four years old during one of our vacations in Florida. A ferocious thunderstorm erupted one night when we were staying in a hotel. Mom came into the bedroom as I was crying. Her trembling arms negated her verbal message of safety. Her incessant trembling transfused her fear of thunderstorms directly into me.

Mom and Dad had taken me to war movies when I was young. To me, the sound of bombs exploding sounded like thunder, increasing my fear of thunderstorms. Temperamentally prone to anxiety when stressed and reinforcing this specific fear over the years, I was primed to feel intense anxiety about the air-raid siren.

Howard comes to mind. He was a polite, articulate man in his thirties with whom rapport was easy. He looked at me with a generous smile as he sat down, leaning back in his chair, appearing to be relaxed. He had thin black hair and large brown eyes that cast a soft gaze toward me.

In his first session, Howard spontaneously told me his story. "I was hospitalized six years ago with a bacterial infection that was spreading through my body. I was very sick. The doctors gave me heavy doses of an antibiotic that eventually cleared the infection. A few days after I came home, I began to experience these horrible episodes of nerve pain everywhere in my body. I was working as a construction worker and had to stop. The pain was just too intense." Howard became teary. He sat up and wiped his eyes with his hand. He continued. "I can barely do anything at home. My wife and three sons do everything. We depend on long-term disability and my wife's income. She works as a receptionist at a dentist's office. My older son helps me out as well. I feel terrible that I'm dependent on my wife and son. I should be working. But I just can't go back. Just talking to friends leaves me exhausted."

Howard told me that over the years he had completed batteries of medical tests and that nothing had shown up to explain his disabling and body-wide nerve pain. "My doctor told me that since all the tests are negative, there is nothing physically wrong with me. I guess it's all in my head." Howard began to weep.

"That's a very upsetting message—telling you it's all in your head like it's not a real problem. I have a different understanding of your nerve pain." Howard wiped his eyes with a tissue and looked up at me. "Of course it's all in your head because every experience we have is in our brain and every experience is real." Howard's gaze became more intense. "There *must* be something going on physically that is causing your nerve pain, Howard. There is something going on physically in our brains and in the rest of our bodies whenever we experience any kind of sensation. Medical tests are not precise enough to detect every physical process going on inside of us. Even though we don't know which process in your body is causing your nerve pain, you can do a lot to help yourself and to feel better. But first, you need to accept that the nerve pain is real."

How ironic! As a psychologist, often my first intervention when treating patients with health problems was to confirm that their problems must have a physiological basis and were real. When physicians did not understand the origin of symptoms, they often concluded that the patient must have emotional problems and required psychological treatment. This message created more emotional turmoil as it implied that patients were imagining their symptoms. Patients felt anguish that their problems were not believed and self-blame for failing to cope better. Many came to doubt the reality of their symptoms.

Howard was open to learning a variety of coping strategies and took copious notes in each session. He practised thinking differently and coping better at home. Instead of reacting to flare-ups of pain by thinking, "I can't cope with this," he began to think, "I can cope with this even though it is really hard. What can I do to feel better right now?"

Treating Howard was smooth and easy. Or so I thought. Six months into treatment, another side of Howard emerged from the shadows.

One day Howard came into my office in obvious distress. He flung himself into the chair while breathing rapidly. He gulped air as if he was drowning. Wringing his hands, he shifted position continuously while he spoke. He had difficulty getting the words out in between gulps of air and frequently swallowing. He was in the throes of a panic attack. "Doctor, I pray the Rosary every morning when I get up. When I got up this morning, I couldn't find my Rosary beads. I always put them on my night table." Howard took time to gasp for more air and stood up stiffly.

I asked Howard if it would help to walk out of the office and down the hall with me while breathing more slowly. He jumped up and was out of the office a moment later. "You are safe, Howard. Breathe more slowly with me. These anxious feelings will pass." After a few minutes, he turned and quickly walked back to my office.

I spoke softly. "You should be proud of yourself, Howard. You are calmer now. Have you had other panic attacks like that one?"

"Yes, but not often because I usually do the right things. This morning, I still said the Apostle's Creed, Our Father, and Hail Mary. Maybe I will still be okay."

"You calmed yourself down effectively, Howard, by walking, breathing more slowly, and believing you are safe. Perhaps you also reassured yourself that you will probably find your Rosary beads at home. You caused the panic to pass. You can help yourself that way whenever you feel anxious."

"I really have to find those Rosary beads, Doctor. I have to hold them when I say those prayers."

"Why is that?"

"If I don't hold them and say the prayers in the right order, the pain will get worse."

I was surprised that Howard linked his saying the prayers correctly with his pain. This was my first glimpse into his world of compulsive rituals aimed at establishing a feeling that he had a measure of control over his episodes of pain.

"I'm wondering why your panic attacks and the way you pray never came up before, Howard. Of course, it's okay that you did not discuss these topics before. I'm just wondering why."

"Because it was working. I was doing everything right. The reason it came up now is that I don't know where my Rosary beads are. I need to go home, Doctor, and search for them now."

"That's fine, Howard. Keep breathing more slowly, loosen your muscles, and reassure yourself that you will be safe as you return home."

In subsequent sessions, Howard disclosed an elaborate and disabling network of rules that he had constructed for his day-to-day life. He disclosed that he felt that he must wear certain clothes on specific days, store certain items in a particular way, and perform personal hygiene tasks in a specific order before bedtime. "There are many more rules than those," he told me.

Whenever a flare-up occurred, Howard was always able to identify some way in which he had not precisely followed his rules and concluded that this was the cause. Since he created complicated rules, imperfection was guaranteed. When a flare-up did not occur, Howard ignored any imperfections and concluded that he had prevented it by following his rules precisely. It was a perfect system for maintaining his illusion of control, which he desperately needed.

Over time in treatment Howard came to understand a great deal. He understood that his compulsions grew out of his desperation to prevent flare-ups; that his thinking was irrational; and that there was no magic in his rituals. He understood that when he failed to perform a ritual, he felt great anxiety that increased his symptoms and perhaps actually triggered flare-ups. He also understood that he had ensured that it would be impossible for him to perform all his rituals perfectly on any day and that, despite this, his flare-ups did not occur every day.

What impact did Howard's intellectual insights have on his behaviour?
No impact at all.

Despite understanding all the downsides of trying to follow his rules, Howard chose to cling to them and to his conviction that they protected him. "I know it's irrational, but I've decided to keep following my rules." Howard was aware that he was making a choice.

This was progress.

Changing our thoughts and behaviour cannot occur without self-awareness of the choices we are making. But self-awareness by itself does not guarantee change. It is only when we take responsibility for our behaviour that we can consider making better choices. Choosing better self-care is often one of the most difficult decisions facing us.

I am thinking of my irrational beliefs that I allow to co-exist side by side with my identity as a scientist. I am bothered when the toes of my shoes do not point in the same direction when they sit in my closet;

when the spoons, forks, and knives in my cutlery drawer are not sorted properly; and when a patient's note begins in blue ink and continues in black ink after the pen with blue ink has run out. It is a reflex for me to say "Heaven forbid" after speaking about a terrible event that I fear might befall someone. True, I can tolerate the disorder of the shoes, cutlery, and colour of ink and resist the urge to say "Heaven forbid." Nonetheless, I feel more comfortable when I don't resist. Like a child holding onto a security blanket, the order I believe that I bring to my life gives me comfort, even though I know, intellectually, that it is all illusory.

Another focus of Howard's treatment was his phobia about taking any kind of medication. He was certain that the antibiotic that he had taken during his hospitalization was the cause of his nerve pain even though his physician repeatedly assured him that the drug was safe.

A few sessions after this discussion, Howard disclosed that one of his teenage sons had been diagnosed with strep throat and was prescribed an antibiotic. Despite his anxiety that his son might suffer a serious side effect, he had encouraged him to take the drug.

"Most of you believes that the antibiotic will help him get better."

"Yes."

"If you wish, you could choose to love yourself as much as you love your son. Your experience with the particular antibiotic you took in the hospital does not mean that all medications will cause harmful side effects. You believe this or you would not have encouraged your son to take the antibiotic."

Howard readily agreed that he had a double standard.

Not long after this session, there was news that the Food and Drug Administration in the USA and Health Canada were warning physicians to avoid prescribing the specific antibiotic that Howard had taken during his hospitalization. They reported that it could cause disabling and permanent neurological pain. Howard heard this report. While he was relieved that the cause of his pain had been validated, his fear of taking medication increased.

"This antibiotic was supposed to be safe. Now it turns out that it is so dangerous that doctors are being advised not to prescribe it. The same can be true for other drugs."

"It is easy to believe that all drugs are dangerous. But this is not true. Refusing to take all medication could put your life at risk, Howard. Taking medication can be risky but going without it can be even more dangerous. When you encouraged your son to take the antibiotic for his strep throat, you thought that he might get worse without the drug. Right?"

"That's right."

"You decided that the benefits outweighed the risks. Today, you did the same thing for yourself when you chose to come here."

"What do you mean?"

"There was no guarantee that your drive here would be safe. Perhaps you didn't think about this consciously, but you decided that the chances were good that you would arrive safely. You decided that the benefit of attending the session outweighed the risk of an accident. I made the same decision. We are always making risk-management decisions because life does not come with any guarantees. In the future, when your doctor recommends a medication, it would be better if you asked about the risks and benefits before deciding. That's probably the way you'd like your sons to decide when they are older. One rule for you and those you love."

When Howard graduated from treatment, he was coping better with his nerve pain. His mood and outlook were brighter, and he was enjoying more time with his family and friends. He was fully aware of the mixed feelings that he had about reducing his compulsive rituals and taking medication.

The time to graduate came when patients felt that they possessed the knowledge and skills that they needed to continue to move forward without me despite the unresolved problems that always remained.

James worked as a garbage collector. He was a tall, young man in his twenties with deep black skin. I recall his gentle smile and gleaming eyes. He was referred by his nurse from the Worker's Safety and Insurance Board with the goal of returning to work.

James began our first session pouring out his regret about having moved from Trinidad to Toronto. "Lookin' for new life. Look what happen! Need back to work but I too scared. Dat machine, hell. Yuh understand, eh?" I nodded, taking time to get used to the quick flow of his language. I had difficulty understanding his Trinidad vocabulary and dialect. His language was super-efficient. Complex thoughts were distilled down to a few words spoken rapidly.

"I may have to ask you to repeat something if I don't get it, James. I hope that's okay."

"Yeah, ax what yuh need."

"I load dat truck—jus normal. Push button start compactor. I go walk away. Den, boom! All hell happen." James exploded out of his seat. Sitting back down, he shouted, "Boom! Bomb gon off. Thrown on back, ankle bust, back pain, cans, bottles, soaking bags, muck all over me, like flood of shit in a hurricane."

James's body was tense. Sweat formed on his forehead. His breathing was laboured. Reaching down he caressed his ankle as if it had just been fractured.

"It was a year ago, right?" I said, hoping to bring him back to the present. "You are safe here now, James. How are your ankle and back?"

"They better. Can walk okay. Dat machine never explode, never. Yuh get it?"

"Yeah. It never happened before, and you got badly hurt and really scared."

"Scare me to death! Thought I die. I wash my clothes at home use my hands. Can't turn on washing machine. Scared!"

Bang! The noise coming from the reception room startled both of us. James's entire body shook, and he bolted out of his seat. "It's okay, James. My secretary must have dropped a book out there. Take some slow, deep breaths with me. You are safe here."

"Scare me—any loud noise, I jump."

"I understand. The loud noise reminds you of the accident. That was one year ago. You are safe here now. Loud sounds are often just loud sounds, not signs of danger. When you turn on your washing machine, does that sound remind you of the accident, too?"

"Yeah. Think it will explode."

James told me that most nights he had nightmares about the accident. "See me dead."

When I asked James if he knew what caused the explosion, he told me that the cause was an almost empty carbon dioxide cannister that someone had thrown into the trash.

"Scared go back to work. Should be brave! Big coward."

"No, James. You are not a coward at all. If you were, you wouldn't be here, trying to get back to work. It's natural you are scared."

"Yeah. Need money! Workers comp not forever." James felt trapped by his fear. Living on his own and having little formal education he needed to return to work but was too fearful to return.

"James, you want to go back to work. You and I together, we can make that happen. When you go back, what would you do to make it safer for you?"

James squirmed in his chair, clearly uncomfortable when he imagined being back. After a few moments, he appeared thoughtful and calmer. "Back away from truck after push da button."

"James, would you like to start with the goal of using your washing machine again?"

"Yeah. Tiring washing my clothes."

"I bet. You know, James, when you think about starting the washing machine, part of your brain remembers the accident and wants to protect you, so you feel scared and wash your clothes by hand. Just thinking about it now, do you believe it is safe to turn on the washing machine?"

"Yeah, it never explode."

I led James through a relaxation procedure and then we drew up a plan that James believed he could manage opening and closing the door to his washing machine. At first, he would not turn it on. He would listen for the click and the beep to tell him the door was locked. "Perhaps after you practise that a number of times, you might get up the courage to use your machine to wash your clothes. But it's perfectly fine if you don't feel ready for that before our next session in two weeks. You need to go forward at your own pace. The important thing is you *are* moving forward."

In his next session James told me that he had used his washing machine for the first time since the accident. "That's great, James. You should be proud of yourself. That's a really big step! As you practise relaxing your muscles, breathing more slowly, and reassuring yourself that you are safe, the easier it will get."

In subsequent sessions, James was able to relax his muscles to some extent and breathe more slowly while imagining that he was at work standing near a garbage truck with the compactor on.

Along the way, I frequently encouraged James to congratulate himself for his courage and motivation to decrease his fear. This was a new concept for him. It was for many of my patients.

We are often taught to pat others on the back for achievements but all too rarely to pat ourselves on the back for ours.

James's case manager expected him to return to work within a few months. When she read my progress report, which indicated that his sessions were occurring every other week, she called me. "Why not weekly? Spacing the sessions out is slowing his progress."

"James is highly motivated to return to work," I told her. "He needs time in between our sessions to practise strategies to reduce his fear. He is making steady progress. If it appears that weekly sessions would be more helpful, I assure you that I will see him weekly."

A few weeks later, James said that he was ready to go to his workplace and stand near a garbage truck but not alone. "Is there a friend or relative who could go with you?"

"No one here. They' all in Trinidad."

"Would it help if I came with you?"

"Yeah man."

James gave me permission to contact his employer to let her know our plan. "I'm glad he's making progress," she said.

At the garbage collection site, James and I stood some distance from a garbage truck for about fifteen minutes. During that time, he calmed himself by relaxing his muscles as he had practised during our sessions and reminded himself that it was almost certain he would be safe. "We need to be honest with ourselves, James. No matter what we do in life, we need to accept that we are never one hundred percent safe. But we can say that the chances are very high that we will be safe as we are now."

I asked James whether he wished to end the session or move closer to the truck even though the compactor was operating. "Go wit you," he said as he pointed at the truck.

As we walked closer, all at once we were surrounded by many trucks and their deafening crushing and dumping sounds as they spewed mounds of trash into gaping holes. As far as I could see, the land appeared to be desert-like with piles of garbage scattered at random intervals on the barren terrain. I felt like I was standing on another planet.

Still breathing more slowly, James inched toward a truck while it was compacting trash until he was quite close. I joined him.

Having heard James's account of the accident many times, I must admit that I felt some anxiety myself.

James practised his relaxation strategies and coping self-statements for about twenty minutes after which he turned to me and smiled broadly. "Did it!"

"Yes, you certainly did, James! You felt scared and you calmed yourself. You told yourself that you were very likely safe. You should be proud of yourself."

James returned to the worksite on his own a few times in the following two weeks. Although we drew up a gradual return to work plan that spanned two months, James decided it would be better for him to start by returning full-time.

James had little formal schooling and minimal insight into his thoughts and feelings. Even so, he readily implemented the techniques that I introduced to help him decrease his post-traumatic anxiety. He returned to full-time employment after a relatively short time in treatment.

Working with James reminded me of the critical role motivation plays in enabling people to make lifestyle changes.

I am also reflecting on the roles that acceptance of fear and rational thinking play in helping us decrease emotional pain. Neither one by itself is sufficient. Upon graduating from treatment many of my patients with post-traumatic anxiety accepted their emotions as natural, without self-condemnation. Thinking logically, they chose to believe that the odds were that they would be safe.

Despite their significant progress, anything that reminded Howard and James of their trauma continued to trigger some level of anxiety, automatically, without any conscious thought. For me, it was sirens and thunderstorms. For Howard, medication. For James, the sound of garbage trucks compacting garbage. Our inner guard remained vigilant, ready to alert us to possible danger. This appears to be an automatic adaptive response. *But then, why is it that only some of us react to trauma in this way?*

35

Educating Angela

I felt ecstasy with every little kick from within but I was also anxious. How would Dr. Wilson react? I had only been at the hospital for two months and in just a few more, I would be off on a maternity leave. When I was in my fourth month, I could no longer hide my ever-expanding abdomen.

Dr. Wilson began one of our supervisory sessions with a compliment. "I am very happy with all the work you are doing here. I've received positive feedback from the medical departments. Keep it up."

I just blurted it out. "Dr. Wilson, I need to tell you that I'm pregnant." I was too nervous to look at his face.

"Congratulations!" he beamed. "When are you due?"

"At the end of August. I am planning to take only three months maternity leave." My tone was apologetic.

"It won't be a problem at all. I will hire someone to cover the time. Tony Lees, our administrator, will be happy about this because it will save the hospital money."

I had never considered that my maternity leave might be a good thing for the hospital and for Dr. Wilson.

Angela entered the world on August 14, 1981. I had a detailed birthing plan that involved using a birthing chair and a Leboyer bath for her. After thirteen hours of what the obstetrician called "unproductive labour," I was induced and eight hours later Angela was born. I spent my first few days at home sitting on ice packs and marvelling at Angela as she breastfed and slept.

Angela was easy to love. She slept through the night after only a few weeks. She had a calm and even temperament and was curious about everything. I woke up to her beautiful little cooing and gurgling sounds every morning. I couldn't wait for this joyful music to transform into speech. *Oh, the conversations we would have!*

Every day during my three-month maternity leave, I created puzzles and games for her. She focused on them for longer and longer periods. I filled the house with classical music, especially Beethoven's symphonies, which I had also played during my pregnancy, hoping that she would be moved by the music as much as I was.

Mom was enraptured with Angela. After I told Mom that I wanted to help Angela learn how to use her hands, she knitted little bracelets with bells on them. After only a few occasions, Angela smiled joyfully, understanding that when she moved her hands, the bells jingled. She quickly became adept at using her hands for exploring everything.

Whenever I played simple tunes on the piano with Angela sitting on my lap, she reached out and tried to copy me. When she was three years old, she often climbed up on the piano bench and laughed when she pressed the keys. I decided to arrange piano lessons for her when she was four years old, the same age when I had started. I wanted to save her from the pressure and anxiety that I had experienced. I searched for an approach that was different.

A friend told me about Nora, a piano teacher who employed the Suzuki method. Nora explained that the Suzuki method required the child to hear recordings of the pieces to be learned over and over again. She also told me that a parent would be required to attend each lesson and take notes as to how the child should practise. This was dramatically different from my musical education, which had not required anything from my parents except their payment.

I asked Luke if he would assume this role. He agreed. Despite my best of intentions, I feared that my perfectionistic strivings would culminate in criticism and unreasonable expectations for Angela. I worried that I might sabotage the Suzuki method.

It was the highlight of my day to listen to Angela's practising with Luke's guidance. The weekly lessons and daily practice sessions assured that Angela and Luke had time together. Angela steadily improved her musical skills and, at the same time, her relationship with her dad was growing closer.

I could not resist becoming involved when Angela practised on her own. I encouraged her to think about a story that the music was telling and to infuse her playing with her emotions. I was impressed to hear the beginner pieces come to life as music. At recitals, I was nervous for her, but Angela was calm and eager to perform.

Angela was precocious. She was sensitive to social cues and empathic. At age five, when we were at the grocery store one day, as I placed a frozen chicken in the shopping cart, she asked, "Isn't that a chicken?"

"Yes, Angela."

"Oh," she said sadly. "A dead chicken."

I looked at the frozen chicken in a new way. I had regarded it as a product much like frozen peas. Now, as I looked at Angela's sad eyes, I thought about how the chicken had looked when it had been alive. Glancing at the meat counter, I imagined the cows, pigs, and lambs that had produced the meat in the packages, which were lying neatly in rows. After a few moments, I put the frozen chicken back in the freezer.

After this shopping trip, I spent several months reading scientific papers about the negative impact of eating meat. I was horrified by the description of factory farming and repulsed by the unethical treatment of the animals. I read about the huge amounts of greenhouse gases that result from animal agriculture and the many forests that were devastated to clear land for grazing. I learned about the health benefits of eating less meat. My decision to become a vegetarian was a natural outcome.

"I've decided to become a vegetarian," I told Luke. "I respect your decision to eat whatever you wish, but I am no longer buying meat, poultry, or fish. You can if you wish. From now on I'm going to prepare vegetarian meals."

Angela added that she wanted to stop eating meat as well.

Luke did not have an issue with my decision. He adjusted to the meals that I prepared.

Angela excelled at school. She learned everything quickly and loved to read and write stories. In grade four, along with her classmates, she was given a standardized intelligence test. A few days later, her teacher, Ms. Bronson, sent a note home requesting that Luke and I meet with her. Luke told me that he could not take time off work so I went alone.

"I have some very good news for you, Mrs. Miller."

"Yes?"

"Angela's intelligence test results indicate that she is in the gifted range."

I recalled the intelligence test that I had taken along with my classmates in grade six. One week later, I was asked to leave the regular classroom in the middle of the afternoon, as were several other students from different classrooms. From that point on, we left our regular class and attended an "enrichment class" for one period every day. I enjoyed that class a lot. Each of us worked on a single research project for the entire year, culminating in a book. My project focused on animals in Canada. I loved spending hours on the weekend at the library reading about animals and taking notes as I went.

I paid a high emotional cost for attending the enrichment class. Whenever I returned to my regular class, I heard snickering and whispers of "Here comes the browner!" At recess no one wanted to play with me. I tried unsuccessfully to befriend the other four students in my enrichment class, but each came from a different class. They still had friends to play with at recess and did not include me. Instantly, I had become an outsider. The loneliness was painful, and I felt helpless to do anything about it.

I did not want Angela to experience this pain.

"What are you proposing, Ms. Bronson?" I asked.

"Angela will go to Givens next year. Givens is the school for gifted students. Here's the paperwork. All you need to do is sign." She presented me with a document, an envelope, and a pen, and smiled as if congratulating me.

I did not feel that I merited congratulations. Although I did my best to provide Angela with as many learning opportunities as I could, the intelligence test results reflected her achievement, not mine.

I was proud of Angela, for sure, but mindful of the possible downside of her going to a different school, one that was for gifted kids.

"Ms. Bronson, I need to think about this and talk to Luke and, most importantly, to Angela about this. All her friends are at Shoreham. She hasn't been bored, has she?"

"No, but why would you hesitate about this? She would receive far more stimulation at Givens than we can provide for her here. Not many students have this opportunity." Ms. Bronson looked at me incredulously.

Angela's social and educational needs were both being met. I saw no benefit in uprooting her and risk her losing her friends. I reflected on the enrichment that comes from interacting with classmates who have different levels of skill. I did not want Angela to come to see herself as superior.

I explained the opportunity to Angela and Luke that evening. I tried my best to present the pros and cons, but I'm sure my preference must have come through. Angela was unambivalent.

"I do not want to leave my school. All my friends are there." Luke supported Angela's decision.

I can never know whether Angela would have benefitted more from Givens or from the type of music education that I received. I made these decisions in reaction to my own experiences. We know that our children thrive when we provide unconditional love and support them through hardship. But other than that, there are very few signposts to help us along our way. We are often guided by our own experiences.

36

I Always Knew

Michael announced his entrance into the world with loud incessant cries. "Michael, we're so happy to see you!" exclaimed Luke as he cut the umbilical cord. It was February 26, 1985.

During those first few weeks with Michael, I felt confident. This was my second child after all. I was an experienced mom. I did everything that I had done with Angela. I expected Michael would respond in exactly the same way. *How strange for one who is well aware that each child in a family is unique.*

I looked forward to the thrill of watching Michael's little brain begin to make sense of the world, culminating in the miraculous dawn of communication. Each day that passed, I anticipated the ecstasy of seeing Michael's first smile back to me—the responsive smile that defines each of us as a separate, conscious human being, communicating pleasure.

I sang to Michael and read him stories. I gave him toys that Angela had enjoyed. I played the same games with him. Angela cuddled him tenderly and told him stories. Luke was loving and attentive. Michael's environment could not have been more enriched and nurturing.

Michael slept a lot, breastfed a lot, and wanted to be held a lot. He was oblivious to what was going on around him and often fell asleep in the midst of songs, stories, and games. I was not concerned. Children develop differently, I reminded myself.

Day after day, Michael looked at everything I showed him with a blank expression. He was obsessed with breastfeeding. No matter how often I fed him, he would cry for more. His only needs were to eat and sleep and be held.

I waited as the weeks flew by for his first real smile. I recalled my thrill when Angela smiled back at me for the first time at six weeks of age. "Luke! There's someone in there!" I cried out to him, waking him from a sound sleep. She was sitting on my stomach, her back nestled against my bent knees, looking at me, and responding to my laughter with smile after smile. It was clear that we were truly communicating.

Six weeks passed. Seven. Eight—the average time a baby smiles back. Michael continued to look at me blankly no matter how much I smiled and laughed. To comfort myself, I touched the side of his mouth softly to encourage a smile. Sometimes it worked. Sometimes I saw him smile when he was asleep. I was not fooling myself. The moment I saw one of those smiles, I felt sad. We were not communicating.

That's when I first knew.

"There's something wrong with him," I nervously told Luke, wanting him to agree and disagree.

"No. He's okay. Don't worry," was his response. "Just be patient. He'll be fine." As much as I sought reassurance, Luke's words only provoked more anxiety. I felt alone with a serious problem that was clearly evident despite my attempts to wish it away. My anxiety escalated to the point that I was awake most nights along with Michael, whose need for breastmilk seemed insatiable—or perhaps it was his need for comfort. Breastmilk and cuddling gave him comfort.

There was no comfort for me.

Nearing the end of his ninth week, I was at Dr. Graham's office for another regular checkup. He examined Michael and gave him a perfect bill of health.

"Dr. Graham," I began, "There is something wrong with my baby. There is no responsive smile. It should have happened by now."

Dr. Graham's immediate response was just as reassuring as Luke's. "Yes. He is a little slow, but he may catch up later. Some children develop that way. Because you are a psychologist, you are worried. If you didn't know so much, you wouldn't have noticed. There is a problem sometimes in knowing too much."

Dr. Graham was correct. Because I was a psychologist, I knew there was something wrong. *But what exactly was the problem? How serious was it? What could I do to fix it?* The problem wasn't that I knew too much. The problem was that I knew too little.

I thought about the pregnancy. What had I done wrong? I had a rum punch when we had travelled to Barbados during my first trimester. Could that have been the culprit?

As the weeks passed, there was not much change in Michael. I was becoming more and more concerned. It was not just the lack of a responsive smile that worried me but Michael's blank expression no matter what I showed him, or what sounds he heard, or how we played with him. He continued to spend his days breastfeeding, sleeping, and seeking cuddles. During the nights, he continued to wake frequently and only went back to sleep after he was breastfed. Unlike Angela when she was an infant, he rejected a pacifier. Despite my increasing anxiety, I persisted in singing to him, showing him different objects, reading to him, talking to him, and playing with him. Never give up was my mantra. Ten weeks. Eleven weeks. No change.

One day during his twelfth week of life, it finally happened. I was lifting Michael up and down and there it was. He smiled at me, clearly enjoying the movement. There was no question that Michael was responding to me. As I laughed, and lifted him high and then down low, he smiled again. Over and over, we repeated the game. I was overjoyed. There was hope in that responsive smile. *Michael will be fine. He will achieve the same milestones as every other child, maybe just a little later. It's just like Dr. Graham had said.*

My attempts to reassure myself as I lifted Michael up and down only partly subdued my fears. Deep inside there was a dark seed of knowledge. I could not pretend that his delay in smiling back at me and his other abnormal behaviours were insignificant. I knew that Michael was not fine.

And so, I always knew.

37

Just a Little Slower

Michael is just a little slower. I was confident that Michael could learn anything. *It will just take him longer.*

My research training determined my course of action. I read all I could in lay and professional books about child development. The ideas I gleaned inspired me to create games, songs, and movements to capture Michael's interest even if for only short periods of time. His attention was fleeting like a precious butterfly but beautiful to behold. Each time he listened to my words as I read to him, or smiled back at me, or attended to a song or giggled when I lifted him high or rocked him back and forth—I felt joy. I was encouraged and optimistic about his future. *Don't worry. Michael will be just fine.*

Lurking underneath, barely perceptible, my gnawing anxiety persisted.

I attached the knitted bracelets with bells on Michael's wrists. They had helped Angela find her hands. I knew that they would help Michael, too. *It will just take him longer.* I celebrated with smiles and hugs the day when Michael discovered that moving his arms and hands made the bells ring.

I took a four-month maternity leave. When it was time for me to return to work, I introduced Michael to Auntie Gloria, the warm and lovely owner of the home daycare that Angela attended. She eagerly agreed to take care of him. "Michael is a lot different from Angela," I said apologetically, anticipating that caring for him would be more taxing. Gloria immediately responded, "Of course he is different from Angela. No two siblings are ever alike—at least not in my experience." Gloria should know, I thought. She had six children, ages twelve to twenty.

"But I mean, well," I hesitated, "he's coming along *more* slowly."

"Don't worry, Rickey. I will take good care of Michael and he will learn a lot by watching the other children." Gloria's comments were only partially reassuring. I tried hard to believe her.

I couldn't stop myself from using Angela's developmental history as a standard against which Michael consistently came up short. Angela slept through the night in her second month and continued to do so most of the time throughout her childhood. During the last few months of Angela's first year, I was joyfully awakened every morning by her beautiful cooing sounds while she waited in her crib for us to greet her. She started to use words to communicate before her second birthday and then rapidly acquired a large vocabulary. She loved to read books and enjoyed listening to music. At four, she was rapidly progressing through the Suzuki piano books. Spending time with Angela was easy. Helping her learn and problem-solve, supporting her creativity and her love for music all came naturally and filled my heart with many moments to treasure.

Spending time with Michael was rarely easy. Michael consistently woke up through the night for his first two years. No matter what I did, whether it was breastfeeding him, rocking him gently, and reassuring him that he was safe, his sleep, and mine, continued to be disrupted. A sleep deficit accompanied me to work every day. I waited in vain to hear delightful cooing sounds coming from Michael's crib in the morning. I was awakened only by loud crying.

Despite his slower development, most of the time Michael was a happy little soul. He giggled when lifted high and brought down low. He smiled often and was amused by Angela who took up the challenge of teaching him through play. She never failed to entertain him. I appreciated the much-needed breaks that she gave me when she held his attention. Otherwise, I supervised Michael or played with him. When left on his own with toys around him, he would run over to Luke, Angela, or me and cry incessantly if we did not interact with him. He was unable to play on his own.

As Michael approached three years of age, I was most concerned about the delay in his speech. There was still no evidence that he understood that words had meaning. At every opportunity, I labelled everything, sounding out words slowly, and keeping the number to a minimum. He'll catch up, I thought. Finally, a light shone in his eyes as he said "Na-na" when I pointed to his cup of milk. Later he said "Eee-ah" for Angela and "Ma-ma" and "Da-da." I was relieved that he achieved this critical milestone. At the same time, I was anxious about his limited vocabulary and his problem saying consonants.

Luke was affectionate with Michael but naturally enjoyed his interactions with Angela much more. He appeared to tolerate the time I spent every day helping Michael and, at times, joined me when I read, sang, and played with him.

Dr. Graham referred me to Dr. Larry, who coordinated the Hanen program at the Hospital for Sick Children. The eight-week group program, *It Takes Two to Talk*, would teach us how to help Michael improve his verbal skills.

"Rickey, this program requires a significant amount of time from both parents." Dr. Larry looked at me rather sternly. "Are you and Luke willing to commit to spend time every day working with Michael? Will you commit to attend every group session?"

"Absolutely."

Over the course of the program, Dr. Larry taught us to simplify our language whenever Michael made any sound that indicated that he was interested in something and was attempting to communicate. We learned to encourage Michael to take turns with us to create little conversations so that we were not just talking at him.

"Uh."

"That's a t-r-uck."

"Uh!"

"T-r-uck. You want the truck."

"Ee-ah."

"That's An-ge-la."

"Ee-ah."

"Yes, that's Angela."

Sometime after the fourth week, I was thrilled when Michael put two words together for the first time and the consonant "t" emerged from his lips.

"On tay."

"You w-a-n-t the t-r-ain?" I said in disbelief.

"On tay!"

"You want the train!" I exclaimed. When I gave Michael the train, he immediately smiled, and started to roll it back and forth on the floor, acknowledging that I had understood him. "You are playing with the train," I said, with tears of joy in my eyes.

Although Luke had less time to spend with Michael because his hours at work were longer, he employed the strategies that we were taught and completed the homework sheets as I did. We both attended the group sessions. Slowly over the course of the eight-week program, Michael was saying more words and putting two together more often. Our little conversations became more frequent.

At age six, Angela eagerly copied us as we employed the Hanen strategies. She created games with puppets that greatly entertained Michael and encouraged him to say more words. Her lessons almost always ended with laughter. I was impressed with her creativity and the ease with which she learned the techniques that we had to work so hard to acquire. She never lost patience. I tried my best to copy her.

After the program was completed, I received an unexpected call from Dr. Larry. He said that he wanted to provide me with detailed feedback. I took time off from work to meet with him.

"Rickey, you and Luke have done an excellent job in the Hanen program. Over the eight weeks you have helped Michael to say more words and begin to string them together. The consonants are coming." Dr. Larry paused.

Muscles tightened throughout my body. I was gripped with fear. I knew that he had more to say. I did not want to hear his words. I glanced at the door to his office. Escape was possible. But not from this reality. I knew that his words would be announcing nothing new, yet they would be excruciating to hear. There was no running away from what I always knew.

"Rickey, Michael has more than a speech delay. There are delays in other areas as well. I think he would benefit from a referral to an occupational therapist to help him with gross and fine motor skills."

More than a speech delay. I was overcome with the familiar sickening anxiety that I tried as much as I could to dispel.

"Go ahead and arrange the referral, Dr. Larry," I heard myself say.

I left the appointment reeling from hearing confirmation that there was more wrong with Michael than a speech delay. Then I thought that helping him with speech must come first. Communication is everything. Occupational therapy will wait.

I arranged for Michael to receive speech therapy at the hospital where I worked. Every week, behind the one-way mirror, I watched the therapist coach Michael to say consonant sounds and to string together new words. She gave me homework to do. I taped large printed labels onto most objects in the house so that Michael could see the letters that made up the words he was learning, and repeated the words every time Michael looked at them. I reinforced any approximations to the correct sound that he made with a lot of cuddles, which Michael loved more than anything.

I tried as much as I could to emulate the patient and calm manner of the therapist. This required all my strength after a full day at work, making supper, and discussing what was happening in Angela's life, and Luke's day. When I was unable to hold Michael's attention long enough to do anything productive, I became exasperated with him and with myself. I heard the impatience in my tone. "Why can't you get this, Michael?!" I shouted. *I should stop now. He's done. I'm done. But what if I try this? Maybe this will work and we'll get somewhere. Let's try again. Never give up.*

It would take me multiple unsuccessful attempts before I would finally give up. When tucking Michael into bed, I would try once or twice more with a consonant, "B-ed. This is your bed. B-l-an-ket. This is your blanket." And then, "I'm sorry I shouted at you. I will try to be more patient. I love you." It was a sincere apology even though I knew that my patience would wear thin again the next day. Many more apologies were to come.

One of the most challenging tasks for Michael was drawing simple objects. Squares, circles, triangles, even simply crossing two lines to make an "X" were impossible for him to copy for many months. *How could Michael learn to print letters if he was unable to draw simple shapes and cross two lines?* There had to be a way to teach him. I had to think creatively to find the best approach.

One Saturday in the summer when he was three and a half, I tried repeatedly to show Michael how to make an X using different coloured crayons on various types of paper. I crossed two lines on paper while putting my hand over his, pushing it the right way. I showed him how to cross his arms and asked him to copy me. No matter what I did, he persisted in drawing lines that did not cross on paper. Then it occurred to me—perhaps a much larger background would help.

I spent some time taping together many sheets of construction paper of various colours to create a gigantic square. I told Michael to follow me into the backyard after I grabbed two black markers. He giggled when he saw me unfold the gigantic square of different coloured paper, which filled a large portion of our backyard. I led him to one corner and said with confidence, "You are going to make an X by crossing two lines, starting from one corner to the other one way over there." I pointed to the other corner and handed Michael a marker. He started to draw as we crawled together from one corner to the other one diagonally opposite. He was laughing as we went.

"Now, let's head over to the other corner. You are going to do the same thing. Make a line from this corner to that other one down there."

I made a point of omitting the word "cross" because, after all our unsuccessful attempts, I thought that the word itself might set him up to fail.

We crawled together from one corner to the other and as Michael crossed the line with the marker, I congratulated him. Now that he had accomplished this, I emphasized the word "cross." "Yes! You made that line cross the other line! Good for you, Michael!" Once at the other corner we stood, and I repeated my congratulatory message. We walked around the huge square to look at the X from all angles. "You did it! You made the lines cross. You made an X."

Hesitantly, I tore two of the pages out and invited Michael to sit on the grass beside me. On one page, as I made an X on the page, I said "See, Michael. That one over there that you made is a big grown-up X. This one that I made is a baby X. I bet you can make a baby one, too." I handed Michael the marker and held my breath.

"Wow! Look at that, Michael. You made a baby X from corner to corner on one side and from corner to corner on the other side. Good for you! There is nothing you can't learn, Michael. It just takes you a little longer." We both laughed with delight as I gave Michael his favourite ride through the air.

Later that day, we sat down at the dining room table, and I gave Michael a lined page from his printing book. I made a small X with a pencil that fit between the lines. "You see, Michael. This isn't a grown-up X and it's not a baby X. It's a teeny-weeny X that isn't even a baby yet. You make a teeny-weeny X between these two blue lines." Joy and hope filled my heart as Michael took the pencil and made the X between the two lines for the first time. We celebrated as he filled in more lines with Xs.

Michael will be able to learn to print, I thought. *He'll just be a little slower to get it.* "You can learn anything, Michael," I said, reinforcing my conviction that this was true. "It just might take you a little longer. But you must never give up. There must be a way. We just need to find the right way for you." It was no longer just my mantra. It was the affirmation Michael heard day in and day out that became a part of his very identity. There must be a way. Never give up.

Teaching Michael demanded creativity. All that was certain was that the obvious way of teaching a concept would fail, even if the method was broken down into small steps. As usual, Angela was especially adept. She devised imaginative ways of engaging Michael, holding his attention, and patiently guiding his thinking towards the light in the most entertaining way. As I watched Angela work her magic, I observed her intellectual skills grow. My heart was also touched by the love Angela and Michael shared.

One of Michael's favourite activities was dancing and singing while naked in front of the mirrors of the laundry room just off the kitchen. He entertained himself for hours in this way. His performance in the nude afforded me time to rest. The only problem was that it was difficult to stop Michael from removing his clothes when we had company. Angela was embarrassed at one of her birthday parties when Michael ran through the house naked when I was not watching him. While most tasks took Michael a great deal of time to complete, he was able to take off his clothes in seconds.

When I was driving Michael anywhere, he engaged in his disrobing pastime. This became especially frustrating during the winter when it took me a long time to get Michael dressed.

While driving, I was aggravated every time I looked in the rear-view mirror to see Michael taking his clothes off. "Don't take your clothes off, Michael. Stop doing that!" My words had no impact except to increase my frustration. Looking in the rear-view mirror minutes later, I would see Michael smiling back at me from his car seat, completely nude, his clothes strewn over the back seat. No matter how tightly I harnessed him into his car seat, he was able to engage in his feat of stripping. There were many cold winter nights when I froze standing outside by the open car door while dressing him again. "Now I am going to have less time to make dinner. We are going to have less time doing any of your books. I will have less time to spend with your dad and with Angela. This is all because you took your clothes off and I must dress you again! I am not happy." My exasperation was clear. Michael was calm and quiet, not appearing to be affected at all by my frustration.

I did not stop, not for one moment, to consider the message that he might be sending me.

How could I not see that Michael was aggravated with me because of all the work that I was imposing on him? I was doing it with the best of intentions, but it was hard work nonetheless. I did not feel compassion for Michael. I did not understand his frustration and his strong motivation to delay going into the house.

One frigid winter night, when Michael was five years old, I drove home from his speech-therapy session, practising words with him as usual. I drove into a gas station, parked, and turned around to face him. Michael was still dressed. I was exhausted. I had worked all day, had driven a long way through heavy traffic to pick Michael up at Gloria's house, had driven all the way back to the hospital, had attended his one-hour speech therapy session, and had driven through more rush-hour traffic toward home. I feel exhausted just thinking about those trips that I often took for years.

"Good, Michael, you are dressed. Please keep your clothes on all the way home. It's cold outside. There's a lot of snow." Michael was looking at me as I continued. "I don't have time to dress you. If you take your clothes off, you will go into the house naked and you will be *very* cold." I paused. Always leave with the desired choice, the one that would be better for him, I reminded myself. "But you will be *warm*, if you keep them on."

When I parked in the driveway a few minutes later and turned around, naked Michael was smiling back at me. Without hesitation, I got out of the car, went around to his side, opened his door, and grabbed all his clothes and boots. I undid his car seat. Michael stopped smiling when his body was hit by the influx of freezing air and falling snow-flakes. He looked shocked. He gazed at the path towards the front door and saw the deep snow.

"Okay, Michael. Time to get out of the car and go into the house." I said in the same way that I would have if he had been fully clothed.

Michael cried and reached for the clothes that I had packed in my work bag. "No, Michael. I don't have time to dress you. Come on. I need to make dinner. You are going to be cold because you took off your clothes. If you had kept them on, you would be warm."

Michael lingered for a while. I stood by the door with my hand held out for his. Finally, he took my hand and I led naked and screaming Michael through the snow to the front door. While I was unlocking the door, I turned to see a neighbour across the street who had been shovelling snow scowling at me.

Would he call Children's Aid?

I was anxious for the next few days. Fortunately, I did not receive that call.

Michael never took his clothes off again in my car. Of course, he persisted in dancing naked in front of the kitchen mirrors because I did nothing to stop him. I could not give up the few precious breaks I had.

When Gloria moved to Winnipeg, I researched daycare centres to find the best fit for Michael. I chose a Montessori one. The teacher felt Michael would do best in the four-year-old's room. She reassured me that she would teach Michael at his level and modify tasks and games to meet his needs. The Montessori approach has a child-centred focus. I felt this would make it a perfect place for Michael.

After three days, the supervisor called me and told me that Michael was not a "good fit" for her daycare. "He wanders around the room, talking to himself, and disrupts the rest of the group. He doesn't stay focused on any activity for any length of time. This is not the place for him. I will provide you with a full refund."

I was disturbed and surprised by this failure.

At the New Foundations daycare, Michael was placed in a class of three-year-olds with Anna, a superbly patient and caring teacher and her equally warm and competent assistant, Mary. From the outset, Anna reported that Michael was doing well interacting with the other children. She told me that Michael was benefitting from the extra one-to-one attention that Mary was giving him throughout the day. That's what he needs—one-to-one attention, I thought. *With that kind of help, Michael can learn anything.*

Amani told me about a set of phonics books that had helped her child learn to read. I quickly purchased the set of 50 books. *For sure, Michael will learn to read.*

When Michael was four years old, we attended our first summer music program at the Suzuki Music Institute at the University of Hartford in Connecticut, where Angela received individual piano lessons, attended group programs, and had opportunities to perform.

While Angela was attending one of her group lessons, Michael and I passed by a classroom that was bursting with the lush sounds of violins. Michael tugged on my hand and motioned to go inside. I peeked in and saw that parents were sitting in the classroom. We walked in and sat down. Michael was mesmerized. The teacher was creating musical games while playing his violin and the children were responding in unison on their violins.

After that whenever Michael heard the sound of a violin, he would stop and listen. The sound held his attention like nothing else. I began to dream that he would become a violinist. *Playing the violin will be his salvation and mine.*

At the age of five, when I asked Michael if he wanted to learn to play the piano, he shook his head. "No. Iolin." I located a Suzuki teacher, Ms. Dunn, and Michael began taking lessons.

As I watched Michael's lessons and helped him practise, a strong yearning was creeping into my awareness. I longed to create music once again. A deep sense of loss and emptiness had been haunting me. I asked Ms. Dunn if she would teach me to play the violin at the same time as Michael. She enthusiastically agreed.

Learning to play the violin was the most humbling experience of my life. While Michael played with perfect intonation from the beginning, I struggled to play in tune. While his vibrato was effortless and natural, mine required hours and hours of work.

Every morning and evening, the house was filled not only with the Suzuki recordings of piano pieces but with violin pieces as well.

Before breakfast, Michael and I were in the basement. I struggled to encourage him to play the sections as Ms. Dunn had instructed. I was tired. Michael was tired. Most of the time only the first few minutes of our time together were productive.

"Michael, hold your bow like this. Ms. Dunn told us to hold it this way. No. Not that way, this way. Your pinky goes here. Michael, are your listening to me? Michael, this isn't time to dance around. We have only a little time. Please, come back. Come back! Now!" Eventually Michael danced back to me and held the bow correctly. "I'm sorry I shouted, Michael. Please work with me. You play so well in tune. Better than me. Just a few more minutes to practise this part." Michael played a part of the piece a few times over. I corrected the errors he was making, pointing to the music. After a few correct repetitions, I congratulated him. "That was a good practice, Michael. Good job! What colour star should we paste on the board?" As I pasted a blue star on the large white board hanging on the wall, I felt it wasn't really star-worthy. But it was the best he could do. And the best I could do. Michael clearly didn't care about the stars that framed the board. For me, they were powerfully rewarding, marking each day that I had succeeded in some way to help Michael move toward becoming a violinist.

Despite our daily control struggles every morning, I noticed that Michael was often playing by ear, reproducing the pieces that he had heard on the audiotapes that he heard morning and evening. It was as difficult for him to read music as it was for him to read words. His capacity for playing by ear, however, was impressive.

Every day after dinner, I sat with Michael and showed him the phonetics reading book: "Cat. C-a-t." I sounded out while pointing to the word and the picture. "M-a-t. Mat. The cat sat on the mat. R-a-t. The rat sat on the mat. The cat and the rat sat on the mat."

I resented Michael's yawns, which signalled that his level of energy was waning. *We can't stop now. We've barely achieved anything.* My tone would become more and more angry as Michael squirmed and refused to cooperate. My frustrated attempts to re-engage him were always futile.

I am angry with myself for pushing both of us beyond our capacity to achieve any benefit. Most of my teaching sessions with Michael left both of us with high levels of tension and disappointment. At their conclusion, Michael would run around the house, inevitably ending up in the basement where I kept his stuffed bears. I would hear him shouting at them and throwing them against the wall, "You do what I say! Do it!"

I feel ashamed to admit that his tone was the same as mine at the end of our sessions. Back then I always came away thinking that I should not be working him so hard. After calming down, I would join him in the basement. Always forgiving me, Michael would climb into my lap as I sat on the floor and snuggled.

"Let's go upstairs, Michael. I'll put on one of your movies." The television became my saviour most evenings. Michael would fall into a trance watching Disney movies. A fragile and short-lived peace would descend upon our home but not upon my heart. I was disappointed with myself every time I lost my temper and shouted at Michael. I was disappointed with him for his short attention span. I kept thinking that he was capable of learning so much more. I remember thinking that Michael's limitations were elastic—they could be stretched—but how far? It was this unknown limit that fuelled my motivation to keep going.

Even though I was faced with constant and clear evidence to the contrary, I clung to the expectation that Michael would act like other children his age. He didn't look like other five-year-olds. He was much shorter. Indeed, he looked like a two-year-old.

In my empty office, my quiet laughter is mixed with embarrassment as I remember that I sneaked Michael into an amusement park for free as a two-year-old when he was five. At the time, I justified this as a little bit of compensation for my hardship.

I was working non-stop to help Michael in every way that I could. My primary mission was to force normality out of him; as if normality, whatever that is, was hiding somewhere deep inside of his brain, just needing to be coaxed out.

He is normal. He is just slower in developing.

Still, I was haunted by reality that persisted in coming to the surface in nightmares and disturbing thoughts and feelings during the day.

Sometime in Michael's fifth year, my gut tied itself up in knots and called my attention to my folly with intense unremitting abdominal pain. I suffered for months and lost a lot of weight. I underwent a multitude of gastrointestinal tests before gastroparesis was finally diagnosed. It was the inevitable outcome of my chasing an impossible dream.

Despite my self-inflicted pain, it would take me many more years before I finally accepted what I always knew.

38

Special Education

Michael attended kindergarten at the same public school as Angela. In grades one, two, and three, Michael was in a regular class with three teachers. There was no end to the problems his teachers reported.

Throughout grade one, Ms. Meadows, the lead teacher, reported in his homework book that Michael was interrupting lessons by pretending to be Jafar, from the Disney movie *Aladdin*. "He stands up and shouts—'I am the most powerful sorcerer in the world!' Mrs. Miller, this must stop. He isn't learning anything. I can't teach him or the rest of the class when he does this."

I remember immediately thinking, well, what do you want me to do? I'm not there when he does that. You are.

"You need to help him refocus, Ms. Meadows," I wrote back. I was appalled by her comment that Michael wasn't learning anything. *Whose fault is that? There are three teachers there. If they only spent more time with him, one-to-one, he would learn. That's how I teach him. Why don't they?*

When Ms. Meadows suggested that placing Michael in a special education class might help him, I was even more upset. There was no question in my mind that segregating him from his 'normal' classmates would damage his self-esteem. He would come to think of himself as inferior. I was worried that he might copy other types of disruptive behaviours that children in the special education class might display. It was also obvious to me that in a special education class, the usual curriculum would be simplified and only partially included. Once in a special education class, I expected that he would be required to continue in that stream. By the time he reached high school, he would certainly be at a significant disadvantage. If Michael had the intellectual potential to benefit from a college or university education, I believed that placing him in a special education stream beginning in elementary school would likely destroy that possibility and limit his career options.

Moving Michael out of the regular stream would certainly make life easier for his teachers. He would become another teacher's problem.

I strenuously argued with Ms. Meadows. "He needs more one-to-one attention. There are three teachers in the classroom. I suggest that one of you spend more time providing Michael with some accommodations. He needs more instruction when you give him work sheets to complete. When I help him at home, he often does not know how to begin. But once I explain it in a simplified way and I repeat the instructions, he understands and can find the answers." I laid out my concerns about placing Michael in a special education class.

I'm now certain that Ms. Meadows felt that I was not understanding the extent of Michael's problems and how frustrated she was about his disruptive behaviour. As much as she dug her heels in, so did I. I was unable to consider the possibility that Michael might benefit more from a special education teacher especially since it was clear that he was not learning much in the regular class. At my insistence Michael remained in the regular stream for grades one, two, and three and as a result, teaching him to print, write, read, add, and subtract became my job.

Maybe it would be my job in any case.

One time when Michael was in grade two, Angela walked by his classroom and saw him quietly lining up chairs at the back, pretending that they were a train, while the three teachers at the front were teaching a lesson. They had given up at any attempts to redirect him. Every day Michael came home from school with his backpack filled with sheets of work that he had not completed. He did not even know how to start.

Each weekday, on my way home from work, I imagined patiently sitting with a cooperative Michael, helping him to read, to understand the instructions, and complete each of the homework sheets. My fantasy of being the patient parent helping her cooperative and motivated son was just as unrealistic as Michael's fantasy of being Jafar.

Each night, sitting with Michael after supper at the dining room table, I started out by patiently encouraging him to sound out the words of the instructions on one of the homework pages. Michael slowly read one or two words and printed a response. He repeatedly yawned and dug his pencil into the paper making big, deep black circles above the *i*'s and where the period should be, creating dents in the dining room table.

"Michael, stop making the dots so black. It's not necessary. It will take us a lot longer to finish this if you keep doing that. If you leave the dots alone, we'll finish faster, and you will have time to play."

No matter how many times I urged Michael to leave the dots and periods alone, he continued to grind his pencil into them. At the same time, he was moving his chair back and forth, creating deep scratches into the wooden floor.

"Mom, read it to me. That will make it easier."

"I know. But Michael, you need to practise reading and understanding the words yourself."

The inevitable control struggle surfaced. As my fatigue set in, I did as he requested, and resented giving in.

When we were both exhausted and it was clear that no further learning of any kind was possible, we stopped. Michael fell into my arms immediately. Hugging him, I kissed his forehead, stroked his hair, and uttered the same words that I said night after night. "Michael, you can learn anything." I needed to reassure myself as much as him.

Partway through grade two, Ms. Meadows called me to set up another meeting with her. I was upset when Luke told me, again, that he could not take time off from work to attend. As usual, it was me, alone, against the school system.

Ms. Meadows, Ms. Loomis, Ms. Earl, his three teachers, and Ms. Plenner, the principal, were sitting close together around the table. My chair was across from the four of them. After listing many examples of Michael's 'inability to learn,' they all joined in their recommendation that Michael be placed in a special education class. I voiced my strong opposition and once again provided all my reasons to keep him in the regular stream. I also repeated my suggestions that Michael receive the extra help and accommodations that he required. "Bring in another teacher from time to time if the three of you are unable to help him," I added.

"We don't have the staff to do that," Ms. Plenner immediately snapped. "We are arranging an assessment by a school psychologist. We all believe that your son has a learning disability. He would learn much more effectively in a special education class. We have Michael's interests uppermost in our minds."

How dare she?! I thought. She thinks that I don't have Michael's interests uppermost in my mind! The rage inside threatened to spill out. I breathed deeply and slowly to contain it.

"We are arranging this at no cost to you." Ms. Plenner added.

"No thank you. I will pay for this to be done privately," I said while standing up. I felt the need to leave to prevent my anger from bursting out in words that I would regret.

Back in my car, my rage erupted into a seemingly endless stream of tears. After some time, I began to think about which child psychologist I could contact. I was concerned that Michael's teachers and the principal might bias the psychologist by discussing their negative feelings about Michael before the first assessment meeting.

A colleague recommended Dr. Rockman. I dreaded the psychological assessment. What hidden, serious problems would it reveal?

Dr. Rockman diagnosed Michael with a learning disability, verifying his teachers' impression. I hated the label even though it was clear to me that Michael had significant learning problems. The diagnosis did not change my adversarial relationship with the school. I kept up my strong opposition to placing Michael in special education. Michael continued in the regular classroom in grade three. However, near the end of the year, I was called into another meeting with the teachers and principal. This time the special education teacher, Ms. Fox, was present. I was told by all of them that Michael would be entering Ms. Fox's class in grade four. The decision had been made.

I felt that I had been defeated, that there was no point in opposing all of them. Perhaps, I was too exhausted to continue the battle. Perhaps, their arguments were making some sense to me. Most of all, I was exhausted by the daily grind of teaching Michael grades one, two, and three curricula, leaving me with precious little free time for myself and time to spend with Angela and Luke.

In grades four and five, Ms. Fox made frequent use of Michael's homework book, which Michael and I came to hate. It was a book of emotional release for Ms. Fox and a book of pain for Michael and me. Each page was filled with Ms. Fox's detailed complaints about Michael and her exasperation with him. I replied with detailed suggestions about how she could help Michael refocus and learn. Our respective communications created a perfectly useless circle, fuelling only resentment and frustration on both sides, drifting down to Michael. Ms. Fox and I became more irritated and disappointed with him. And he hated school more with each passing day.

Ms. Fox arranged a meeting with me when Michael was midway through grade five. I attended alone, as usual. "Mrs. Miller, Michael cannot learn here—not even in a special education class. There are residential schools for children with severe learning disabilities in three different cities in Ontario. I am recommending that he be transferred to whichever has an opening for him. He will get the help he needs."

I could not contain my shock and fury. "No, Ms. Fox. This system is failing Michael. He learns when I teach him. He is learning to read and write and do arithmetic."

"Mrs. Miller, Michael can't even tie his shoelaces!" Ms. Fox glared at me.

"I am totally opposed to sending him to a residential school. Such a move would harm him emotionally and set him back intellectually. It would be a disaster. Ms. Fox, you must not give up on trying to teach Michael in your class." With that, I excused myself from the meeting, ran to my car, and wept for a long time before I could drive home.

I recall my shock when Ms. Bronson, Michael's grade six special education teacher, wrote in Michael's homework book, "Please keep Michael home tomorrow. I need a break." *How was it that a special education teacher was requesting me to give her a break from Michael?* When the shock and anger dissipated, intense anxiety burned from deep within. *Was Michael that impaired that a special education teacher was unable to teach him and needed a break from him? I was teaching him every evening—one-to-one. Why is she unable to teach him?*

I wrote back. "I am very upset that you are asking me to keep Michael home so you can have a break. It is your job to teach him. I know that he is challenging. I am teaching him every evening. Michael can learn. You need to break down the instructions into small steps and repeat them while speaking directly to him. We must not give up on him. Please don't ask me to keep him home again."

Thinking back, I understand Ms. Bronson's need for a break. Michael often lost focus and started talking out loud, playing out scenes from movies or making up stories of his own. It was frustrating and exhausting to redirect him each time. I can imagine how much more difficult it was for his teachers to redirect him when he disrupted their lessons repeatedly and distracted the other students. No wonder his teachers put Michael at the back of the class to block out his self-talk.

At the time, all I felt was that the school system was failing Michael and that it was up to me to make up for it. The furthest thing from my mind was that learning to help Michael could be of any benefit in my work with patients. Over time I was developing more compassion for parents who were struggling with their children's learning and emotional problems. I was becoming more skilled in helping people of all ages who had learning and developmental disabilities as well as brain damage from injuries and disease. When working with them, I helped parents accept their limitations and the limitations of their child. I helped parents manage their frustration and make it a priority to take care of themselves. I helped parents effectively advocate for their child within the constraints of the school system. With patients who had learning problems or brain damage, I became more skillful in meeting their cognitive and emotional needs. It was easy to teach approaches that were extremely difficult to implement myself with Michael.

Charlene comes to mind. Her mother called to tell me that she had significant developmental disabilities and was living in a group home. "I've heard that you help people with these kinds of problems," she began. "Charlene is sixteen. She is having problems getting along with another girl. Nothing violent but she has been yelling at her. The staff tell her to stop but she keeps at it."

"Do you know why she is angry with this other girl?" I asked.

"No. She says that the girl is a liar."

Charlene was tall and slim. She rushed into the office and threw herself into the chair with a big smile. Her large velvet brown eyes seemed to smile as well. She had short blond hair that bounced about as she rapidly turned her head, gazing about the office, and finally looked directly at me. Sinking down into the chair, Charlene stretched her legs out in front.

I can't recall another patient with whom rapport was as easy. It seemed that we had a genuine connection as soon as I asked her for her address, phone number, birthdate, and the other information on my routine patient information sheet. She told me that her mother always answered questions like those. "You know the answers, Charlene, so we don't need your mom's help. Right?"

"Right on!" She responded enthusiastically, and clapped her hands a few times.

Gauging from the questions she asked, I simplified my speech when I explained the limits of confidentiality and emphasized that I would not be sharing anything she told me with her parents or anyone else unless there was a danger to her life or to others.

Charlene disclosed that she was in love with Stan, a child and youth worker at her group home. She told me that she had seen her friend, Joy, staring at Stan and smiling. While telling me her story, she spoke loudly and slowly, emphasizing her words by moving her arms and hands. Her thinking was concrete. I knew that I needed to adjust my responses to be concrete to enable clear communication. Underneath her words, I felt her anger and jealousy toward her friend and her affection and sexual attraction toward Stan.

"I get it, Charlene. You love Stan."

"Yeah, he's w-o-n-der-f-u-l!" She said with a deep, warm smile that lit her entire face.

"What do you like about Stan?"

"He's won--der--f-u-l!" She repeated exuberantly, lifting her arms up, and gazing at the ceiling.

"Stan is wonderful so everybody likes him?"

"Yeah. Everybody."

"Then I bet everybody smiles at him sometimes or maybe a lot?"

"A lot."

"And he smiles back?"

"Yeah."

"Joy smiles at him, like everyone else."

"Yeah. She loves him. I can tell." Charlene jumped up out of her seat and then fell back into it, looking dejected.

"You love him. What does that mean?"

"I want to be his girlfriend."

"Is he the first you've loved?"

"Yes."

"I understand, Charlene. Stan is wonderful so you love him. You wish you were his girlfriend. Have you told him how you feel?"

"No."

"Why not?"

"I'm worried he'll say no."

"Why would he say no?"

"Maybe he has a girlfriend."

"Maybe he does. He may say no for other reasons." Charlene squirmed in her chair.

"For other reasons? But he likes me. And I love him."

"Yes, he likes you. And you love him. He works at your home, right?"

"Yes. He's a child … and… youth worker." Charlene smiled with satisfaction after finding the correct words.

"You and Joy are both residents. Right?"

"Yeah—we are both residents."

"But Stan is not a resident."

Charlene laughed loudly. "No. He's not a resident! That's silly! He comes in the morning and goes home at night."

"The rule for all group homes is that a worker and a resident cannot become boyfriend and girlfriend. Did you know that?"

"No. Why?"

"That's a good question." Charlene sat back and peered at me with inquisitive eyes. I sat back, too. "What kinds of things does Stan do as part of his job?"

"He tells us what to do. He tells me to go to my room to calm down when I'm yelling. He makes sure we follow the house rules."

"He's in charge. He makes sure the rules are followed. He's a leader or a boss."

"Yeah, like a boss but a nice boss."

"A nice boss. But the residents—they are not the boss. They don't make the rules. There's a big difference."

"Yeah. So, what?"

"Let's say that a worker in a group home became a resident's boyfriend. That worker would start treating his girlfriend differently than the other residents—like maybe letting her break rules or giving her special treats. So, he would no longer be caring for all the residents the same. How do you think the other residents would feel?"

"Mad."

"Mad at the worker and mad at the resident and jealous that she was getting special treatment. The worker is supposed to care for everyone the same. There's another problem. A worker like Stan is like a boss."

"He's a nice boss."

"A nice boss but still a boss. If a worker has a resident as a girlfriend, he might boss her around in their girlfriend-boyfriend relationship because he is her boss in the house. He might tell her what to wear or what to eat and get upset with her when she does not do what he wants."

"Stan is too nice to do that."

"You don't really know. It could easily happen because he is your boss. Right now, he can tell you what to do but you can't tell him what to do. And since he is in charge, if you were his girlfriend, you would be afraid of upsetting him and losing him as your boyfriend if you argued back."

"No, you're wrong. I tell him when I'm mad at him now."

"Yes, but he's a worker and comes back every day to work even when you are mad at him because it's his job. But if he was your boyfriend, and you were mad at him, he might not want to be your boyfriend anymore. So, you would not be as free to say how you really feel." I paused. "Can we talk a little more about your friend, Joy?"

"Ok."

"Joy is your friend?"

"Sometimes." A tiny smile escaped at the corners of her mouth.

"What do you like to do with her?"

"Well, we watch videos—have you seen this one?" Charlene whipped out her phone and, in a flash, the loud sounds of hard rock music filled the office. She bobbed up and down in her seat to the banging of the drums, which caused my seat to vibrate. She began singing loudly.

"That's really got a strong beat," I wasn't sure she could hear me. After a few more minutes, I began again. "Charlene, I see you love that kind of music. Could you please turn it off just for now so we could talk some more? Is that ok with you?"

"Sure." Charlene turned the music off for a second and then turned it back on. She continued to move to the music.

"Could you please turn it off now *and keep it turned off*? It's hard to talk with the music." Once it was off, I asked what else she liked doing with Joy.

"We love dancing to the music. We play cards. We just talk."

"Isn't it cool, Charlene, that her name 'Joy' is part of the word 'enjoy'?"

"Yeah. Look at that! Joy and enjoy. Joy enjoy! Enjoy Joy!"

"They go together, don't they? Sometimes you enjoy your friend, Joy."

"Sometimes."

"Sometimes. It's like that with friends, Charlene. Sometimes we enjoy them. Sometimes we get upset with them. When she smiles at Stan, what do you do?"

"I yell and scream. Stop staring at him! Stop it now!" Charlene shouted at me as if I was Joy.

"Is there anything bad that happens to you when you yell and scream?"

"Yeah. The house staff tell me to stop. They get mad. They tell me to go to my room and be quiet."

"What do you do in your room?"

"I listen to music."

"That's great. You listen to music and that helps you calm down."

"Yeah."

"Is there anything else bad that happens to you when you yell and scream?"

"My throat hurts after."

"What does Joy do when you yell and scream at her?"

"She yells and screams back."

"And how do you feel then?"

"More mad!"

"Yelling and screaming are bad for you because the staff get mad at you, your throat hurts, and Joy yells and screams back at you. A lot of bad things. Much better to go to your room and listen to music when you are mad and not yell and scream."

"Go to my room, listen to music before screaming. That's hard."

"Yeah, you're right. Easiest thing is to yell and scream when we are mad. Hard to take care of ourselves and get away to calm down. It's worth the effort."

"I can try. Will be hard not to yell first."

"You should pat yourself on your back when you go to your room first instead of yell first or even after you yell first. Maybe it's just a short yell and you go to your room. Better if no yelling." At my suggestion, Charlene began to pat herself on the back. "Yes, Charlene. Just like that. Feels good?"

"Yeah, like I did something right."

In her next session, Charlene came in and patted herself on her back again and again while exclaiming loudly, "I went to my room, put on music! The staff were happy. I got a certificate—look!" She stood up and thrust the paper into my hands. "It says I practised ex-cell-ent self-control!"

"What an achievement, Charlene! Congratulations!"

"I only screamed at her once or twice or maybe three times, not sure, but one time, I went into my room—no yelling hardly at all!"

As I worked with Charlene, she made steady progress toward controlling her temper and gaining more understanding about the limits of her relationship with Stan. After every session, I was left with questions as to whether Michael would be able to control his temper as well as Charlene. *Could I be as effective in helping him achieve that goal? And what about controlling my temper better?*

From ages six to twelve, Michael would often run into the basement, flooding the entire house with his loud, angry screams. Sometimes he imagined that he was a teacher shouting at disobedient children. Sometimes he had no target but simply poured out his fury to the universe.

I knew that he was frustrated with the demands of schoolwork and the demands that I was placing on him. The invisible and ever-present obstacles standing in his way at school stoked his anger and frustration.

I felt sad that his life was hard and tried desperately to suppress my guilt for contributing to his stress. He was learning to read, to write, to count, and play an instrument. *But at what cost?*

The question of means versus ends reverberated within me. I pretended that I had not resolved it. A distant memory from my childhood would occasionally break through my awareness. It was Dad's voice: "The ends never justify the means." If he was here now, would he tell me to stop? I shuddered to think that he might. But then again, when it came to his grandson, would he have made an exception?

To encourage Michael to vent his rage in a constructive way, I bought a small trampoline, put it in the basement, and introduced Michael to the idea of jumping his frustration out.

Michael continued to scream and throw his stuffed animals against the wall every evening.

I, however, put the trampoline to good use.

Working with Michael taught me a lot about compassion—compassion for people with cognitive challenges and compassion for their parents, caregivers, and teachers. As the years passed, I came to appreciate that taking better care of myself enabled me to take better care of Michael. It was a lesson learned only after I had suffered the pain of subordinating my own needs too often. Striving to save others this pain, my emphasis on self-care in treatment sessions took on a more sincere and passionate tone.

39

The Question of Acceptance

Sitting at a round table, I was filled with the hope of receiving emotional support from this group of parents with children who had a learning disability. Feeling emotionally isolated on my mission to parent Michael, receiving support was a priority for my self-care.

Each participant in the parent support group looked relaxed. There was friendly chatter. This was the first time for Luke and me. It had not been easy for me to convince him to take time off work to attend.

"This is a total waste of time. Michael doesn't have such serious problems for us to have to go to a learning disability parent support group. And you realize this is costing us big time because I had to leave work for the entire afternoon," Luke said before we left the house.

"Let's give it a try," I repeated as we made our way to the car. I yearned to receive support and reassurance from others who understood. I longed to hear that others felt exhausted, too, that all the homework and remedial work and music work that I was doing every day was the right thing to do, and that my efforts to help Michael were commendable.

The leader was an older woman. Her wrinkled face conveyed years of experience. She spoke confidently and softly in welcoming tones as she introduced Luke and me to the group. The chatter stopped and everyone looked at us with warm smiles. I felt immediately comforted.

"Rickey and Luke, since this is your first time, why don't you tell us about yourselves and about your son, Michael."

Luke immediately deferred to me. "Thanks, Charlene. Michael is nine years old. He is in a special education grade four class. He's a really happy kid most of the time and very affectionate. He is close to his eleven-year-old sister, Angela. She teaches him all kinds of things by making a game of it." I took a deep breath. "Every day after dinner, I help Michael complete homework sheets. We do as many of them as possible, but I always try to leave time for the remedial books as well. These are arithmetic and phonetic reading books. Michael is slowly learning to read by sounding out words. In his school, they have a method called whole language, which requires memorizing how words sound." I paused. Leaning back in my chair, I looked up. I had everyone's attention. "The whole language approach hasn't helped Michael. He needs the phonetic method."

I felt myself relax more, like a weight was being lifted. "Michael is also getting better at adding and subtracting. We are using the Suzuki method to help Michael learn to play the violin. At 6:30 every morning, he practises violin with my help. He plays everything in tune and has an excellent vibrato." I paused. I sensed increasing tension from Luke.

I recalled our usual evening argument. "You shouldn't be doing the teacher's work. We don't ask them to do our work."

"Michael isn't learning anything at school. If I don't teach him how to read and write, he will never learn," was always my response. "He just needs one-to-one help, that's all."

It surprised me to feel tension rising in the room. Some parents were no longer looking at me but gazing downwards. Others were sitting stiffly.

"I think you are overworking yourself and your son." A father from the other end of the table commented. I saw other parents nodding. "Why are you putting him through all that?" Almost inaudible, his last comment came crashing down on me. "That poor child."

I heard a mocking chuckle from Luke, which cut even deeper and intensified the pain of the blistering attack on me.

One of the mothers joined in. "You should be accepting his limitations. You are working him way too hard, forcing him to do homework and remedial work every evening and every weekend and getting him up at 6:30 a.m. every day to practise violin. Why on earth are you adding music on top of all the other work? This is the wrong thing to do to a child with learning problems and bad for you, too." There was no concern in her tone, only anger.

I was shattered. *What kind of support group is this?* I looked up at the leader, who stood silently, looking down at the round table, clearly taken aback by the mounting tension in the air. She hesitated, not knowing how to respond. Finally, she began, "Well, every parent must figure out the best way to help their child. Every parent and every child are different, so we should not judge."

It was too late for that.

What was going on here? I was clearly a threat to these parents. They were reacting as if I was criticizing them. Were they feeling guilty that they weren't spending more time helping their children?

The leader quickly turned to another set of parents. "Paul and Mary, let us know how Cindy is coping with that bullying problem at school that you told us about last week." All eyes focused on Paul and Mary as the tension in the room dissipated.

I sat frozen in my seat, all my energy focused on holding back tears of anger and grief. The group had failed me. The leader had failed me. Luke had failed me.

Luke sat back, stretched his arms out in front of him, clasped his hands, and placed them on the table. His posture was one of vindication. All those times that he had admonished me for doing the teacher's work had been validated. *How ironic! Luke had resented my pressure to attend. He was totally confident in his views and did not need any support. Yet, here he was receiving unanimous powerful support.*

There was a deep betrayal in his relaxed, victorious posture, and in his silence. Instead of being commended, I had been condemned.

Words were exchanged about bullying. My mind drifted to the scene at the school yard that had happened a year ago. I had an appointment to meet with Ms. Meadows, Michael's grade three teacher, during recess.

As I approached the school, I saw Michael sitting alone on a step by the door and saw a boy approach him. I paused. This was a rare opportunity for me to observe Michael interacting with a peer. I discretely hid along the side of the building, anxious to hear how they would interact. I heard the boy shouting at Michael in a menacing tone.

"Hey, Michael!" A large group of boys drew close to Michael who was sitting alone on a step by the door. I knew that Michael did not have a friend to play with. It broke my heart to see him sitting alone, waiting for recess to be over. He hated recess. He hated school.

"Hey, Michael!" The boy repeated, louder. The boys crowded around him. I held my breath. *Should I intervene?* "Hey, Michael. You are stupid and dumb! You can't do anything! Why don't you just suck my dick!"

Michael stood up and paused, seeming to consider this deeply. "Ewwww. That's gross." Michael's tone was not angry or afraid, but rather curious. "Who would want to do that? That's disgusting." Then, to my amazement, Michael started laughing. Ripples of laughter moved through the crowd of boys, embarrassing the antagonist. More children gathered around.

The boy who had started the altercation was inflamed by the laughter and shot back at Michael loudly, "I'm going to beat you up, Michael!"

Michael walked toward the boy. His reply was immediate and confident. "If you touch me in any way, I am going to report you to the principal and he will call the police. And do you know what will happen to you then? They will put you in jail. And in jail you will only get bread and water. You will suffer in jail if you touch me. You just try and see!" I held my breath. *What would happen next?*

The boy laughed loudly at Michael and walked away with his group in tow. Michael sat back on the step.

Michael had not been shaken by the bullying. He was able to turn the tables and embarrass that boy. I was proud of him. I basked in great pride and relief, chasing aside the worries that threatened to surface. *Would he always be able to defend himself like that?* Then my pride turned to anxiety. *Would he always be without friends and alone?*

As the discussion about bullying continued, I recalled the meeting that I had with Michael's Special Education teacher one year later. Ms. Fox launched into repeating the complaints that she had recorded in Michael's homework book. "Michael can't focus on anything. When I am not talking to him directly, he starts talking to himself and distracts the class. Several times he has moved chairs together in a line at the back of the classroom, pretending that they are a train that he is driving. Time and again, I have to stop teaching to redirect him. You know, Ms. Miller, I have twelve special education students. I can't give all my attention to Michael." She let out a long, exasperated sigh as she stared at me. I feared that her message was that I should withdraw Michael from her class.

"I know it is difficult to redirect him. Michael needs one-to-one help."

Ms. Fox continued as if I had not spoken.

"Ms. Miller, either he is unfocused or he is over-focused. He can't shift from one thing to another. He is totally disorganized and can't even get organized enough to eat lunch. He can't manage grade three French at all and this is grade four. You have to accept his disability."

My attention was drawn back to the support group by the leader asking if anyone had any comments or questions to ask. Luke straightened up in his chair, ready to leave. A mother turned to me and spoke softly, "I spend, at most, one hour each day helping my daughter with homework. You should do no more than that. You should accept your son for who he is."

I left the meeting, trying with all my strength to suppress the inevitable self-doubt that kept resurfacing. *What was I? An abusive taskmaster of a mother, overworking her son because she couldn't face up to the truth about his limitations, or a loving mother who was committed to helping him realize his full potential?*

What about the other parents? To me, they epitomized not acceptance but resignation. Although they reported helping their children learn, in my view, it was a lot less help than they likely needed. I felt that they were rationalizing their resignation as loving acceptance.

What is acceptance? For me, it was accepting that Michael needed a lot of help to learn and, therefore, that I needed to work tirelessly to help him learn as much as possible. For them, it was accepting their child's limitations, and, therefore, limiting their help.

I left the meeting feeling more alone than ever.

40

This Is How It Ends

I did not know the man who told me that I had to hold my hands out, cupping them together to receive it. He looked down at me with stern, accusatory eyes. His expression was more than one of personal offense. He looked at me as if I was a criminal. His unspoken condemnation fell as heavily upon me as the single piece of paper that dropped into my quivering hands, wet with my tears—a mere piece of paper, yet it felt like lead. My hands fell towards the floor as if it had enormous weight. I grasped the paper lightly, barely keeping it from flying away.

I scarcely heard the words uttered by the rabbi who watched the ceremony to ensure that it was being carried out in accordance with Orthodox rules. I wept for the part of me that had died long before. Her epitaph was written on this piece of paper. *Here lies the one who believed it would never end, the one who never gave up, the one who had the dream of forever.*

At that moment, holding that piece of paper by my side, in that cold, hollow room filled with religious men, the events of twenty-three years ago flooded my mind.

"You are betrothed to me with this ring according to the law of Moses and Israel." Luke's gaze met mine in a loving, tender embrace as he slipped the ring onto my forefinger. My words echoed his, in the sweet tones of love, "You are betrothed to me with this ring according to the law of Moses and Israel."

"Look at the love in your eyes," our rabbi said. "May you always love each other as you do now." The rest of his words receded into oblivion. Our eyes held each other in that loving silence that only two lovers share.

A loud chorus of mazel tovs resounded as Luke stomped on the glass.

The rabbi handed us the ketubah, the traditional Jewish marriage contract that I had spent months creating. I had translated our friendship, our commitment, our understanding, and all our dreams into Hebrew and English words. It was a beautiful ketubah reflecting the union of two hearts, forever joined as one.

The first argument that Luke and I had flashed through my mind. It was 1976. Luke and I were enjoying our first year living together and studying at university. He continued to be supportive and empathic as I began to climb out of my pit of grief and guilt. One day he came home after shopping in the mall and said that we should buy a tax shelter.

"Luke, we are both students and don't pay taxes. Why do we need a tax shelter?"

Luke showed me a pamphlet that a salesman had given him. "You don't understand, Rickey. In one year, I will be earning a lot of money. A tax shelter is a really good idea." As he went on, Luke became the salesman.

"Maybe that's true in the future, Luke, but we don't need this now. When the time is right, we should get financial advice from someone who does not have a vested interest in selling us anything."

My words made no difference. As Luke continued to try to persuade me, he became more insistent, and I became more frustrated. I shouted at him, saying that he was being irrational and gullible. The more I shouted at him, the more he tried to convince me that he was right. He shouted back, accusing me of being close-minded. I left the apartment without saying anything. I was conveniently unaware that my sudden and silent departure was a snub that added fuel to the fire. Luke ran after me. When he caught up, he grabbed my arm hard.

"You haven't heard anything that I said! I know much more about money matters than you do!"

I pried his fingers from my arm. "You hurt me, Luke!" I ran down the street in tears. Luke went back to the apartment.

Our first argument ended hours later with Luke agreeing not to buy the tax shelter.

I was too self-absorbed to consider the pain that I had caused Luke by losing my temper. I did not think how easily Luke had been persuaded by the salesman.

I should have known that this first argument was a template for all the conflicts that would follow. Had a patient disclosed such an argument to me, I would have focused on the underlying issues that could surface again. At the time, forgiving Luke came easily. Examining my role was just as easily dismissed. I was too impatient to feel enraptured again. My heart longed to bask in the beauty, sweetness, and promise of love. And so, we made up.

Mom and Dad had plenty of arguments. Their respect and love for each other grew over time despite their conflicts. I had no doubt that the same would be true for Luke and me. In my mind our love was a garden of roses that would bloom forever and never be threatened by the arguments that would only temporarily divide us. I did not want to take notice of the weeds that were already taking root.

Sitting in my office, I think about my skill in helping patients accept and defuse their rage. I would lean in and respond softly and gently, accepting their right to feel their tumultuous emotions, coaching them to focus on taking care of themselves by breathing more slowly, perhaps walking around the office, perhaps taking a sip of water, focusing on embracing their inner pain with compassion. I would encourage them to commend themselves for cooling their inner fire.

I recall the many times I had hurled verbal barbs at Luke who naturally flung them right back at me ensuring that we both ended up feeling hurt and justified as the injured party. Despite all my knowledge and skills, it was a major challenge to do better. Many times, I failed to say, "Excuse me. I need a break to calm down," before leaving the room. Many times, I failed to take care of myself by breathing more slowly, sipping some water, embracing my pain with compassion, focusing on drenching my inner flames. Rather, I actively stoked my inner fire by replaying over and over Luke's hurtful comments and behaviours like a movie on an endless loop, feeding ever-increasing flames of rage. *How is it that with all my knowledge and skill, I engaged in such self-destructive behaviour?*

The arrival of Angela flashed through my mind. It was a joyful time. I recalled our first night with Angela in our apartment in Mississauga. Our new house was three weeks late and Angela was three weeks early. We were in our box-filled apartment, ready to make a move to our house.

I nudged Luke awake that first night. "I'm scared."

Luke asked softly, "Why are you scared?"

"I don't know how to take care of her," I admitted. I had already messed up at the hospital by putting Angela's diaper on backwards and by calling the nurse when she was inconsolable. My baby was lying in her little crib next to my hospital bed, just as I had requested on my detailed birth plan.

"Why is she crying?" I asked the nurse. "What's wrong with her? I tried everything and she's still crying!" I felt like a total failure as a mother and it was only day one.

The nurse picked up tiny Angela and wrapped her in a blanket. Angela stopped crying. "Why, she's a little popsicle! That's all. She was lying here practically naked and frozen. Do you want me to take her back to the nursery so you can get some sleep?"

"Yes, please!" I was desperate.

Luke turned to me. "Haven't you ever babysat anyone's baby?"

"No, never."

"Well, don't worry. I have. There's nothing to worry about. Go to sleep. She'll be fine." Luke put his arms around me in a reassuring and loving embrace and he instantly fell asleep again.

Through that night and many more, I got up to make sure my little Angela was still breathing.

The beautiful moments we shared continued to flow through my mind. There were those lovely Saturday nights when we danced the night away to the music of the trio at the Inn on the Park. We talked and talked about everything. Our conversation flowed easily, naturally, lovingly. It always did back then.

This paper in my hands, how could this be?

"You have to get a ghet," my lawyer had tried to use his sense of humour to lighten the darkness of his words.

"Why?" I asked, even though I already knew the answer.

"Because if you don't, Luke's lawyer will use this against you in court. He will say that you are blocking him from getting remarried. The only place you can get the ghet is at an Orthodox court. I know that you won't want him to be there. Don't worry. Someone else there can give you the ghet."

There was no question that the marriage had died. Even so, the thought of going through this religious ordeal filled me with dread. It was a funeral for our marriage.

The beit din was in a building in the heart of the Orthodox community. At my initial appointment I was ushered into a room filled with Hebrew books and a small desk. A rabbi with a thick beard wearing a kippah greeted me politely but coldly. I felt that he had branded me a loser, a failure, a bad woman. His judgment was clear in his face and in his tone.

I looked around the room and read some of the Hebrew titles out loud without thinking. It was a futile attempt to distract myself from the pain mounting inside and from his accusatory gaze.

"Oh, you are learned, well educated," the rabbi said, obviously impressed with my knowledge of Hebrew. But even this compliment was dripping with condemnation, the unspoken, 'You should have done better.'

"What is your Hebrew name? And the Hebrew names of your parents?" I answered all his questions, one after the other, struggling to hold back my tears. Then I requested that a substitute for Luke act for him. The rabbi nodded, without looking up as he made another note on the page.

A word spilled out from my lips, "Sad."

"Yes, it is very sad," he said, in icy tones, "when two people don't have the sense to work things out." His words cut through my heart.

I am recalling the moment when I saw Luke slumped over the computer back in 1996, twenty-one years after we had embarked on our lives as one. Luke was crying.

"What's the matter, Luke?" I asked as I rushed over to him and put my hand on his back. Peering over his shoulder I saw the computer monitor filled with numbers, and at the bottom, one number, underlined, sitting by itself: three hundred thousand dollars. "Why are you so upset?"

"We have a big financial problem," he began. "We are three hundred thousand dollars in debt."

My hand flew off his back and onto my mouth as I gasped. "How can that be?" What followed was his painful account of his business overheads and lower incomes, which I barely heard. We had so many arguments about his overheads. Many times, I had questioned and later demanded that he cut back his expenses. Justin, his long-time friend and accountant, had echoed the same advice. Luke never deviated from his grandiose plans of opening multiple locations and making a lot of money.

Over the years, Luke's businesses often failed to be profitable. No matter how much evidence to the contrary, he pursued his dream, a dream that would forever elude him. Luke continued to overinvest, overspend, and live in his own version of reality. When I voiced my concerns he would say, "You have to spend to succeed." Every time I urged him to focus on only one location, he already had his sights on another.

Luke was adept at interpreting the numbers in his financial statements in a way that substantiated his belief that all was well. I participated in supporting the same illusion by consistently ignoring the brackets that framed certain key numbers. *Was this the blinding power of my love or my anxiety? Perhaps, it was both. It still amazes me that my perception of reality was distorted to such a degree that the brackets became virtually invisible, year after year.*

The crumbling of Luke's dream empire was inevitable. The magnitude of his debt—our debt—came crashing down upon both of us. The illusions that we had nurtured could no longer be sustained. The brackets could no longer be wished away.

Looking at Luke slumped over and crying, my shock dissolved into compassion. His dream was lying in ruins. I cried for him and with him. I put my arms around him.

"Don't worry, Luke. It's a money problem. There must be a solution. We will get financial advice and work it out. We will budget and save money. Money problems can always be solved."

Lurking just beneath the surface was rage that Luke had not taken my advice over the years, advice that I was convinced would have prevented this disaster. I was not yet angry with myself for all the arguments that I had fuelled, for failing to appreciate the terrible toll the arguments were having on our relationship. Every time Luke had acted against my advice, I had erupted in rage, unleashing a torrent of criticism. Over and over, I lectured him about the importance of making financial decisions collaboratively, as partners. Each time Luke agreed. *How naïve I was to think that these repeated lectures would change the pattern that both of us maintained. It is still a challenge for me to accept that I was doing the best that I could at that time.*

Hindsight is easy, I have often told my patients. Regretting some of the things we did in the past is natural. Judging ourselves critically for them is unfair and irrational. We are not the same person now as we were back then. And now we have the benefit of knowing how things turned out.

I think of Monica, a woman in her forties, with soft dark brown curls, framing a downcast face. She walked into the office slowly, hunched over, and slumped into the chair, carrying an aura of sadness and great pain with her.

Monica's eyes welled up with tears as she described her relationship with Peter. "It didn't take long for us to fall in love. I was happy to leave my home. I love my parents and my brother, but they were always telling me what to do. Peter was handsome and had a good job working on computers for a big company. In the beginning he was kind and gentle."

"When did that change?"

"After Tim our son was born. Now he is seventeen. Peter is always shouting at me, criticizing me. When I come home from work Peter screams at me. 'What kind of wife are you?! You are a lazy, good for nothing, slob of a wife—the house is dirty, the food stinks. I thought I was getting a good wife. Look at what I am putting up with all these years!'"

"How painful. What do you do when he attacks you verbally like that?

"I yell back and then go to the bedroom and cry."

"What happens next?"

"Peter comes in and yells at me more. 'So now you are feeling sorry for yourself! What about feeling sorry for me? And for your son? You are useless.' He slams the door and leaves the house. When Tim comes home from school, he is very rude to me. 'Where is dinner, Mom? Why isn't it ready? What have you been doing since you came home from work?' He sounds like Peter."

"You're being criticized and attacked verbally by both your husband and son. That's so hurtful."

Monica wept. I leaned forward and gave her the time she needed to let her tears and pain flow.

"Sorry," she said after a few minutes.

"No need to apologize for your feelings, Monica. Does this pain remind you of hurtful feelings you experienced when you were living at home?"

"Yes. My brother, who is five years older, and my mom would always tell me what I should say and do."

"And your dad?"

"My dad was terrifying. When I was little, he would yell at Mom and hit her. I was afraid of him and would hide."

"Home was often a scary place for you. What did your mom do when your dad shouted at her and hit her?"

"She'd back away, cover her face, and hide. She would try to make him happy after that. But he was never happy."

"When Peter shouts at you, do you feel scared like you did as a little girl when your dad yelled at your mom and at you?"

"Yes, I feel scared like that."

"Has Peter hurt you physically?"

"No."

"What would you do if he did or if he threatened to hurt you physically?"

"I would call 911. I would go to my parent's home if I needed to leave."

"What prompted you to come to see me now? It sounds like you have been feeling a lot of pain for a long time."

"I can't go on like this, Doctor. I just can't take it anymore." Monica pulled more tissues out of the box and cried. "I deserve better. Love and respect."

"Yes, you deserve love and respect and especially self-care and that's what you are doing right now by coming here for help."

"Yes."

"Have you considered marital therapy?"

"I have brought it up with Peter. 'There's nothing wrong with me,' he screams. 'You need to be fixed.' That was just last week."

"Are you thinking of separating?"

"I've thought about it many times."

"What stops you?"

"I keep thinking that things will be better if I stay. If I leave him, my family will hate me. I worry that Tim will hate me."

"You keep hoping things will improve. You worry that your parents and brother will blame you and that Tim will be very angry with you if you separate. It is a huge ordeal to separate and courageous of you to even consider that possibility. If you move toward separating, I recommend that you obtain legal advice."

"My parents have a big house. I'm thinking that they might let Tim and me move in if I decided to leave."

"Living with your parents would be a big adjustment but you're thinking that might be better for you and Tim. Earlier you said that Tim is rude to you."

"He fights with me all the time."

For the next few months, Monica focused on improving her relationship with Tim. She took breaks to calm herself when she felt her temper flaring rather than shouting back. I recall the session when Monica said that she was proud of herself for the way she had communicated with her son. "I told Tim that his words had hurt me. I said that I was hoping he would apologize for losing his temper. Then I apologized to him for losing mine so many times. I said I was sorry for any pain I had caused him. I asked him to take a break to calm himself down like I did the next time he felt mad. Then I told him that I love him."

"You should be proud of yourself, Monica. You took the time to calm yourself and then you told Tim how you feel and exactly what you wished him to do. How did that feel?'

"It felt good and also a little scary."

"What was scary?"

"I was letting him see that he had hurt me."

"He knew that already, don't you think?"

"Yes, I guess that's true. I was also scared that he might not apologize but lash out at me again."

"Yes, that's the reason speaking to him this way took courage. You did not know what you would get back. How did he respond?"

"He said that he was sorry, too." Monica cried. "We hugged."

As Monica's relationship with Tim improved over the next few months, she felt more positive about herself. At the same time, she was critical for having acted as a passive victim many times in her life. "With Peter, I acted like I was a little scared child just like I felt when my dad yelled at me."

As she progressed, Monica was able to embrace the little girl she had been with love and tenderness and accept that acting passively was a survival strategy back then. It would have been dangerous for her to act assertively. But now as an adult, she understood that acting assertively was in her best interests. She also came to accept that she could not have done better in her relationship with Peter until now. She embraced her past self with compassionate understanding. She was feeling more respect and pride for the person she was choosing to become.

"The most important question you need to ask yourself every day, Monica, is, 'How can I help myself feel better?' When you take better care of yourself, everyone you love benefits."

One year after beginning treatment, Monica decided to separate from Peter and moved into her parents' home with Tim. She clung to the hope that Peter would change.

In a telephone call, Monica asked Peter to seek treatment for anger management. Her request triggered another outburst. "You think I need treatment? Look at how you are acting! I am a good provider. You are ungrateful for all I've done for you and left me!"

"You lose control of your anger and say hurtful things. I can't take that anymore, Peter."

After each hurtful interaction, Monica came away feeling more confident that her decision to separate was best for her and Tim. But as time passed without contact with him, Monica began to doubt her decision and imagined Peter as the partner she wished him to be. For another year, Monica reached out to Peter by telephone and in person, hoping to see her dream of love and respect fulfilled only to come away with grief. She needed to re-experience this pain before she was able to accept reality and confirm her decision to separate.

Unlike me, Monica had the courage to move out of her home. Not for a moment did I consider that option. For me, separating was admitting personal failure. I could not see that I was faced with a relationship failure and that giving up should be seriously considered.

It was not long after discovering the three-hundred-thousand-dollar debt that Luke told me that he had a solution to our financial problems. He announced the plan with obvious relief and as a *fait accompli*. "Yesterday I met with Mr. Kingsley, my financial consultant at my bank. He recommended that we consolidate all my loans and get a mortgage on the house. The house is worth more than three hundred thousand dollars now and that will clear the debt. We will pay off the mortgage over time."

"This does not make sense, Luke. The reason this problem occurred is that your overheads exceed your income, and this has been going on for years. If we mortgage the house, and this problem continues, we could lose the house. Our savings would be at risk. We need our house and savings for us, for Angela's music education, and for the tutoring that Michael needs. The solution is cutting back our expenses at home and your expenses in each of your businesses and paying off the debt."

"I don't want to live like a pauper!" Luke angrily shot back.

I was surprised by his outburst. "I am not suggesting that we should cut out everything that we enjoy. But we need to cut back on some of our expenses to pay off the debt."

Luke was defiant. "Look, Rickey, this is the perfect solution. We will save money this way if we consolidate all the loans and debts and pay them off all at once. Don't you think that the financial consultant at the bank knows more than you? Why don't you set up a meeting with him yourself?"

The next morning, I arranged a meeting with Mr. Kingsley. I brought along a page on which I had written all the loans and debts that comprised the dreaded three hundred thousand dollars.

Mr. Kingsley stared at the list for a long time before commenting. I was uncomfortable with his silence.

"I did not know anything about the three hundred thousand dollar debt until just a few days ago. Should we mortgage our house?"

Mr. Kingsley's response was instant. "No. Absolutely not!" His voice was so loud that others standing near his office turned to see what had happened. He lowered his voice as he went on. "You could lose your house. I did not know that Luke was three hundred thousand dollars in debt. I see a loan here for sixty thousand dollars from Luke's parents. I did not know anything about this. It was not on his loan application. He was supposed to disclose all his loans to our bank."

I was shaken. *Had I disclosed a deep dark secret? Would Luke be angry with me?* Luke had told me that he had revealed everything to Mr. Kingsley—another naïve assumption on my part. Luke had kept many secrets from me, purchases he had made, employees he had hired, new locations he had investigated, hoping that I would not find out. *Since he hid things from me, then why not from the bank?*

"It's not just about this additional loan, Luke's income has been unreliable over the years. I have advised Luke not to borrow money to invest in mutual funds. I told him that he should give priority to paying off his debts."

A secret had been delivered back to me. I did not know that Luke had borrowed money to invest in the stock market. *What other secrets would come to light?*

Mr. Kingsley continued, "What if he has to declare bankruptcy at some point? What would happen with your house?"

As soon as he asked, I remembered our meeting with our lawyer, Tim Birnbaum, in 1993. I told Mr. Kingsley that Justin, Luke's accountant, had told him that, in view of his falling income, he should consider putting the title of the house in my name. That way, if Luke had to declare bankruptcy, the house would be protected from his creditors. Luke had agreed. The legal process was simple. The title of the house was put in my name. In the years that passed since then, Luke had reassured me that his businesses were profitable, or they would be very soon. I had believed him.

I left the meeting with Mr. Kingsley fearful that Luke would be angry with me for revealing the loan from his parents. As I drove home that day, I could not help but relive the shock that I had experienced upon accidentally discovering that loan.

That day, Angela had asked me to proofread one of her essays. When I turned the computer on, a loan agreement between Luke and his parents jumped into view. I drove to Luke's parents' home.

I walked into the den and asked them if we could talk. They both looked worried.

"I just saw a document on our computer, a loan agreement between you and Luke for sixty thousand dollars. I did not know anything about that. Why didn't you tell me? I am responsible for that loan, too." I spoke as calmly as I could.

"We are helping you out, that's all," Tom began. "Why are you so upset, Rickey? He needs our support, and we are here for him and for you. He can pay that loan back any time. We thought that he told you about this."

Lauren looked at me with irritation. "You should be thankful for our generosity," she said. There was no point in arguing. I left their house with more anger and frustration.

Later that evening I pleaded with Luke, yet again, to be open with me and not keep any secrets, still believing that pleading would make a difference.

I am recalling the day that Luke had greeted me after work exuberantly. "Rickey, I have some exciting news. I did a lot of research into this fantastic investment with Camping World. I've bought a recreational vehicle, a motorhome. Every time the motorhome is rented, we will get a share of the rental."

I exploded. "How could you purchase a motorhome without discussing it with me first? This is unbelievable." *Yet, as I see it now, it was totally believable, totally predictable.*

I cried and shouted and screamed, scarcely hearing my own words let alone Luke's justification. It took me hours to calm myself sufficiently to think and speak rationally. Once again, I lectured him about our need to work together as partners. "The motorhome might work out to be profitable or it might not, but you should have discussed it with me first."

"I've done research into the profitability of the motorhome," Luke countered. "You should trust me."

I had lost trust long ago.

It did not take long for my worst fears to materialize. Over the next few years, the motorhome was not rented enough to make up for its purchase price. Luke reluctantly informed me about the loss that was accumulating. I advised him to sell it as soon as possible. "We will have to budget to pay off the accumulating debt. The sooner we sell, the better. We must cut our losses."

Several weeks later, Luke quietly told me that he had solved the motorhome problem. "I told the rep that I wanted to sell the motorhome. He told me that he was surprised that the rentals had been down. He showed me a houseboat and said that people rent houseboats much more often than motorhomes. He said that he could get me a good deal on a trade-in. The profits from the rental of the houseboat would more than offset the loss caused by the motorhome. So, I bought the houseboat."

Hearing this, the earthquake inside rattled me so powerfully that I could not utter a single word. Tears were streaming down my face. I left the house.

Refusing to give up on our relationship guaranteed that I would experience shock and profound disappointment again and again. The weeds in our garden of love had spread uncontrollably, the blooms were fading, and yet I refused to give up. Lethal tendrils of disgust toward Luke were beginning to poke through the surface.

Our conflict concerning finances totally overshadowed other problems in our relationships that simmered just under the surface. I failed to see the widening chasm between us that my successful career was creating. Luke consistently supported my career and was happy with my increasing income. At the same time, my lucrative practice contrasted with his unsuccessful business. *How could that not gnaw at his self-esteem?*

Then there was the resentment that I felt because I was weighed down with the load of helping Michael. I felt as if I was a single parent. Every time Luke criticized me for doing the teacher's work, I felt more angry, hurt, and isolated.

My focus on Michael left me with little time and energy to meet Luke's emotional needs. My next priority was caring for Angela. Luke came third. I was a distant fourth. *My priorities were all wrong.* Self-care must come first. That was the recommendation that I made to every one of my patients. *How is it that self-care was last on my own list?*

My strong belief that Luke and I could improve our relationship was reinforced by the couples I worked with who effectively resolved issues, especially financial ones. *If they could do it, then of course we could, too.* Robert and Devon come to mind.

"Our main problem is money," Robert began. "Devon spends too much and doesn't think about our budget. He doesn't want to make a budget. He just wants to spend."

"All Robert wants is to save money. He's so worried about running out. I understand he came from a family where his father gambled on the stock market and lost piles. Robert had to go without. But we are not in that situation at all."

Robert and Devon were a handsome young couple. Robert was clean shaven, had deep brown eyes, and curly hair. He appeared to be athletic. Devon sported a short beard, a round face, with blue eyes. He often squinted as he spoke, his narrowing eyes expressing his tension. He sat straight up in his chair, whereas Robert sat back with his legs stretched out in front of him.

"Please, when you speak here, can you both look at and speak directly to each other rather than to me?" Even though I always placed couples' chairs facing each other, Robert and Devon, like most couples, turned toward me, and spoke to me about their partner as if the other person wasn't present. I repeated the suggestion several times until Robert and Devon finally addressed each other while I listened. This was a challenge for most couples. It was often the beginning of genuine communication.

Partway through a discussion of their conflicting views about saving and spending money, Robert accused Devon of having been dishonest. "You need to tell me what you want to buy before you buy it. The worst thing is when you say you didn't buy anything when you actually did—like that camera, remember? And I happened to find it. You lied to me. I lost my temper. What did you expect?!"

"You have a problem trusting Devon."

"Exactly! It's not like in the beginning of our relationship. In those first few years, Devon, you and I were completely honest and open when we had those other affairs with guys. Remember? Then, later, we decided to become exclusive."

"That's right, Robert. But in this case, I'm afraid to tell you when I buy something because I know you'll be angry. You scream at me and call me stupid."

"Devon, can you tell Robert what you wish he would do differently when he is angry."

"I would like you to calm down first and then talk to me."

"What do you think about that, Robert?"

"I can do that if you are honest with me. I hate it when I'm surprised and find out later that you bought something and especially when you lie! Of course, I get mad."

"So, what would you like Devon to do?"

"I want you to be honest and open with me before you buy something."

"Before I buy something? Like when I buy a coffee? I need your approval for that?!" Devon spoke softly but his resentment bubbled to the surface for the first time.

"No not for a coffee," Robert replied. "For something more expensive. Like that camera was over one hundred dollars—anything over one hundred dollars."

"Robert, you will trust Devon more, the more open he is about spending money and especially when it is for something over one hundred dollars. Is that correct?" Robert nodded. "And Devon, it will be easier for you to be open with Robert if he manages his anger better, if he takes a break to calm himself, when you talk to him about a purchase that you would like to make. Is that correct?" Devon nodded.

"I will be open with you, Rob, if you can talk to me calmly and stop calling me names. That hurts me. The more you tell me off for spending money, the angrier I get, and the more I want to buy things behind your back to get back at you."

"It feels good to hurt him back, Devon, but then Rob loses his temper and hurts you. It's a cycle you both keep going." Robert and Devon nodded. "You have seen how destructive dishonesty is; how easily trust can be lost."

Leaning forward, Devon looked directly at Robert and spoke. "I will be open and up front with you, Rob, from now on, before I buy something. I won't do it behind your back. You need to control your anger. Stop calling me names. Stop shouting at me."

"I will have an easier time doing that, Devon, if you are open with me about purchases."

Devon and Robert were highly motivated to improve their relationship, and over the next few sessions, worked out a budget for spending and saving.

What enabled Devon and Robert to improve their relationship while my relationship with Luke continued to fall apart?

I'm thinking back to the day in 1991 when Luke came home with a variety of soaps, household cleansers, and jewellery that I had never seen in any store. "These products are excellent," he announced. "I will earn money by selling them and getting other people to sell them." Luke sat down at the kitchen table with a pile of documents with the name *Cashflow Net* at the top. I had never heard of this company. He showed me a diagram of a pyramid and explained that the person at the top earns millions of dollars. "The more people I can persuade to join, the more money I will make," he said after a long discourse. Once again, Luke was a salesman delivering a pitch.

Luke assured me that he would not cut any hours from his work to pursue his *Cashflow Net* business. I took the *Cashflow Net* window cleaner and sprayed it on the bathroom mirror. It worked just as well as my usual one. I did not see the anxiety and anger in the eyes that stared back at me, only the spotless mirror.

Not long after that, ten-year-old Angela told me that riding with her dad in the car had become a strange experience. "Dad is playing audio tapes with people talking about making lots of money. He always tells me to be quiet so that he can listen to these tapes."

The next time Luke drove us to the grocery store, he inserted a cassette, and we were listening to a man and a woman who took turns speaking in evangelical tones, praising *Cashflow Net* and the vast amounts of money that they had earned. They spoke about the intimacy that they shared as a happy couple by virtue of their successful *Cashflow Net* business. Their religious fervour was palpable. Luke had been converted.

"I would like us to go to the *Cashflow Net* convention in the States," Luke announced. Angela was immediately excited about going on a trip. "There will be thousands of people, lots of music, and fun things to do. It will not be an expensive vacation."

It was strange to think about a company hosting some kind of convention. The only conventions that I had attended were psychology conventions in which research and clinical papers were presented. I would not characterize them as 'fun.'

When we crossed the border, Luke told the customs officer that we would be attending the *Cashflow Net* convention. He understood. I thought that I must be the only person who had never heard of this company.

A rock concert at the mega-church of capitalism—that is how Angela described it. We sat in an enormous indoor arena, every seat filled with enthusiastic people who cheered as each speaker took the podium. Each proclaimed that all who work for *Cashflow* Net make massive amounts of money and live a happy life. There were tubes and bags of confetti on each of our seats. Angela and Michael were delighted when they pushed on the bottom of the tubes and colourful streamers flew out into the air over the heads of the people in front of us. Sparkling confetti rained down from all sides throughout the evening.

One after the other, two men wearing elegant business suits were introduced to raucous cheers and applause as having achieved the third and second highest earnings in the last year. The climax of the evening was accompanied by a drum roll and an announcement that the Number One golden trophy would soon be awarded to a couple who had earned more than any other that year. A man in a tuxedo and his wife, in a sparkling blue gown, strode onto the stage, hand in hand, as thousands rose, applauding, shouting accolades, stomping their feet, creating a deafening standing ovation that seemed to go on forever. A singer and choir took the stage and, accompanied by a small orchestra, filled the huge hall with songs celebrating *Cashflow Net* and the winning couple, echoing the religious tones of the evening. Luke joined them in their zeal.

After our return, I told Luke that he should stop playing the cassettes in the car when the children were riding with him. "I think you should talk to them about their day instead." Angela told me that Luke continued to play his tapes.

Several weeks later, I received a most unwelcome call from Ms. Dunn, Michael's violin teacher. She told me that Luke had called her to ask if she would sell products for *Cashflow Net* and become part of his business. She said that he had kept her on the phone for a long time explaining the benefits of joining him. I apologized repeatedly and told her that I did not give him her phone number, nor did I know that he had contacted her. I was furious with Luke.

"How could you call Michael's violin teacher? It is inappropriate to pressure people we know to join you in this business. It is hard for them to say no."

"It's not hard. They are free to say no. They may want to make money, too, and say yes." I asked him who else he had contacted and was shocked to find out that he had approached friends of mine as well as relatives.

Luke continued to bring home boxes of *Cashflow Net* products. His obsession with all things *Cashflow Net* began to fade over the next six months until all that was left were empty spray bottles and a banker's box full of cassette tapes. I preferred to think that he had not amassed a large debt because of this failed excursion. I did not ask.

The evening after I met with Mr. Kingsley, and Angela and Michael were in bed, I sat down at the kitchen table with Luke.

"So, did you meet with Mr. Kingsley?" Luke asked, certain that I had been persuaded.

"Yes, I did. He told me that we could lose the house if your businesses did not generate enough income to cover the mortgage. He said that we should not mortgage the house."

"That's not what he told me," Luke said without hesitation, implying that I must be remembering incorrectly. Luke genuinely believed that his version was correct. Doubting myself, I replayed the conversation in my mind. Then I pushed aside all doubt.

Luke shouted in frustration. "What is wrong with you, Rickey? This is the way out of our problem. We must mortgage the house."

There was too much at stake. I would not be persuaded.

"No." I was calm and certain. "We need to secure our savings and the house for Angela and Michael. We cannot risk losing everything. We need to cut our expenses. That's the way out of this hole."

To Luke my words were a declaration of war. I could not have known that the most traumatic battle of my life had just started.

On July 17, 1996, while I was preparing dinner, Luke presented me with a letter. Angela and Michael were sitting at the kitchen table. I turned off the stove and unfolded the paper.

Luke was proposing that we each hire lawyers to create a marriage contract 'which would spell out for each of us the rights and obligations that you and I both have in this marriage.'

My tears spilled onto the letter before I reached the end. *A marriage contract? After twenty-one years of marriage?* "This is not the way a married couple works out problems. I am committed to working things out with you, but not with lawyers. Are you?"

"Yes, I am," Luke said.

The next day, fifteen-year-old Angela asked Luke for the reason that he had consulted a lawyer. She was about to attend an overnight music camp for several weeks. Luke told her, "Don't worry, Angela. Most divorces don't end in court."

Luke's response guaranteed sleepless nights for Angela. She had heard him say that he was committed to working things out with me. Why then was he talking about divorce? While she was away at camp, she was consumed with worry that when she returned, we would have separated. Her safe and secure world was crumbling.

I told Mom about the letter. "You need to get a lawyer," she said.

"Why should I do that?" I asked.

"Because he has consulted with a lawyer. You need to protect yourself," she explained.

I did not appreciate the wisdom of her words. Hiring a lawyer was, for me, an admission that our marriage had failed; that I had failed.

I told Luke that we should seek marital therapy. Luke agreed.

My hope was rekindled as we entered the psychologist's office. We performed our usual dysfunctional dance in the session. I chided Luke for making financial moves behind my back. He chided me for shouting criticisms at him. I blamed him for our debt. He rebuked me for putting pressure on him to pay for household expenses that he could not afford and blamed me for the debt. The psychologist asked a few questions but listened for the most part, offering no suggestions or insights. She appeared to be at a loss as to how to intervene. As the hour proceeded, I began to weep in frustration and desperation. Luke reacted to my tears with indifference. This, more than anything else, brought home to me the enormous chasm that had opened between us. The session ended. We left without hope. We both agreed not to return.

In the first few weeks of September 1996, there was an uneasy peace between us, but peace nonetheless. Angela had returned from music camp feeling relieved that we were still together. Her mood was even more buoyant when she saw us hug and kiss. She later told me that she felt guilty to have even considered that her father might leave and scolded herself for thinking badly of him. She knew that I would never consider separating.

I recall Yom Kippur, the holiest day of the year, September 23, 1996. Angela, Luke, and I prayed through the day at synagogue as we had on every other Yom Kippur.

After dinner at Mom's, we visited Luke's parents briefly, and then returned home. I told Angela that I did not understand the reason for my exhaustion. She said, "Praying all day, really praying, is exhausting." She was right. My prayers were about forgiving others, forgiving myself, committing to doing better in my relationships, in my community, and in the world. It was heavy stuff but full of hope for a better year, for a better me.

I appealed to Luke to help reign in Michael as I got ready for bed. Luke shouted at Michael. I did, too. I took over as I often did when Michael was rambunctious. I rubbed his back and sang him a song. It took an hour or so until he fell asleep. Then I returned to our bedroom.

It was approaching midnight. Luke was unusually silent as he lay in bed. His eyes were wide open.

I went over to Luke, riding high on the wave that had carried me through my prayers all day. At synagogue, I had apologized to Luke for having hurt him in any way. He had said the same to me. It was an expected script on Yom Kippur but I had felt that our atonement was genuine. We were ushering in a new year of love between us.

I was delusional! How could I have been so out of touch with reality?

"I'm feeling stressed out because of Michael's behaviour. I would love a hug." My request was met with a menacing silence. I waited. "Why are you hesitating?"

"I don't know how I feel about you." The words were devastating, shocking.

"What do you mean, you don't know how you feel?" I stood up and moved away from the bed. Luke got up.

"I'm all mixed up," he began softly. "I don't know how I feel about you," he repeated. My heart was breaking.

"Luke, we've had our problems, but I'm committed to our marriage. I'm sure that we can improve our relationship this year. Don't you think so?" I heard my voice quiver, fearing his response.

"I'm not sure."

I heard my words pose the critical, fearsome question. "Are you thinking of leaving me?"

"I'm not sure." The truth shot through his passive-aggressive haze like a bullet and took my breath away.

"When will you be sure?"

"Soon. I think I've said too much already."

I knew that he had said exactly as much as he had intended.

"What do you mean, you think you've said too much already? Luke, I can't live with you in this atmosphere of uncertainty." My tears were flowing.

Talking through the night, I made a futile effort to persuade Luke to stay and work things out. I told him that it was important for Angela and Michael. I told him that after twenty-one years, surely we could resolve our financial problems and improve our communication; surely, we could be happy together again as we had been in the beginning. "Let's not throw it all away," I said.

"You are too good for me, Rickey."

Anger boiled up within me at this inverted compliment. "Yes, I am too good for you," I blurted out. "I did not give up. I would never have given up on us. It sounds like you have." I did not want to believe it though. Perhaps he will feel differently in the morning.

Seeing my tears from a great distance, Luke said, "Talk to Amani. She will help." His recommendation that I turn to my close friend and business partner for emotional support made it clear that he was departing. He was consoling himself. He did not have to worry about me. I had a good friend who would help me cope.

Although we talked for many more hours, nothing more was said. Luke told me that he had to go to sleep. I went into the den and cried the hours away until dawn broke and ended the first of many traumatic nights to come.

Luke was up at five-thirty in the morning and said that he was leaving. Really leaving. I told him that he must not go this way without giving us a chance to explain what was happening to Angela and Michael. When I opened the door to Angela's room, I saw that she was crying. She had heard everything that had been said through the night and was devastated. As I hugged her, I heard Luke open the front door.

"I feel so guilty," he said as he walked out.

I focused on getting the children ready for school and tried my best to minimize the catastrophic upheaval that the morning had brought with it.

"Dad and I both love you and always will. And neither of you had anything to do with our problems. They were only about money." This would be my frequently repeated script. I told it to myself over and over, convincing myself that it was, after all, only a money problem.

I was a psychologist who understood the multi-layered complexity of human relationships and yet there I was, attributing the cause of the breakdown to a single cause.

When I arrived at work that morning, I hastily wrote a note to Amani informing her that Luke had left me. I added, "Perhaps he will change his mind."

A few weeks before, Amani and I had enjoyed lunch together at a restaurant for her birthday. On the way back to the office, Amani asked how things were going between Luke and me. I had told her about our debt and conflicts about money.

"Things are still tense between us," I told her. "Somehow we'll work it out." *It was my eternal refrain.*

"You've been through a lot, Rickey," she began. "Do you ever think of leaving him?"

"Never!" I said with great emphasis. "I don't have to worry about Luke. He will never leave me. He depends on me to organize everything at home and with the kids. He relies on my income as well."

After my first two patients of the morning, Amani and I had some time to talk. She came into my office. I struggled to hold back my tears.

"Did you read my note?"

"Yes," she began tentatively. "I am not surprised." I gathered that she had assumed that we would separate at some point. "Luke came to see me a few weeks ago."

"He came to see you? Why? Was it before we went out for your birthday?" The shock and pain of her disclosure were numbing. *Why had she kept this meeting a secret from me?*

"He told me that he was going to leave you. He said that he wanted me to know so that I could help you cope after he left." Amani looked down at the floor and then up at me and then down again, anticipating my hurt feelings.

"Why didn't you tell me that?" My already tattered heart was being ripped apart. *How could my close friend have been complicit in keeping this secret from me?* I felt foolish for having told her with certainty, one week earlier, that Luke would never leave me.

"I didn't know what to do," Amani began. "I felt that if I told you, you would be horribly hurt. And I thought that Luke might change his mind. I thought that I would save you the pain if I didn't tell you and he didn't leave." Luke had put her in a no-win position.

"When did he come to you?"

"Sometime in August. He told me that he had decided to leave you back in May after seeing a lawyer and that he no longer loved you. He said that he had looked for an apartment over the summer. He said that he had delayed telling you because he was worried about how you would react. He said that he had planned to tell you in June, July, and then August while the children were at camp. When he spoke to me in August, he said that he might tell you in September or October. I thought that maybe he would change his mind and try to work it out with you. I was hoping that he would. I told him that it was up to him to tell you if he decided to separate. He left saying that everyone deserves a crack at happiness."

The almost intolerable pain of the day only deepened. Luke had made his mind up months ago. He had been too cowardly to tell me directly. He was waiting for me to put the words in his mouth to achieve the clarity I needed and at the same time abhorred.

I immediately called Luke. "It sounds like you have decided to leave me. Is that correct?"

"Yes," his answer soared on a deep sigh of relief.

"Well then, the sooner you move out, the better so that you cause as little disruption to me and the children as possible. Do you have a place to stay somewhere else tonight?"

"Yes. I will stay in a motel and then I'll live with my parents for a while."

In the evening of the first day of my new reality, I prepared dinner as usual and reassured Angela and Michael that they were not responsible for the problems their dad and I had. I told them again that we loved them and always would. I also told them that I would be letting their teachers know that they were going through a difficult time and to give them extensions to complete homework.

When I walked into my bedroom after Michael was asleep, I stood and stared at the bed. All I could think of was the pain of the night before. Luke's words came crashing down again. I felt a relentless storm of sorrow and devastation and anger. I stood transfixed. I did not like sleeping alone when Luke was away attending his many professional conventions. During those nights, I worried about an intruder breaking in. I doubted my ability to keep Angela and Michael safe. *It will be my responsibility every single night from now on.* I felt alone, rejected, abandoned, unsafe, vulnerable.

As my tears were falling, I heard Angela enter my room. "Mom, I think it would help you if we moved the bed to a different spot."

"Yes. That's a good idea."

Angela and I moved the bed so that the headboard was against a different wall. The moonlight drifted onto the pillow, splitting the darkness with a swath of brightness. We lifted and moved the dresser and the two night tables. Standing back, I told her that the room looked altogether different. It would become a suggestion that I would share with many of my patients who were coping with a new separation or loss.

I fell asleep with thoughts about how blessed I was to have Angela and Michael.

41

Onto the Battlefield

*L*ess than a week after he had left the house, Luke wrote to me: 'I know that you are still very angry and hurt about what I have done to you and our family. I never wanted it to happen this way. I have respected your wishes and not called or come to the house, not because I don't care but because I do not wish to create any more pain. This is a very difficult time for me as well. I feel a great deal of shame and guilt for being the primary cause of this situation. The sooner you hire a lawyer, the better.'

Hiring a lawyer was the farthest thing from my mind. Helping Angela and Michael was my priority. Despite my attempt to keep our daily routine going, it was impossible for me to conceal my grief. My dream of forever had died. My life ahead looked bleak. All I could see was growing old alone.

Mom encouraged me to seek legal advice. I resisted. I was hoping that Luke would change his mind, as if only Luke was in a decision-making position. I still believed that if Luke returned, our relationship could become the loving marriage of my dreams.

It was upsetting for Angela when Luke came into the house unannounced. I considered changing the locks. I needed to obtain legal advice. I contacted the Law Society's referral service and was given the names of three family-law lawyers. I chose one at random.

The lawyer's office was in a high-rise building in downtown Toronto and occupied an entire floor. Large glass doors met me as I exited the elevator. The receptionist directed me to sit in an enormous waiting room. Everything was immaculate. A vase filled with a large bouquet of fresh flowers sat on the table in front of me. The receptionist pointed to the marble table adjacent to the wall and told me to help myself to a hot drink and cookies. It was all very welcoming. Looking out of the floor-to-ceiling windows, I saw the city sparkling in the early morning sunlight. All seemed peaceful outside. I longed for some of that peace to enter my torn heart.

The lawyer was a tall man, likely in his fifties, and partly bald. He was dressed in a grey business suit. He ushered me into his office, which was just as immaculate as the waiting room. Sitting down in his high-back leather chair, he picked up a pen and a pad of lined paper and looked up at me. "Tell me your story."

I handed him the pages that I had prepared, which provided the basic facts. I told him about the letter that Luke had given me while I was cooking supper, in which he had suggested that we meet with lawyers to draw up a marriage contract. I told the lawyer that Luke and I had an argument about that letter.

"Were the children present?" he asked, glaring at me.

"Yes. Luke gave me the letter while I was cooking dinner for us. Angela and Michael were sitting at the table when I read it."

"You are a psychologist? And you had an argument about that in front of your children?" His criticism triggered a tidal wave of self-doubt and guilt. Then my self-doubt dissolved into waves of anger. He was supposed to be my advocate. Starting out with criticism, it was clear that that he could not function as my lawyer. I left the meeting politely.

When I returned home, I was in deep despair. Who could possibly help me? I called Mom to tell her what had happened.

"Maybe you should call David Bloom, Terry's friend," she began. "He's a lawyer." The very mention of his name rekindled an old, warm glow in my heart.

I had not seen David for over thirty years. I summoned the courage to call him, worried that he might not remember me.

"Of course, I remember you, Rickey." His words felt like a tender embrace. I told David a little about my situation. "Can you recommend a lawyer who can help me?" I asked.

"Yes. Me," he said. "I have family-law experience, Rickey. I would be happy to help you."

And so it was that David came back into my life.

David's office was in a narrow building on a busy main street. I walked up the dingy stairs to the second floor and found his office off the hallway. I knocked on the door and a woman's high-pitched, friendly voice loudly sang out, "Come in!"

When I opened the door, I was confronted with chaos. There were papers strewn on the floor and more papers crammed into banker's boxes, which took up almost all the space in front of me. A narrow passage led to two office chairs. I had to move a pile of papers from one chair to the other before I could sit down.

Who had invited me in? The desk in front of me had mountains of files and papers sitting on it. I could not see clear space anywhere. The entire office looked like a disaster zone.

I have made a big mistake. How could anyone who occupies an office like this be of any help to me? I stood up, ready to exit, still not seeing the source of the friendly welcoming voice that I had heard moments before.

Just then a head popped up from behind the piles of papers on the desk. I knew that this was Darlene, David's wife, although I had never met her. Mom had told me that she worked with David. She was full of energy and cheer, clearly happy to meet me. Her eyes were sparkling and her face radiant. She smiled broadly as she spoke, infusing the air with warmth.

"Hi, Rickey. So nice to meet you! David will be with you soon." Sensing my anxiety, she said, "Don't worry. I'm certain that we will be able to help you, Rickey."

When David opened the door to his office, I was greeted by the same sweet smile that had touched my heart when I was twelve years old. He was almost completely bald, and his face was wrinkled but David's eyes sparkled as they had years ago. He shook my hand and then held it in his, gently placing his other hand on top. Then he hugged me.

I dissolved into tears but quickly regained control. I desperately needed his advice and could not allow myself to indulge in the warmth of his embrace for more than a moment.

David's office was the same disaster scene as the reception area. Books, papers, and banker's boxes were strewn everywhere.

I handed David the same pages that I had presented to the other lawyer. David listened closely and took notes. Just as he had done years ago, every time I used a word that wasn't precise, David corrected me. I was irritated that he was obsessed with such precision. I just wanted him to understand my situation, no matter which words I used.

After the fifth correction, I asked David the reason he was so particular. David recounted his experience when he was a little boy in the Hospital for Sick Children. "After my tonsils were removed, a lady asked me if I wanted to go outside to play. I said 'no' because I knew that it was not time for me to leave the hospital. Later, I found out that she was asking me whether I wanted to leave the room to play in the playroom down the hall. I had lost out on playing because she had not used the right words!" Despite my compassion for him, his corrections remained irritating. Trying to find more precise words used up precious energy from my already exhausted reserves.

David paused. "Rickey, is there any potential of reconciling?"

"No. We tried marital therapy. It was not helpful. I suggested that we cut back our expenses to pay off his debt. Luke said that he did not want to live like a pauper. He insisted that the only solution was to mortgage the house. His bank manager disagreed with that plan. There is no possibility of reconciling." I was finally making the decision.

David handed me financial statement forms to complete. "Bring me all the financial documents that you have. The equalization law in Ontario states that the couple's assets and debts are equally divided unless there is evidence that one partner has been irresponsible with money."

When I presented Darlene with several large bags of papers at my next appointment, she exclaimed joyfully, "You have filled one banker's box already!" This hardly seemed a reason to celebrate.

During our second meeting, I asked David for his advice about changing the locks to the house. "Angela is upset every time she comes home and is surprised to find that Luke is in the house." David did not advise me to change the locks. Instead, he suggested that I work out a schedule with Luke for Angela and Michael to spend time with him.

"Angela doesn't want to see him at this point," I said.

"Since she is fifteen years old, Angela can't be ordered by a court to see him, but Michael is eleven and …"

"… and learning disabled," I quickly added. "I think it might help him to cope better if he sees his dad. I would like his routine to remain as stable as possible."

Luke and I worked out a schedule for regular visits with Michael. Luke wrote letters to Angela urging her to call him, telling her that he loved her and hoping that she would reach out to him soon. Angela's turmoil was palpable every time we spoke. "It's not your fault," I said repeatedly and in many different ways but to no effect.

Luke sent me a letter to say that he would be arranging for a van to move items out of the house that belonged to him. We agreed about the specific things that he would be taking. After the move, I noted that Luke had left several large banker's boxes full of papers in the basement. Thinking that they were unimportant to him, I planned to throw them out at some point in the future.

At the end of each of my appointments with David, he asked me to look for more documents. Every time I brought in more papers, I was rewarded with Darlene's enthusiastic response. I declined to scrutinize any of them, too fearful to discover what they might indicate. Each time I told David that there were no more to be found, he urged me to look again. He never stopped and neither did I. Each time I looked, I found more. It did not take long before we had filled many more boxes. By the time we filled box D, I was certain that the task was done. I did not know that it was still just the beginning.

One weekday evening when I was alone in the office, a man walked in. He asked me to say my name. I thought that was odd.

"Here are your divorce papers," he said almost joyfully, with a wry smile, clearly understanding that his delivery would be distressing. There was an air of satisfaction in his tone, as if he were divorcing me and happy to do it.

"Thank you," I responded politely as if he had delivered legal briefs pertaining to a patient.

After he left, I opened the envelope and was met with my introduction to an affidavit, a type of legal document that I had never seen before. I read the affidavit but did not understand the implication of any of the words. I called David.

"That's it!" he announced. "That's what we have been waiting for."

The war had formally begun.

The next morning, I was at the office early. I showed the document to Amani, who, like me, had never seen this type of document. Her comments were reassuring. *This divorce will proceed smoothly and quickly.*

I met with David and Darlene later that day. Their home was in disarray just like the office. Papers were piled up on the right side of each step leading to the second floor. There were enormous piles of newspapers covering much of the living room floor. A few cats wandered around, not showing any interest in me, and a little white dog with curly fur jumped up on my legs, yapping loudly. David told the dog to go into the kitchen. He welcomed me warmly with a reassuring smile. Hearing his kind voice, for a moment, I felt that I was twelve years old again.

Darlene exuberantly shouted, "Hi, Rickey! Come in! Have something to eat!" A large pizza was sitting in its open delivery box on a folding TV table in the dining room. David and Darlene sat on chairs behind the TV table. I declined. The messy house and the stress of reviewing the legal document ensured that I had no appetite.

While eating, David began discussing the contentious issues in the affidavit. He began to dictate, and Darlene went to her computer and began typing furiously. She added comments and suggestions as he went on. I contributed my ideas as well. My first affidavit began to take shape.

We wrote about the history of the marriage. We included details about the financial issues and our need to obtain full financial disclosure from Luke. David said that we would be going to court to obtain an interim separation agreement that would provide me with child support and clarify the schedule for Michael to see Luke.

"The debt he came to you with, it was three hundred thousand dollars, right?" David asked.

"Yes."

"The house is probably worth six hundred thousand. You refused to mortgage the house. He sought legal advice and learned that he was entitled to half of the value of the house and half of your combined savings. He learned that you are responsible for half of his debt. The solution to his debt problem became obvious. 'Divorce her and your debt will be cleared.' The facts that you have given me suggest that he may have acted irresponsibly with money. If we can prove that, we may have a chance to challenge the equalization rule. We will know better when we get his financial disclosure. We can't do anything without that."

David said that he would be notifying Luke's lawyer about moving the action to Newmarket. "Motions are heard there twice each week. In Toronto this action would proceed more slowly."

Motions? A loving song drifted up from my memory accompanied by the clear image of Mom singing to baby Angela, "Let me see your motion. Tra-la-la-la-la. Very pretty motion. Tra-la-la-la-la." Then just as clearly, I saw myself as a teenager sitting in the meeting room at the B'nai B'rith house, raising my hand to be the seconder of a motion introduced by our president to accept the minutes of the last meeting.

What is a legal motion in a divorce proceeding?

It would not take me long to find out. I did not know it yet, but I had become an unwilling student of the Ontario family law system.

The night before my first day in court, I hardly slept at all. David told me that our case would be heard at ten o'clock. As for all appointments, I made certain that I was there early.

The brown brick court building was intimidating, as were the police officers coming in and out and the security guards who checked my purse.

A typed list was posted on a pillar not far from the front door. I read the names on the list and stopped when I found ours. 'Eisen vs. Miller, Court Room 4A. Eisen versus Miller, Eisen fighting Miller, Eisen attacking Miller. This is what it has come to, I thought, holding back bitter tears.

It was nine o'clock. I took slow, deep breaths to calm myself. I stood by the window awaiting David's white car, which had to pass by the front of the building on his way to the parking lot.

Nine-thirty, no David. Nine-thirty-five. Nine-forty. My heart began to pound with anxiety as the time continued to pass with no white car driving past the window. Nine-fifty. I rushed to the pay phone, inserted a quarter, and in a panic called Darlene.

"Where is David? It's almost ten o'clock!"

"Don't worry, Rickey. He's on his way. Your case will probably not be the first." Darlene was calm, but her words were confusing. I assumed that our case was the only one that was to be heard at ten. I returned to my vigil by the window. Ten o'clock came and passed and still there was no David.

Fifteen more panic-stricken minutes passed and finally I saw David's white car make its way slowly around the curve towards the parking lot. I watched him exit the car pulling a trolley loaded with two banker's boxes. He had a black coat of some kind folded over his arm. His pace was slow and relaxed. His nonchalance increased my panic. David showed a card to the security guards and came towards me, smiling warmly as ever.

"What room are we in?" David asked calmly.

"Room 4A. I thought you said that we would be heard at ten. It's almost ten-twenty now." My voice trembled as I spoke.

"Don't worry, Rickey. Come with me." David led me to a room on the fourth floor that was labelled "For barristers and solicitors only" and ushered me in. Upon opening the door, I saw a large room with couches, chairs, and desks scattered here and there. Many men and women wore black robes with floppy white tabs emerging from their collars. Some were snoozing on couches. Others sat at desks and were busy typing on their computers. Many more milled around, chatting. Some looked at me oddly not knowing the reason for my presence. I was clearly not a barrister or a solicitor. I didn't know what I was doing there either.

David came up to me, wearing the same strange garb as some of the other lawyers in the room. He looked intimidating in his robe. As we approached Court Room 4A, I saw Luke sitting by the door and, beside him, a man dressed in the same robe as David. This was Mr. Garner, Luke's lawyer. David shook hands with Mr. Garner and introduced him to me. It was an odd scene. We were shaking hands with Luke's lawyer as if we were meeting at a party.

Luke and I exchanged curt hellos. I saw Luke's eyes focus on the banker's boxes. Instantly, my anxiety dissolved into sympathy for him. *He would be found out. All his financial mistakes would come out.* The banker's boxes were a Pandora's box that I knew he was seeking to keep forever sealed and hidden from view even though I did not yet know the particulars of the contents.

"David, your client pays mine two hundred thousand dollars and we go home. Okay?' Mr. Garner's question was an announcement as if he was certain that the answer would be in the affirmative.

"No," David responded. "We need financial disclosure before we can settle anything."

David whispered in my ear, "Our matter has been moved to another court room. Follow me."

We entered Court Room 4B. The judge was speaking to a lawyer. David pointed to where I should sit. He took a seat closer to the front. Luke sat some distance away from me. We did not look at each other. As David had predicted, the judge said that as Angela was fifteen years old, she could not order her to see her father on any schedule.

"The boy is eleven and he has a learning disability. The father should see him every weekend and one night each week."

There was discussion of an amount to be paid by Luke for child support based on his income in the past year. David commented that he had no issue with this as a temporary arrangement. He then told the judge that Luke's petition did not include his tax return. Before he had finished the sentence, Mr. Garner handed the document to David.

Smooth sailing ahead. All we need now are the rest of Luke's financial documents to calculate the child support that he should pay. After that, we will move towards a fair division of the assets. This should all be over soon.

The financial documents that we needed did not arrive in the months that followed. David wrote numerous letters to Mr. Garner asking for the documents that were missing. The few that arrived came only after three or four letters and they were always incomplete. The documents raised question after question.

I continued to find copies of financial documents in the house that I delivered to David's home, where we met most of the time. When I arrived early in the morning on a weekend day, I would find David scrutinizing the documents. This was the same scene when I left late into the night. Every time I told Angela that I would be going to David's home, she would remark, "That place is like a black hole." She was correct. My time there was never brief.

I did not stop to think about the toll my absence from home was taking on Angela and Michael. I was single-mindedly focused on resolving the legal issues as soon as possible.

There was a trickling stream of secrets beginning to flow from the analysis of Luke's documents, more and more financial moves that he had made that I had known nothing about.

Every time I went back home to search for documents, I dreaded finding more. For David and Darlene, each piece of the puzzle that I delivered was a treasure. For me, as each piece fell into place, a hideous picture of betrayal and financial loss emerged. The nightmare of discovery was only just beginning. I continued to hunt for documents but prayed that I would not find any more. They continued to surface.

In March 1997, Michael came home from a visit with Luke and shouted angrily. He said, "Daddy told me that you are fighting him for money and you have all the money. You should be sharing your money with him. He said that he can't afford to keep taking me out to restaurants because you have all the money. He said that you are forcing him to fight with you in court."

I could not believe that Luke had brought Michael directly into our conflict. "Daddy and I are having a problem with money but should not be discussing this with you. We will sort it out. In the meantime, I will ask Daddy not to discuss our money problems with you so that you can just enjoy your visits with him. We both love you and always will." I hugged Michael and helped him get ready for bed. Angela had overheard the commotion and our conversation.

"Dad should not have upset Michael like that," Angela said angrily.

I called David and let him know what had occurred. "That's totally unacceptable and insensitive," he began. "Michael has problems understanding things. Thinking that he is going to lose out on going to restaurants with his father and that you are doing something bad will of course upset him. I am going to write a letter to Mr. Garner and tell him that he needs to advise Luke to keep Michael out of the divorce-related issues." He paused. "You should start recording the conversations that you have with Luke." David's advice caught me off guard.

"Record them? Why?"

"Because there may be other things that Luke says that will help us. He should never have said that to Michael. He knew that he would upset Michael and was hoping that would pressure you into ending our financial investigation."

"Isn't it illegal to record a conversation when the other person doesn't know?" I thought that besides being illegal, it was also unethical.

"No, it is perfectly legal. It is only illegal if a conversation is recorded and neither person knows."

"It still seems unethical to record our conversations," I countered.

"Look, Rickey," David began in a patronizing tone, "this is going to be an uphill battle for us. The legislation is clear about no-fault divorce. We will need evidence that because of Luke's financial decisions, there should not be a fifty-fifty division of assets."

I was reluctant to follow through with this suggestion, but David was insistent. The next day I bought the recording device.

I questioned what kind of person I was becoming.

I still regret my decision. It was a self-betrayal motivated by the pain and anger I felt toward Luke and my willingness to be directed by David. I felt betrayed by Luke for leaving me when I had been committed to stay with him. I felt betrayed by his decision to sue me for money after he had caused us to lose hundreds of thousands of dollars. Despite my mixed feelings, I was too willing to do as David advised.

I called Luke and our conversation became the first of many that were recorded and transcribed by Darlene. Listening to the conversations again was always painful. I heard Luke's voice, but the words seemed to be spoken by a stranger. Hearing the outpouring of my pain and anger, I sounded like a stranger myself. Each time I listened to a recorded conversation I came away feeling more disturbed. I shuddered at the deception that I was engaged in. When I told David that I wanted to stop recording the calls, he became more insistent than ever that I continue.

We were only into the first month of the battle and I was ready to end it. I was still reeling from Luke's leaving and suing me. I was exhausted from my ongoing work with Michael, complicated by his more frequent rages in the basement and his greater difficulty focusing. I was stressed by Angela's guilt and anger about the separation. I was struggling to do my best to help my patients.

Mom advised me to obtain an independent opinion from my accountant, John. Knowing my financial situation in detail, John went through the math. He told me that if I settled with Luke, it was not likely that I could afford to pay for a music program for Angela and tutoring for Michael.

I left the meeting with John with a renewed commitment to fight. I was fighting for Angela and Michael. The same tenacity that had kept me in the marriage propelled me forward onto the battlefield. The truth will come out in the end, I told myself. *Angela and Michael will have the education they deserve.*

It was March 1997, six months after Luke had left, when Darlene called and asked me to look in the basement for more financial documents.

Upon entering the furnace room, I noticed the boxes of papers that I had planned to throw out. Dreading to find what lurked inside the boxes, I had conveniently forgotten about them. David picked them up the next day.

A few days later, Luke called me. "David's letters are very disturbing. He's trying to escalate a battle that is going to hurt everybody. Honestly, sweetheart, you are making a big mistake. We should come to an arrangement so that the lawyers do not make piles of money. He should stop writing letters asking for more information."

"Luke, if you were concerned about the piles of money that our lawyers are making, you would provide us with the financial information that we need. Your initial petition didn't even include your tax return."

"The tax return was handed over to him."

"Yes, in court." I went on trying to contain my frustration. "Neither was your year-end financial statement included."

"He's making a lot of fuss about a tiny oversight. David is fighting instead of being reasonable."

"Why does he have to write six letters before he gets your complete tax return? Why isn't the information forthcoming?" I asked.

"Because it's his style. If he wants to go through everything with a fine-tooth comb, he can do this whole investigation, but you're the one that's going to be paying for it. You don't have a winnable case. There have only been eleven cases of unequal division in all of Ontario. It's such a long shot. I'm trying to prevent you from wasting the family's money."

"Luke, please provide the financial information that we need. Then we can calculate the amount of child support. Then I can consider negotiating some kind of settlement with you."

How could I expect Luke to disclose the truth about his finances now when he had not done so throughout our marriage?

Luke continued. "What do you think you will find? You are aware of everything that we've done. I think that David advised you to take those records out of the basement and bring them to him. Did David advise you that those records are going to help you win your case because of mistakes I've made in the past? It's all irrelevant. You knew everything that I did with money throughout our entire marriage."

"How can you say that?" I asked truly in wonder. Luke seemed to believe his assertion.

Luke's tone rose in anger. "Fine. This is the most expensive route to go. This is it. This was your last chance."

I was more relieved than frustrated when the line suddenly went dead.

A few hours later Luke left me a voicemail. "It's not right for you to pump Michael for information and ask him what I said. This is not something that your lawyer should be writing to my lawyer about. It's irrelevant."

"I'm very upset about the message that you left on the machine. Michael's feelings are not irrelevant. He was upset after you told him that I was fighting you for money. You need to keep him out of our conflict, Luke."

"I will be very careful about what I say to the children." Luke sounded sincere. I wanted to believe him.

I went on. "I cannot believe that you said that I knew what you were doing with money throughout our marriage. You must remember when I accidentally learned about that sixty-thousand-dollar loan from your parents."

"It was no surprise. You knew about it." This was a blatant distortion of reality.

"How can you lie directly to me like that? You know that I did not know. You know about the many arguments that we had because you did things with money behind my back."

"Do you really want to relive that now?"

"So much of what you did behind my back is only coming out now. I am so hurt. I feel betrayed."

"Rickey, this is all irrelevant. Do you want to relive it?"

"It is not irrelevant. You remember how upset I was about the motor-home and houseboat that you bought behind my back."

"All of those things won't mean a thing in court," Luke stated with certainty. "All of the money that I wasted, all the money that you say I squandered, is peanuts compared to what you are squandering now on this case. David is selling you a bill of goods. He is taking advantage of you."

Luke's attempt to weaken my trust in David inflamed me, but I returned to the main betrayal. "I did not know what you were doing all those years." I tried to control my tears.

"I know, sweetheart. I know. I'm sorry. I know, Rickey, that I lied to you in the past. I hid things from you because I was ashamed. I did not hide things from you because I was making money and putting it away and hiding it from you."

Yes, indeed. I knew that Luke was not making money behind my back. His secret schemes were losing propositions. *I don't want to endure the agony of a thousand cuts. Tell me all the secrets now.* "What do you mean, you hid things from me?"

"I hid things from you like that loan or the fact that I lost money on the houseboat, which you knew but I didn't let you in on the full details of it. So, you are finding out now and you're reliving it and you're going through the hurt all over again but amplified."

"Yes, I am. You betrayed my trust many times."

"I understand how you feel, and I don't deny that I made mistakes and I did things that were bad. You got me into this mess, Rickey, and you're going to be held responsible for your part of it. David should have explained to you that for you to win your case on the grounds of reckless depletion of family assets, there's got to be intent. It's got to be so obviously reckless. But Rickey, living through this again will not accomplish anything for you. It will only make David rich. You may be forced to sell the house to pay your legal costs. It will only make you upset and me upset and the children upset. This process is going to ruin our family."

"You have ruined the family." I asserted.

"I accept the blame, Rickey. But this mistake that you're making now is worse."

"It's not a mistake to find out what you are worth. How can I sort anything out about child support, how can I come to any kind of fair settlement with you if I don't have your financial information?"

"Rickey, don't let your emotions interfere with your common sense. This is all about money and the court is going to look at the current situation. They're not going to look at past history. It's going to be a fifty-fifty split in court. David should have told you that an unequal division is a long shot. It's like going to Las Vegas. If I'm forced to go through this process, don't expect me to settle for two hundred thousand. I won't. I can't. It's going to cost you. I have nothing to lose. I can always declare bankruptcy, but you could lose the house. You're going to pay very dearly." I ended the call.

One week later, David told me that Luke had filed a complaint against him with the Law Society. "On what grounds?" I asked.

"He claims that the files in the basement are his and that we should return them to him. They must have a great deal of importance. Don't worry. Luke had plenty of opportunity to take those files out of the house. He chose not to do so. Since he left them, you are free to keep them."

The Law Society confirmed David's conclusion.

Helping David and Susan organize and analyze the ever-increasing number of documents became my second job. When it was two o'clock in the morning, Darlene reminded me to move my car into the lot down the street where overnight parking was allowed. Each time, David walked me to my car and back again, talking about his latest discoveries concerning Luke's financial situation. At three or four o'clock in the morning when I typically departed, David accompanied me to my car and continued his discussion. Despite the late hour and my fatigue, I cherished those discussions. I treasured David's jokes and laughter, his taking my side, his warmth and empathy, his attention. I did not want to return to my lonely home. Many times, Darlene came out of the house and waved to David to come back.

As I look back, I see a vulnerable, lonely me in love with the kindness, compassion, validation, and attention, conveyed by a man I had felt attracted to as a child and who regarded me with tenderness as his younger sister.

Obtaining proper financial records from Luke and his accountant was a process that took more than two years and even so, plenty of gaps remained.

After one of his visits with Luke, Michael came home and was once again distressed. "What has happened, Michael?"

"I don't know what to do, Mommy," Michael began. He cried for a long time. I waited.

Angela patted his back and said, "We can help you, Michael. We love you."

"Daddy told me things about money. He told me it was private. I'm worried that he's going to be angry with me."

"Michael, you have not done anything wrong. We are discussing money and it's up to us to figure that out. It has nothing to do with you. I will ask Daddy again not to talk to you about money." I held Michael for a long time until he was settled and then helped him get ready for bed.

Michael continued, "Daddy said that you have six hundred thousand dollars and that he only wants two hundred thousand because he has no money now."

I called Luke. "You put Michael in an impossible situation. He is upset about what you told him—that I have six hundred thousand dollars and you want two hundred thousand and that you have no money now. He said that you told him to keep this private. He is worried that you will be angry with him."

"Did you interrogate him again?" Luke asked angrily.

"He told Angela and me about this because he was upset. Luke, are you using him to upset me?"

"I am not using him. He asked me questions. I answered his questions truthfully, which is more than you've been doing with the children."

"A few days ago, you said that you were not going to talk to Michael about money and that you were sorry that you had upset him."

"He asked me questions. Am I supposed to refuse to answer his questions? I told him that he should not allow you to pump him for information, to interrogate him."

"You are trying to make him feel guilty for the sacrifices you are making by taking him out to restaurants. You want him to feel sorry for you."

"Michael is eleven years old. I wanted him to understand what's going on and the truth because he wants to know what's going on. I want him to know that not everything you say to him is the truth. I want this thing to end. You are the one keeping it going so you can hold on to your money. You are afraid of him finding out how greedy you are and how greedy your lawyer is. And don't tell me Michael came home upset after seeing me. When he left me, he was as happy as a lark. You must have given him the third degree when he got home and that's why he was so upset. If you cared about the children, you would settle with me."

"Luke, the money is for the children. Angela has an expensive music career ahead of her. Michael needs help every day from tutors. If I settle with you, I won't be able to afford to pay for what they need."

"The money is not for the children. You're keeping every penny of it for yourself and you know it. Now the children are involved because you're involving them. I can't believe that you've lost such control of your senses. You've just lost it, Rickey."

"He's creating turmoil for the children so you will give in," David said.

I arranged for Michael and Angela to see their own psychologists to help them cope with the ongoing stress.

I kept wondering if the fight was worth the toll it was taking on them.

Angela felt that she could have done something to prevent the separation. In half-spoken sentences Michael let me know that he felt responsible. No doubt he had heard arguments that Luke and I had about the time I was spending helping him with his homework and violin practice. No doubt he could see that Luke preferred to spend time with Angela.

Looking back, I find it most disconcerting that I did not consider the impact my choosing to remain in a conflict-ridden, unhappy relationship had on Michael and Angela. I had assumed that keeping the family together was better. I had advised patients in similar situations to question this assumption. An intact unhappy marriage is not necessarily better for the children than a separation. Again, I failed to consider the advice I so easily gave to my patients.

Neither Angela nor Michael was spending time with Luke. A few weeks after Luke left, Angela told him that she felt angry and hurt about his moving out, after which he told her that she should be "over it by now." In later visits with her, Luke compounded her pain by accusing her of speaking her mother's words, thus blocking any possible real communication she might have with him. Each time Michael returned from a visit and was distressed, Angela's anger with Luke became more intense.

Michael continued to see Luke on a regular basis for months after Angela withdrew from him. Michael's anger intensified when Luke told him that David was a bad person who was out to hurt him and his girlfriend Betty. Michael was repulsed by the fact that Luke had a girlfriend. He saw this as disloyalty towards me and as an indication that Luke's moving away was permanent. After a few months, Michael refused to go on further visits with Luke.

Less than a year after moving out, Luke changed the battle from one focused on money to one focused on parental alienation. He brought motions aimed at forcing Michael to see him again. His claim that I was guilty of parental alienation, that I did not have Michael's best interests at heart, cut through me. *It was another betrayal.*

I felt increased pressure to settle with Luke. David said repeatedly, "That's what Luke wants you to do. He's driving up the pressure on you because he doesn't want us to address his financial situation and get to the truth about all the money that he has lost for the family. That might lead to an unequal division, and he doesn't want that."

David informed me that Luke had hired a new lawyer, Mr. Smithers, and that we would be meeting at his offices to look at new financial documents that Luke had delivered. When we got out of the car, I noticed that Darlene was slightly dragging her right foot as she walked.

"How did you hurt your leg, Darlene?"

"I don't have any idea. It doesn't hurt. It's nothing," she answered in her usual cheerful voice.

Once inside the office, David scrutinized the papers. Immediately he noticed that the documents were incomplete.

David began dictating numbers to Darlene. The numbers coalesced into a thick, dark cloud in my mind. My children's faces shone through that darkness, raising the question in my mind again. *Was it worth it to continue this battle?* The further into the quagmire I slogged, the more difficult it was for me to consider withdrawing.

About one hour later, Mr. Smithers threw open the door. We all jumped. "Well, Mr. Bloom, have you found the smoking gun yet?" A mean-spirited grin accompanied his mocking tone.

Without looking up, David softly responded, "Not yet."

Michael's refusal to see Luke paved the way for him to easily obtain a court order for a custody and access assessment, ostensibly to determine what was in the best interests of the children. Luke chose the psychologist.

The assessment would cause both Angela and Michael anguish. They would be asked questions about our separation, knowing that whatever they disclosed might affect their relationships with Luke and me. They would be required to relive painful moments. It would be stressful for them to be required to meet with Luke as part of the assessment.

The assessment would take a heavy emotional toll on me as well. I would also be forced to relive heartbreaking experiences. The psychologist would meet with Luke and me for at least one session. As I thought about the assessment to come, I felt disgust toward Luke. I recalled my internship year—how Mark's mother had recoiled when I suggested that she sit in the same room as her ex-husband during grand rounds. Now I understood her reaction. I dreaded sitting in the same room with Luke.

Luke launched a motion to move back into the house and live in the basement, claiming that he could no longer afford to rent the apartment in which he was living.

"You need to tell Angela that Luke is asking the court to allow him to move into the basement," David said. "She should ask her psychologist to write a letter stating that he does not recommend this since she is not communicating with her father at this point."

I dreaded disclosing the details of the motion to Angela. I knew that she would be extremely upset to know that her father was asking the court for permission to move back into the house.

Angela asked her psychologist to write the letter. He wrote that Angela was upset after her conversations with Luke and that she felt guilty and depressed about our separation. He concluded by stating, "At this point in time, it is not in Angela's best interests for her father to move back into the house. If he does so, she will likely become more significantly depressed."

At the same time Luke wrote in his affidavit that "I spoke with Dr. Pont who told me that Angela was strongly motivated to see me but was not doing so out of loyalty to her mother."

When David pointed out the discrepancy between Dr. Pont's letter and David's affidavit, Mr. Smithers said that Angela's psychologist must have reversed his position when writing his letter for Angela. Angela concluded that Luke had fabricated something that her psychologist had said, which pushed her farther away from reconciling with him.

Every time we responded to Luke's thirteen motions, there was a deadline. Every time David was late. Time after time we worked through the night after the deadline had passed leaving me in a continual state of high anxiety. I worried that Luke's motion would be automatically granted by the judge because David's documents were submitted too late to be considered. I worried that I would be forced to pay costs.

I asked David, "Why are you always late in producing these documents?"

"You should know by now, Rickey, that I am a perfectionist. This is just how I work." Every time our responses were considered by the judge, David was rewarded for being late.

To make the process more efficient, I learned how to write an affidavit and factum. I hoped that my drafts would enable David to meet the deadlines. Sadly, this remained only a hope.

In the meantime, Luke brought a motion to force Michael to see him. "Your Honour, it is perfectly clear that the Respondent has alienated both children from their father," Mr. Smithers began. "She has refused to allow her eleven-year-old son to see him despite the access that was granted by Justice Heart, access that was on consent of both parties months ago. Justice Heart did not stipulate access for the daughter as she was fifteen years old at that time. However, it should be noted that she does not see her father either. There is a clear pattern of parental alienation here. The Respondent is clearly using her children as a weapon in the divorce litigation. She does not want the legitimate equalization claim of the Petitioner to be granted and is refusing to consider mediation of any kind."

Judge Leland addressed David sharply. "Mr. Bloom, the affidavit of your client and your factum were both submitted too late to the court to be considered. I am therefore granting the Petitioner's motion, and the

Respondent will pay costs. I am ordering the Respondent to ensure that her son resumes access with his father forthwith."

Before he could finish, David stood up and interrupted the judge. "Your Honour, there is evidence that it is the Petitioner who has alienated his son, while the Respondent has encouraged him to resume access. The son has a learning disability and is emotionally unstable. He is receiving psychological treatment. It is in his best interests that he be allowed to resume access at his own pace and not be forced to see his father before he is ready."

"Sit down, Mr. Bloom!" Judge Leland commanded. "You have no idea how seriously I take my role in making these decisions! It is important for the children to have access to both parents. I have to live with my decisions, and I am fully aware of my responsibility, which is to the children. We shall return to the status quo as determined by Justice Heart and that is my final order."

"But, Your Honour ..." David's protest triggered a more explosive response from the Judge.

"That is my final decision, Mr. Bloom! Now, sit down and be quiet!"

I was horrified by the judge's angry outburst, the smirk on Luke's face, and the wide smile on his lawyer's. I was also angry with David for provoking the judge, and for submitting our documents late.

How was I going to make Michael see Luke again?

I explained the situation to Angela and suggested that we arrange a family meeting with Dr. Pont as Michael's psychologist was out of town. Angela resented having to share Dr. Pont in this way but agreed to ask for his help. She felt that she had no choice.

Our fractured family met with Dr. Pont. This time, I did not anticipate feeling anxious about sitting in the same room with Luke. My focus was on helping Michael and Angela. My concern for them left no space for any other feelings.

Dr. Pont spoke gently to Michael and encouraged him to talk to his dad about his feelings. Michael said that he did not want his dad to talk about money, and Luke promised that he would not do so again. Angela and I reminded Michael that he had enjoyed going to restaurants with his dad and that he should visit with him as he had before. The tone of the meeting became soft and gentle among all of us. Michael got up and hugged me, then Angela, then Dr. Pont, and lastly, his dad. And so, Michael resumed visits with Luke.

Dr. Farmstein was scheduled to start the assessment one month later, in October 1997. One of the conditions of Dr. Farmstein's contract was that the litigation be put on hold while the assessment took place. The financial investigation was halted.

In his initial conversation with David, Dr. Farmstein said that he would be mediating the contentious issues. He was announcing his role as providing treatment. David was shocked. He reminded him that the court had ordered an impartial assessment, not treatment. He explained that we could not mediate the financial issues as we did not have financial disclosure from Luke.

On the first day of the assessment I dragged myself into Dr. Farmstein's office. Luke was already there. I could not bring myself to look at him. Dr. Farmstein asked about the contentious issues of custody and access. Luke's answer surprised me.

"I agree that Rickey should have sole custody. I just want her to keep me informed when major decisions are to be made."

"What about access, Dr. Eisen?" Dr. Farmstein asked.

"I agree with Rickey about the scheduled access for Michael. And I will wait until Angela feels ready to see me again. I hope that is soon."

"Dr. Farmstein, since Luke and I agree about both these issues, why are we proceeding with this assessment?"

"Because the court ordered it, Dr. Miller," was his curt response.

The assessment process was as stressful as I had anticipated. Answering Dr. Farmstein's questions meant revisiting many painful moments in the marriage, recounting the heartbreak of the separation, and disclosing the stress of the legal battle.

Angela was furious with her dad for asking the court to order the assessment. The last thing she wanted to do was to dredge up painful experiences and emotions that she was struggling to suppress.

After each of his sessions with Dr. Farmstein, Michael came home and ran into the basement, venting a storm of emotions by shouting and throwing his stuffed animals around.

We received Dr. Farmstein's report in January 1998. Having provided Dr. Farmstein with pages of pleadings, correspondence, phone call transcriptions, and detailed notes describing the history of our conflicts, I was confident that he would perceive the situation accurately.

Darlene read the report out loud as David made notes. Dr. Farmstein acknowledged that Luke and I agreed about custody and access at the outset. He noted that Luke and I agreed that neither Angela nor Michael should be forced to have contact with him.

After reading it through, Darlene got up and limped down the hall to the washroom. "Is Darlene still having trouble with her leg?" I asked David.

"Yeah. It doesn't hurt her. It just kind of drags behind as she walks. We don't know why." David then returned to the report. "You realize that there is a lot wrong with this, don't you?"

I did not see anything wrong with the report. I had been too emotionally drained to analyze the content as the words flew by.

"Dr. Farmstein did not include any examples of Luke's lying. You gave him evidence that Luke lied about what Dr. Pont had told him. You gave him a copy of his sworn affidavit claiming that Dr. Pont told him that Angela really wanted to see him but was not doing so out of loyalty to you. You also provided him with Dr. Pont's letter that proved that this was not true. He didn't say anything about that." David was walking up and down the hall as he spoke.

"You gave him the section in his affidavit in which Luke states that Dr. Pont reversed his position in order to protect his relationship with Angela. You told him that Angela asked Dr. Pont about this and he said that he had not reversed his position. He said that he had never told

Luke that Angela wanted to see him. This is cogent, written evidence of Luke's dishonesty. There is absolutely nothing in the report to indicate that Dr. Farmstein asked Luke or Dr. Pont about this.

"You provided Dr. Farmstein with a transcription of the telephone conversation in which Luke admitted to lying and hiding things from you. He doesn't reference that anywhere in this report either. But look at this." David pointed to a paragraph. "He does write about the telephone conversation in which Luke told him that he did *not* admit to lying and hiding things in that conversation with you. Dr. Farmstein deliberately omitted the transcription of the telephone call but did include Luke's assertion that he did not say what he did. This implies that Luke didn't lie and hide things. Dr. Farmstein systematically suppressed the evidence of Luke's dishonesty. This is clear evidence of bias in Luke's favour. It would have been better if Dr. Farmstein had chosen not to deal with Luke's credibility at all. But he chose to deal with the issue by concluding that Luke did not lie. His report makes it look like your claims are false and only due to your anger about his leaving you. This would not have been Dr. Farmstein's conclusion if he had completed an unbiased analysis of the evidence." David paused to catch his breath.

"Look at this. Dr. Farmstein did not report nor did he investigate Luke's three different explanations for his court motion to move back into the house to live in the basement, even though you brought them to his attention. You told Dr. Farmstein that Luke's motion to move back into the house had a profound impact on Angela as she knew about it and was estranged from him at that time. There is evidence that Luke was intentionally upsetting the children as a pressure tactic in the litigation.

"Dr. Farmstein totally avoided a discussion of Luke's behaviour in explaining the children's alienation from him. He conducted a joint session between Michael and Luke acting as a therapist not as an assessor, and stated that he wanted to try to help Michael and Luke improve their relationship. This meant that he soft-pedalled when interacting with Luke to establish a therapeutic alliance with him. As an objective assessor, Dr. Farmstein's role was to observe and analyze and when appropriate challenge Luke and you about your behaviour. He inappropriately tried to persuade Michael to see his dad again, which caused Michael more distress. He did not know enough about Michael and his relationship with Luke to take on the role of therapist. In any case, this was not his role as an assessor. I had pointed that out to Dr. Farmstein right at the beginning!" David pounded the dining room table.

"To top it all off," David said angrily, "he didn't file his report with the court as he should have."

I was a psychologist. Dr. Farmstein was a psychologist. I felt betrayed by a colleague.

When I look back, it is clear to me that Dr. Farmstein was emotionally moved by Luke's persuasive claims that he was the victim, that I refused to take any responsibility for his financial losses, and had broken his relationships with his children.

I understand that no assessor can be truly objective. Our experiences and beliefs inevitably shape our perceptions. However, it is incumbent on assessors to be aware of bias so that they can produce a more accurate and balanced evaluation. In this regard, Dr. Farmstein failed.

A week later, David called me to say that he had received a motion from Mr. Smithers asking the court to expunge the portions of Dr. Farmstein's report that detailed Luke's offers to settle. Still grappling with the enormity of the assessment process and the report, I failed to see the significance.

"Dr. Farmstein failed to file his report with the court. If he had done that, all parts would be considered relevant. Luke chose to discuss his offers to settle with Dr. Farmstein to show that he was being reasonable, and you were not. You told Dr. Farmstein you could not settle without Luke's financial disclosure. His failure to file the report has led to more litigation for you."

Once again at court, we lost. The judge ordered that all references to Luke's offers be deleted from the assessment report. David urged me to appeal. I told him, "No. We keep losing. This is another losing proposition."

"This time we will win," David stated with conviction. "Luke chose to give this information to Dr. Farmstein. It is not privileged. It is important that it remains in the report."

The appeal went ahead. David called me later that day. "I don't seem to be able to convince anyone of anything anymore." He began ominously. "We lost the appeal. You must pay costs."

I was overwhelmed with a feeling of hopelessness. I felt that I had lost control of the legal battle. I turned to my rabbi and asked him for a referral to a social worker. I told him that I did not feel comfortable receiving help from a psychologist who I might meet at conventions and workshops. He recommended Melissa Davis.

Melissa was an older woman with a refined British accent. She welcomed me into her office with warmth and grace. There was something elegant and dignified about the way she moved to her chair and motioned me to sit across from her.

My opening was far from elegant. It was a direct expression of my desperate need for understanding, compassion, and control. "I'm a psychologist," I began. "I'm going through a very stressful divorce. It is difficult for me to be a patient. I need empathy and support." The courage to seek out her advice and to critically examine my choices would come later.

"No problem," Melissa responded softly.

That first meeting with Melissa took place on the day after we lost the appeal. I cried through the session. I had lost all the motions that Luke had initiated. My dark despair cast its shadow over everything in my life, as though the divorce battle *was* everything in my life. I had allowed it to become my life.

As I stood on the subway platform on my way home from that session, for a moment, a shocking and strangely appealing impulse broke through the black cloud of my hopelessness. I looked out onto the tracks.

The pain could be over in an instant.

My legs stepped back so that I was standing against the wall. A powerful force held me there. A voice inside me shouted, "No!" The faces of Angela and Michael came into view. I felt that they were standing directly in front of me looking at me with sad eyes. Then I felt their embrace. The faces of Mom and Dad emerged. I heard them both speak, "Never give up on life. It is precious. Where there is life there is hope. All this pain too shall pass. I heard Mom's voice. 'You promised me. Remember?' I took hold of myself and thought, "I am *more* than a Respondent. This is only part of who I am right now. My life is *more* than this battle."

Later that day, I called David. I needed to take back control of the legal action. "David, when are you going to launch a motion for the discoveries? Am I right in thinking that if you don't do that first, Smithers may launch a motion for me to be questioned?"

David confirmed this. I urged him to work on the motion as soon as possible. I immediately set about writing a draft of the documents. Working from my drafts, I believed that David and Darlene would surely submit the documents on time.

Sitting down with David and Darlene at their home the next day, Darlene looked up after reading my drafts. Her voice was shaking. "I can't figure out what's wrong with my leg. It is getting worse."

"Does it hurt?" I asked.

"No. It just doesn't work right." When she walked out of the room, I watched her dragging her leg more slowly behind her other leg. I followed her into the kitchen.

"Have you asked your doctor what's wrong with your leg?"

"I have. He said that he doesn't see anything wrong. I'm going back tomorrow. Maybe he'll send me to a specialist."

"It's probably nothing serious,"

A few days later, David called me. "Rickey, Darlene saw the specialist. He did an EMG test. It's really, really bad what she has."

"Is it cancer, David?"

"No. It's worse than cancer. There's no treatment at all for it. It's Lou Gehrig's disease. ALS."

I stopped breathing. My body froze in disbelief. Finally, I asked, "Are they sure? Could it possibly be a mistake?" Please let it be a mistake, I was praying inside.

"No. The doctor said that she has all the classic signs."

David's soft weeping broke my heart.

"How is Darlene dealing with this, David?"

"She isn't. The specialist had to put her out to do the EMG test because it hurt her so much. He told me. I'm the one who has to tell her. I have to get this right." He described the terrible burden as a performance that had to be perfect.

"David, you can't get this right no matter what you say. It is terrible news. Are you sure you don't want the doctor to tell her?"

"No. It's my place. I have to get this right. I have to go now. I just wanted you to know." His voice trailed off.

How could this be? Many images rushed in—the cane to come and then the walker, and then the wheelchair, the slow drop into the hell of losing control of all her muscles except for her eyelids—the horror of suffocating to death.

Perhaps if I don't move this nightmare will dissolve.

I don't know how long it took before I put the phone down.

The tears flowed from rage. She is such a good person, in her fifties, friendly to everyone, bubbly, full of life, always smiling, always encouraging me, telling me when I became tearful, 'First you have to get angry.' *Well, I was angry now. Who decreed that such a beautiful, cheerful, bright light as this should slowly and cruelly be snuffed out? How can we be hopeful when there is no cure? Even hope has been extinguished. There is no treatment. Just an excruciating slow progressive fall towards a terrible death.*

The unfairness, the injustice, burned inside me as I wept.

With much anxiety, I called David the next day. "When she heard," he began softly, "she said, 'Isn't this the illness where you die of suffocation?' And then she ran downstairs to the computer, and started to read and …" His voice was seized by grief. "I will talk to you later."

How were we to go on?

It was Darlene who led the way back onto the battlefield. As her body succumbed to the silent, unstoppable, unforgiving killer, Darlene became more and more focused on the sea of documents and data points requiring analysis. David and I joined her. The mission to see the legal battle through gave Darlene a purpose. It was the only way for all three of us to cope.

Not long after, we were back at court with a motion to obtain an affidavit of documents as many were missing and others were incomplete. This was the first motion that we won. The tide was turning.

As letters flew back and forth between David and Luke's lawyer about the financial documents we required, I was shocked when David called me a few months later with the news that Luke had changed lawyers again. Lawyer number three was Mr. Stone.

David told me that at any time Luke's lawyer could file a motion to have me questioned in discoveries. I repeated my plea to bring a motion for Luke's discoveries as soon as possible.

42

It Has to Come Out

At age eighty-one, Mom was still a voracious reader. Her eye-sight was never good despite wearing thick bifocal glasses. In the spring of 1998, she told me that it was getting harder and harder for her to read. I suggested that she arrange an appointment with the optometrist. She was told that she did not need a new prescription.

In the weeks that followed, Mom was experiencing more and more difficulty reading books and began to take out large-print books from the library. When I told Dr. Bromstein, our family physician, about this problem at one of Mom's visits, she ordered a CT scan.

Dr. Bromstein gave us the results without emotion. "The CT scan shows that you have a tumour. It is probably a benign meningioma, and it is located in your occipital lobe, the part that has to do with vision." Mom and I both cringed at the same time. Bobby had died after surgery for a meningioma.

While I recoiled in shock, Mom asked, "What do you suggest that I do?"

"Well, at your age, brain surgery is risky. We need a neurosurgical opinion. I can refer you to someone that I respect highly."

Mom consulted with Dr. Majorsky who ordered a contrast MRI. After receiving the test results, he began slowly, and in a patronizing tone, "Faye, this is a slow-growing benign tumour called a meningioma. It has probably been growing for a long time. It doesn't threaten any of your vital functions."

He doesn't consider eyesight to be a vital function?

"Faye, you are eighty-one. I think you should leave this alone."

"Doctor, I am having a hard time reading. If I leave it, will I lose my eyesight altogether?"

"Yes, but not for a long time. It is risky to have brain surgery when you are eighty-one and you have a history of high blood pressure and diabetes."

"Okay, Doctor. Thank you." As she always did when she had somewhere to go, Mom stood up and rushed out. She kept up her quick pace all the way to the parking lot. Sitting in my car, she turned to me. "Do you know any other neurosurgeons? This thing must come out."

I had worked with Dr. Farelli, a neurosurgeon who had referred patients for cognitive rehabilitation and emotional support. Dr. Bromstein agreed to refer Mom to him.

After reviewing the scans, Dr. Farelli got to the point immediately. "In view of your health and your age, there is a significant risk in removing this tumour."

"What exactly is the risk? Can you put a number on it?"

"Twenty-five per cent risk of significant brain damage, fifteen per cent risk of death."

"And will I lose my eyesight if I do nothing? What's the number you would put on that?"

"One hundred per cent at some point, but it's hard to say when. These tumours are usually slow growing. Why don't you take some time to think about this?"

"No. I do not need any more time. It must come out. I want the surgery. What's the point of living if I can't read, if I can't see? When can you do it?"

Early in the morning on Thursday, October 15, 1998, I drove Mom to the hospital with Angela and Michael. I accompanied Mom to her hospital room, where she received some injections and was transferred to a gurney. When we reached the doors of the operating room, I said the phrase that would become my standard for many more of these anxious farewells, "I'll see you soon, Mom."

When Dr. Farelli opened the door hours later, I jumped out of my seat and ran towards him, trying to discern from his face whether Mom had survived or not. He smiled. "The surgery went well. She should make a good recovery."

I dissolved into tears. Dr. Farelli was surprised by my reaction.

When she was back in her hospital room a few hours later, Mom told me that she was looking forward to going to her favourite restaurant to celebrate her birthday the following week, on October 22. "Of course we will go," I said feigning confidence. *How could anyone recover from brain surgery sufficiently after one week to go to a restaurant?*

But there we were, one week later, Mom, smiling with delight, with Angela, Michael, and I, beaming with pride, as the waiter took our photo. And so, Mom was able to keep reading.

As I plodded forward through the legal documents with David and Darlene, Mom reinforced my spirit with her strength of steel and courage, while Melissa gave me the gift of warm, empathic support. And Darlene inspired me not to give up.

43

Discovering

For more than two and a half years, at court I was forced to listen to Luke's lawyers' strong arguments accusing me of alienating Michael from Luke. Their stories were presented in the most riveting and convincing way. Every judge believed them. For the longest time it had been impossible for David to even slip a word in about the financial issues. The heart-rending stories describing Luke's longing to see Michael and my alleged blocking access were so effectively highlighted that they were the sole focus of the litigation until the day when we won our motion to cross-examine Luke on his financial statements.

The discoveries were set to take place at a large complex of offices in downtown Toronto. On each of the nine discovery days, David was late. My high levels of anxiety and frustration about his late arrivals made coping with the extremely stressful process even more difficult. While I waited, Mr. Stone, Luke, and the transcriptionist would complain endlessly. I was certain that David's late arrivals made the process more adversarial than ever. Nothing that I said to David made any difference.

On each of the discovery days, David sat at the head of a long table. I sat near him. Luke and Mr. Stone sat side by side across from me. The transcriptionist sat at the other end of the table and typed rapidly throughout the seven-hour sessions. David brought our ten banker's boxes into the room each day. Darlene was ready at home to tell David where to find each document.

On the first day, David turned to me. "It will take days for the official transcript to be provided. I will need the transcript immediately. Based on his answers, I will formulate the next day's questions. Can you take verbatim notes?" David's tone made it clear that this was not a question.

So began my new job as the unofficial transcriptionist. I wrote each word on paper and continued to do so for the next seven hours. I did my best to ignore the burning pain increasing in my wrist with each passing hour. In the evening at home, I retyped the notes that I had written and sent them to David.

This onerous job had a benefit. Trying to capture every word diverted my attention from the disturbing content. I kept my eyes focused on the paper in front of me as it filled rapidly. As time went on, I imagined that Luke was someone I did not know and that my transcription work was just a job.

From the outset, David delved into Luke's financial quagmire by asking a stream of logical and carefully framed questions. As I noted Luke's answers, familiar self-doubt surfaced. Luke often answered a question in a confident tone. When asked the same question a few minutes later, he provided a different answer, just as confidently. I found myself questioning whether I had heard his first answer correctly. Despite clear evidence to the contrary, Luke consistently conveyed the strong impression that he was being straightforward and honest. As I recorded his answers, I was left wondering whether Luke himself knew which of his answers was true and whether he was aware that his answers were different.

During the first day, David asked Luke about entries in his ledgers and various drafts of his financial statements. It appeared to me that David had become lost in a sea of numbers without any apparent goal. As the mundane questions continued hour after hour, Mr. Stone began to snore. David and I exchanged smiles. I felt like I could have dozed off as well.

Toward the end of the second day, David began linking Luke's answers together with discrepant entries on his ledgers. Mr. Stone suddenly woke up. He would not fall asleep again.

Sometime after the sixth day of discoveries, I called David to check if there had been any new developments.

Darlene answered. Her voice was filled with exuberance. "There is great news, Rickey. It's over. Luke has declared bankruptcy. You have won."

"What?" I asked in disbelief. "How does bankruptcy mean that it is over?"

David picked up the phone. "Hi Rickey. We've won. He's given up his equalization claim. You will have sole custody and you and Luke will work out access for Michael. Once he declared bankruptcy, his equalization claim died."

There was an ecstatic feeling of relief. *Finally, it is over.* I drove directly to Mom's. I told her the wonderful news.

"He declared bankruptcy. He's given up his claim of equalization. The house is safe for Angela and Michael and so are my savings for them. It's all over."

Mom was silent. I looked up at her as she sat in the La-Z-Boy chair that had been Dad's favourite. She had been lounging with the chair pushed all the way back, her legs resting comfortably on the footrest. Upon hearing my good news, Mom lurched forward suddenly. It looked as though she was going to fly onto her feet. She held her hands tightly on her lap. Her thick brown hair, freshly puffed out from the hairdresser's, framed intense worry on her face. She looked directly into my startled eyes.

"No," she said quietly. "It's not over."

"What do you mean?" I asked, incredulously. "You are not a lawyer. David is. He said that it's over, Mom."

"I just don't think it's over. I don't trust him. Not after all he has done." Her words shook me. *What if she is right?*

I did not have to wait long to find out.

One week later I received a registered letter from my bank. The letter was a new and more frightening declaration of war. The bank was taking over the equalization claim. They were seeking to recover Luke's huge debt.

How can I do battle with a bank? The bank has unlimited funds for a legal battle. I do not. I could lose everything. Then I thought, if there is evidence that Luke isn't entitled to an equalization claim, then neither is the bank. But this of course means there is a new front to the battle. *The war is not over.*

David told me that he would continue to question Luke and that a lawyer representing the bank might attend. The bank's lawyer would receive a copy of each of the transcripts. I heard in David's quiet tone his anxiety about this turn of events, which he had clearly not foreseen.

44

Myocardial Alarm

August 13, 2000, was a lovely summer day. Mom and I enjoyed watching a movie together. As soon as I began to drive her home, Mom turned to me calmly and said, "Something is wrong with me. My left arm hurts." I was alarmed. Mom always understated her health problems. "We need to go to a hospital." My heart was pounding with terror as I drove to the hospital. My anticipated diagnosis was correct. It was a heart attack.

I ran up to the triage nurse, skipping the initial check-in area. "My mom is eighty-three and I believe that she is having a heart attack."

Mom was quickly moved into an examination room. When I returned, a physician was already reading an EKG printout. "Your mom is having a heart attack. I would like to give her a clot buster, thrombolytic therapy, as soon as possible. I need to know her health history first though."

"She has had hypertension for many years. She has type two diabetes and osteoarthritis in her hips and knees."

Tell him quickly. I must save her.

"Has she had any operations?" The physician was writing everything I said in her chart.

"She had her appendix removed a long time ago and a total hysterectomy in the 1980s. I don't recall which year."

"Anything else?"

"No." Just as the physician was walking down the hall, I suddenly remembered. *How could I have forgotten?* Running after him, I called out, "Doctor, wait. I forgot. She had neurosurgery for a meningioma in October 1998."

"Oh, that changes everything. It would be too risky to give her this medication. It's good that you remembered." At this, I began to cry. *What if I had not remembered? I could have been responsible for her death.* I immediately promised myself to type up a detailed record of Mom's health history and medications and to keep copies in her purse and mine.

I was told that a heart attack was in progress, like a monster creeping up and slowly overtaking her. She would be transferred to a major teaching hospital downtown in view of her age and other health conditions. Mom made the trip by ambulance. Behind the wailing siren, I followed in my car, petrified.

At the hospital, I left a message for Angela who was attending a summer music program in London, Ontario. I called Michael and Terry to let them know what was happening.

Mom was transferred to a hospital room in the coronary-care unit. Telemetry electrodes were attached, and IV lines connected. Painkillers enabled her to settle to some extent. The cardiologist, Dr. Mondale, said, "The prognosis will depend on how much damage has occurred. It's not possible to assess that at this point." From the tone of his voice, I could tell that he felt that her heart had suffered significant damage. Seeing my tears, his voice softened. "We will do all that we can."

I spent the night in a chair by Mom's bedside, holding her hand, trying to transfuse my strength into her. The next day, her breathing became laboured. I saw fear in her eyes. Suddenly, a group of physicians were at the door. One of them came up to her bed. Mom was gasping for air. Oxygen had been administered, but every breath was a major struggle for her. I could hear the ominous sounds of fluids gurgling up and down in her chest with each of her breaths. It sounded like she was drowning. Mom suddenly sat up, gasping for air. Nurses and other medical staff had crowded into the room. Everyone was watching the horrifying spectacle. Mom's face was contorted in panic. No one was throwing her a lifeline. Being a spectator along with them was unbearable torment.

I blurted out to the physician in the most diplomatic tone I could manage, "I don't know if this will help but whenever she's had asthmatic attacks, Ventolin has helped her breathe better. Would that help dilate her bronchial tubes and help her breathe?"

Before I had finished, a respiratory therapist was placing a mask on Mom's face and administering medication. After a few minutes, Mom's breathing slowed down and became deeper, and more regular. The spectators silently dispersed. As quickly as the crisis had occurred, it ended. Mom collapsed from exhaustion back on her bed, breathing more easily, the gurgling sounds fading away. After a few minutes, she turned to me.

"They were all around me, everywhere. But no one was doing anything for me." I held her hand. My eyes met hers in agreement. My heart broke for her suffering.

Sometime later that day, Dr. Mondale ushered me into the hall. "Rickey, you need to let us know if you want to put a 'no code' on your Mom. Do you want her to be resuscitated in all circumstances or not? You do not need to make that decision right now but we need to know soon."

I knew all about no codes, having worked in hospitals for ten years. I went into Mom's room. *Why was he asking me? This was Mom's decision.*

"I don't want a tube stuck down my throat for me to breathe on some kind of machine," she began. "And I don't want to live on if my brain isn't working." I told Dr. Mondale about Mom's wishes, and he added 'no code' to her chart.

Angela took a bus from London and arrived at the hospital the next day. Mom knew that Angela had been attending a music program in London. As soon as Angela arrived at her bedside, kissed her, and held her hand, Mom said, "Angela, I'm okay now. I want you to go back to your music program."

Angela remained by Mom's bedside all day permitting me to take a much-needed break. I was able to go home, shower, and change my clothes. When I returned, Mom again urged Angela to return to her music program. I concurred. That night Angela was on a bus heading back to London.

I slept on and off in the visitor's lounge and asked the nurse to let me know if there was any change in Mom's condition. At around four in the morning, a physician was tapping my arm. "Rickey, wake up."

I bolted. "What is it?"

"She is having trouble breathing again. We tried medication but it isn't enough. This is the time to intubate. Do you want us to do that? If we do, she will breathe much more easily. If we do not, she may not make it."

Mom said that she did not want to be intubated. Even so, I hesitated. In Mom's room, I watched her struggle to breathe again. I asked the physician whether any medication would help open her airway. "That is not the answer. Her heart is failing and fluid is building up in her lungs. She is getting the maximum dosage of Lasix but it is not enough."

'I do not want a tube to be stuck down my throat.' I kept hearing Mom's words. "My mom said that she does not want to be intubated," I told the physician. Hours passed. Mom's breathing improved. The catheter drained large quantities of fluid from her bladder. The Lasix was doing its work. The crisis passed.

In the morning, Dr. Mondale spoke with me in the hall. "The telemetry shows that her heart function is decreasing. She will get better care in the intensive-care unit. I would like to transfer her." His words sounded like death was knocking at the door. I accompanied him as he bent down to talk to Mom.

"How are you, Faye?" His voice was soft and comforting.

"I'm okay, Doctor. How are you?" *Even now she is thinking of him.*

Dr. Mondale smiled, surprised at her response. "I'm just fine, Faye. I see that your stomach is quite distended," he said as he gently lifted her hospital gown.

"Oh that, Doctor—my stomach always looks like that. I always look like a horse. That's just the way I'm made."

Dr. Mondale continued. "You will get better care in the intensive-care unit than here. A nurse will be with you twenty-four hours a day there. So, we're going to be moving you in a little while. Is that okay with you?"

"Yes, of course. It's worth a shot."

"Thank you, Dr. Mondale, for all you have done for Mom," I said as I thought this was bidding him farewell.

"I will still be involved," he said. "I will be consulting with the ICU physician." I felt immediately reassured that he would still be there for us. This soft-spoken, gentle doctor had earned my trust.

I updated Angela. She told me that she would be returning to Toronto on an overnight bus. Angela felt that her place was with her Bubby.

Dr. Donaldson, the chief of the ICU, met me before Mom had been settled into the unit. "I have reviewed Dr. Mondale's notes. Your mom is in critical condition now. I doubt that she will recover. If she has another heart attack or stroke at this point, it is not likely that she will have any quality of life if she is resuscitated. I see that she is a 'no code' already. Is that still your wish?

"Yes, if it is likely that her brain will not be functional, yes," I said without believing his assessment.

"You will see that we put a pacer into her heart to help stabilize the rhythm. She also has a number of medications being delivered through her IV. We are doing everything we can for her."

I entered the ICU in the evening and stayed with Mom throughout a night of torment. She was writhing in agony in front of my eyes hour after hour. I asked the nurse for the reason. She said, "I don't know," as she was attending continuously to the multiple bags of medication hanging from the IV pole and checking the monitors for blood pressure, oxygenation, heart rate, and other data.

Mom uttered confusing words here and there in a guttural voice that I had never heard before. I felt as if I was watching someone I did not know in great pain. Her breathing was irregular and noisy. She was delirious, caught between life and death. I held her hand whenever I could. Her agitation and constant movements in the bed alarmed me. Sometimes she folded her legs and brought them towards her chest. She turned on her side and then her other side and then onto her back again. She could not find a position that afforded her any comfort. The nurse kept making notes in Mom's chart and checking the IV pump. She appeared to be oblivious to Mom's extreme agitation.

Through that long dark night, I kept asking myself and her nurse, "Isn't there anything that can be done to relieve this poor tormented soul?"

At seven in the morning the nursing shift changed. Miranda, the new nurse, entered the curtained cubicle and saw Mom writhing. She heard her delirious guttural sounds. She saw my tear-stained face. She left Mom's bedside and returned after a few minutes with a syringe. "This is Haldol. It will calm her down."

After the injection, the writhing stopped. Mom's breathing became quiet and more regular. An exhausted but calmer expression took the place of the agony I had seen in her face all night. She was sleeping. I could not have been more grateful to Miranda. I fell into her arms and Miranda hugged me. I felt that she was an angel sent from heaven.

Angela joined me at Mom's bedside. As the day went on, I noticed that the urinary catheter was not draining. A physician arrived and identified himself as a urologist. In a gentle voice he explained that Mom's kidneys were failing and that she would die without continuous dialysis. He said that a continuous dialysis machine would be brought to her bedside shortly. He explained the surgical procedure needed to connect it to her body and asked us to leave.

When we returned, we were immediately confronted by an enormous machine. Blood was moving through a series of clear tubes from Mom's upper arm into the centre of the machine and emerging from the other side, moving back into Mom's arm. Angela and I gasped in awe and horror at the machine. Her life depended on this machine.

Our focus on the dialysis machine took our attention away from the nurse who was sitting nearby, reading the manual that was attached to the machine by a cord. Miranda had left as her shift was over. The nurse who took her place looked perplexed as she flipped pages. She studied the machine and the complicated control panel. We heard her mumble about numbers. She took out a pen and began to make calculations on a pad of paper.

I felt intense anxiety. *Perhaps this nurse does not know how to operate the machine.* Angela shared my concern. She reached into her bag and pulled out her calculator. "Do you want a calculator to help you?"

"No," the nurse responded with frustration. Angela and I watched as the nurse pushed buttons and changed the speed at which Mom's blood travelled in and out of the machine. I had no choice but to trust that the nurse knew what she was doing. Her hesitation and her repeated flipping through the pages of the manual were not reassuring.

Angela and I decided to spend the night in the ICU visitor's lounge. As we made our way towards the exit of the ICU near midnight, a physician stopped us. "I need to speak with you." His tone was urgent. Mom's nurse was standing beside him.

"Her vein is collapsing and we can't find any really good veins for the IV medications. We need to know whether you want us to insert a central line. Given her critical condition, inserting a central line carries risks. She might die from the procedure."

"And what will happen if you don't do it?" I asked, struggling to remain calm and think logically.

"Well, we can try to find another vein and see how long that one lasts. If that gives out, we can try to find another one again."

There was a long pause. Angela and I looked at each other, unsure about how best to proceed.

"What do you advise, Doctor?"

"I can't advise you. It's your decision."

I turned to the nurse who had been consistently cold and unresponsive.

"What do you think we should do?"

The nurse looked directly into my eyes with irritation. "As the doctor just said, it's up to you to decide."

"Well, Doctor, if there was no family here to ask, what would you do?"

"I would insert the central line."

"Then do it!" As I turned and walked towards the exit, anger welled up within me. There was no reason for him to cause me further stress by refusing to make that recommendation!

Angela and I spent a sleepless night in the ICU waiting room. It was a dismal, foreboding place. Angela commented, "It's like a funeral home in here." Neither of us had ever been to a funeral home but we were certain that this was how a funeral home would look and feel. The light was dim, only a few lamps with old-style lampshades provided bleak and foggy light. The couches were worn and the carpet was thin and frail. A few people were sitting in chairs, their stillness and silence amplified the pounding of my heart. The room seemed to smell of death. I spent the hours waiting for the phone to ring.

The following day, Michael joined us and we took turns sitting by Mom's bedside. She had been unresponsive for days now, barely opening her eyes.

Throughout the day, my gaze became fixated on the heart rate monitor above Mom's bed. I could not help but watch as her heart rate steadily dropped. From seventy to sixty to fifty and finally to forty beats per minute. As her heart rate dropped hour by hour, so did my energy and resolve to stay awake. Dr. Donaldson came by at around noon. "How many hours of sleep did you have last night?"

"Maybe two or three." I made up the numbers.

"That's not enough. You should go into the ICU visitor's lounge and sleep. We will get you if anything changes." I told him that I did not want to leave her.

It was three-thirty when Dr. Mondale suddenly appeared by my side as I was holding Mom's hand. His voice was soft and gentle. The words were devastating and harsh. "I don't think she is going to make it, Rickey. You should gather together your family. I think it likely that she will pass away by four o'clock."

I suppose it really is over. A voice from within me directed me into the visitor's lounge. I called Terry to update her. The chairs and couch were occupied. Without thinking, I collapsed on the carpeted floor and entered a deep and troubled sleep. I had finally given up.

"Mom, wake up, wake up!" It was Angela's voice commanding me to open my eyes. Was this a dream? Her tone was one of excitement. Forcing my eyelids to open, I saw that Angela's face was one large smile. *Must be a dream.*

"She's better. Bubby's better. Her heart is beating better!"

Then Terry's face appeared in front of my bleary eyes. "She is alive but her kidneys are dead, dead, dead. She will need dialysis for the rest of her life. But she is alive."

Dead kidneys? Mom is alive? Springing up, I rushed to the ICU phone to ask permission to enter. Once inside with Angela, I ran to Mom's bedside and was shocked to see that her heart rate was seventy. Her oxygenation was in the nineties. Her eyes were open and she was smiling. Looking over at Angela, she said, "Sweetheart, go back to London. I'm okay now."

How had this miracle happened? When Dr. Donaldson came by later in the morning, he told me that he had jolted her heart through the pacemaker to see if that would make a difference. He smiled as he told me that as soon as he gave her heart a jolt, it sprung back into a regular rhythm and within a few minutes, rebounded from forty to fifty to sixty and up to seventy beats per minute again. "That's all her heart needed," he remarked. "Apparently, less of her heart tissue was damaged than we had thought based on her symptoms and the test results. Sometimes you can't tell that way."

"Thank you, Dr. Donaldson. Thank you for saving my mom's life!"

As the hours passed Mom slept on and off. Glancing down at the urinary catheter, I suddenly saw a drop of urine. Then there were more. I could not believe what I was seeing. In the early evening, the urologist returned. Upon seeing the bag that contained a small pool of urine, he exclaimed, "Oh, this is wonderful! Her kidneys are working again."

I had never been so happy to see urine.

Mom's kidneys continued to function and the next day we said good-bye and thank you to the dialysis machine. Several days later, Mom was moved out of the ICU into a regular hospital room.

I had notified our synagogue, and our rabbi was kind enough to visit. Each time he entered her room, Mom remarked, "Oh, it's my handsome rabbi!" His visits were more than comforting. His caring manner and familiar voice brought to mind memories of all the times I had prayed on Shabbat, sitting in the third row in front of the rabbi's lectern with Mom and Dad on either side. His many visits brightened Mom's hospital room with hope.

Just before Mom was discharged home, I summoned the courage to revisit her wishes. "Mom, you told me that if you were ever in critical condition, you did not want to have a tube put down your throat to help you breathe and keep you alive. During your hospital stay, there was a time when your doctor asked me about this and I said, 'No.' Mom, do you want me to say 'no' if this ever happens again?"

"Well, if there is a chance to save my life, I would be okay with having a tube down my throat."

Having come close to death and now being blessed with life again Mom's feelings had changed.

In the months that followed, Mom pursued all her activities as usual, doing her best to push aside the nagging pain in her chest that often woke her at night. Dr. Mondale performed a heart catheterization procedure and told her that she had three partially blocked arteries. He recommended that she consult with a surgeon about bypass surgery.

"Okay, Doctor, go ahead and set up the appointment with that doctor." Mom's voice was confident.

We did not wait long for the consultation with Dr. Abel. Angela joined us for the meeting.

After a short introduction, Dr. Abel leaned toward Mom and began. "Mrs. Miller, I agree with Dr. Mondale. I recommend surgery to bypass three major blood vessels. Two are moderately blocked and one is more severely blocked. This is the cause of your angina. You also need to have a valve replaced. Are you Jewish?"

Why ask about her religion?

"Yes, I am." Mom answered with pride.

"Well, do you have any objections if we replace your valve with a natural valve that comes from a pig? It's better than a synthetic valve."

"I have no objections at all," Mom began. "I don't keep kosher. If the pig is healthy and it helps me, I have absolutely no problem."

Dr. Abel's resident knelt beside Mom to examine her leg. I did not understand the reason. *The problem is her heart.* I watched the doctor trace a vein running from Mom's knee down to her ankle with her finger. Angela and I looked at each other in horror, suddenly understanding that this vein was going to be removed from Mom's leg and used as the bypass blood vessel. The image of having a vein pulled out from her leg filled us with dread.

"This vein looks perfect," the resident said.

"Well, Mrs. Miller, you know there are risks associated with this surgery, especially since you will be eighty-five when we operate. Although most people come through it just fine, there is a risk of stroke and there is a risk of death. Take some time to make your decision. If you want, you can also seek a second opinion."

Angela and I looked at each other with heightened anxiety. We asked Dr. Abel further questions about the probability of complications and death. As he began to answer, Mom spoke loudly and interrupted us.

"I don't need any time to think it over, Doctor. I want to go ahead with the operation."

Dr. Abel noted Mom's response and told her that his secretary would let her know the date of her surgery. Walking out of the office, Angela and I spoke at the same time. "Are you sure about this? It is risky."

"I can't live with this chest pain waking me up every night and if I have blocked vessels, it will only get worse. What's the point of living if I can't do what I want to do? It needs to be fixed. Now, let's go to the restaurant for lunch!" Mom smiled as she anticipated the meal. Angela and I tagged along behind her, full of fear.

Mom waited nine long months for her bypass surgery. The angina became more frequent and began to attack during the day at odd times, taking her breath away. When I was with her during those times, I was always ready to call an ambulance. Each time I waited for what seemed like an eternity before the pain eased off after I gave her nitroglycerine sprays.

The day of the operation was a little over a week before Mom's eighty-fifth birthday. Holding her hand as Mom was wheeled down the hall towards the operating room, I said with confidence, "I'll see you in a little while, Mom."

As we waited, I saw numerous physicians walking into the waiting room, greeting other families with good news. When Dr. Abel walked through the door five hours later. I ran up to him. "How is she?" I asked breathless with anxiety.

"Your mother did well and is in recovery. We replaced the valve and did a triple bypass."

Dr. Abel did not look relieved. I knew that something was wrong.

"There is a small sponge unaccounted for. We looked for it everywhere and could not find it. I'm afraid that it is inside your mom somewhere. There is a risk of a stroke because of this problem. If the sponge does not move, then it may not do her any harm."

I did not know what to say. I fumbled for words. "What is the probability of this causing a stroke?"

"I don't know the probability. It depends on where it is and whether it moves."

"Well, let's hope it stays in place." I appreciated Dr. Abel's honesty in admitting that an error had been made. At the same time, I felt a storm of anger. *How could he have lost a sponge inside her body?* It did not occur to me at the time that he had failed to apologize. All I found myself asking next was, "Can I see her?"

Dr. Abel led me to the recovery area, which looked like the intensive-care unit that Mom had been in after her heart attack. Off a long hallway, there were a number of side-by-side rooms all facing a window overlooking the street. Entering the room where Mom was lying, I heard the rhythm of the ventilator pumping air into her body and the beeping of multiple monitors. There were groups of IV bags hanging from poles on either side of her bed. It was difficult to see Mom in that body. Her eyes were tightly closed. Her lovely deep brown hair framed her pale face. The two nurses tending to her told me that she was doing as expected. I held her hand for some time praying that she would survive. The two nurses began to discuss the 'pumps' that were still coming up from surgery. One of them turned to me, embarrassed, and apologized.

"I'm sorry."

I supposed that it helped them cope by depersonalizing the unconscious ventilated bodies that depend on their care by calling them 'pumps.'

Wandering down the hall a few hours later, I discovered an unoccupied small room. Sitting down, I breathed deeply and worked on releasing some of my tension. My aunt and uncle drove Angela and Michael home. I could not imagine returning home before Mom opened her eyes again.

Late into the night, I was still in the waiting room, lying on a couch, when a physician came into the room. I wondered how he had found me. I jolted up.

"I'm sorry to tell you this, but your mom is experiencing seizures. We are trying to get them under control. We think that they might be related to the brain surgery she had previously. Sometimes when people have brain surgery and then they have a major anaesthetic medication and are on a heart-lung machine for hours, the brain becomes irritated because there is scar tissue and seizures occur. We are trying to get the seizures under control with drugs right now."

"Can I see her?"

"I don't think that is a good idea right now. I'll get you when the seizures stop or if her condition changes in any other way."

I could not just sit in this room without knowing what was going on. After a few minutes, I walked softly and slowly towards her room. I overheard one of the nurses tending to Mom.

"What did they expect for an eighty-five-year-old woman? They should never have operated on her. Look at her condition now."

At the time, their comments horrified me. I felt like shouting out in anger that Mom's eighty-five-year-old life was precious and worth saving. I was grateful to Dr. Abel for giving Mom the choice to undergo bypass surgery and I was proud of Mom for having the courage to agree. The complications did not mean that the surgery was a mistake. I understood that the nurses probably preferred caring for younger patients whose recovery was more straightforward.

If the physician judges the benefits to outweigh the risks, is there an age when a person should no longer be given the choice of life-saving surgery?

With a few breaks to get food and drink, I spent the next five days and nights in my little private waiting room down the hall from Mom's room waiting for the seizures to stop.

A slant of bright light cut across the floor of the room announcing the arrival of dawn on the sixth day after the operation. Footsteps coming from down the hall woke me. *Was she still alive?*

Dr. Abel spoke softly. "We finally got the seizures under control. Your mom has regained consciousness. You can see her now." Quickly I made my way into Mom's room.

"Hello, Mom. You did very well. The operation went wonderfully. You are going to be okay. I love you so much. It's so good to see that you are awake."

Mom's eyes reflected enormous frustration. She raised her hand and pointed to her mouth. I knew that she wanted to speak but she was unable to do so with the ventilator connected to her. The nurse gave her a piece of paper and a pencil. Mom wrote, "Take this thing out! Now!"

"Can we remove the ventilator now?" I asked the nurse.

"We need the doctor's order to do that. It hasn't been long since the seizures stopped."

"Please ask the doctor if the ventilator can be removed." I was trying my best to speak calmly and softly, but Mom's agitation was increasing. A heart-wrenching hour passed with Mom writing again and again on the paper that she wanted the tube in her throat to be removed. I told her that we were waiting for the physician's order. I felt like pulling the tube out myself.

A physician entered her room. The nurse spoke to him, "She's fully conscious now. Can we stop the ventilator?"

After the physician agreed and wrote the order in the chart, the tube was removed. The nurse told Mom that it would take a few days for her throat to heal and her normal voice to return. At least she could talk again. She whispered in my ear, "Thank you, Rickey." We hugged.

Mom was moved out of the cardiac intensive-care area to another intensive-care unit where she remained for the next three weeks. During the second week, when it appeared that her condition had stabilized, I returned home in the evening. *What a joy to sleep in my own bed!* A few days later I returned to work and spent each evening at the hospital.

Not long after, I received a call from the intensive-care physician.

"Your mom is having problems breathing. We are going to investigate the cause. I think you should come down here."

As soon as I entered Mom's room, I saw that there was a large mask on her face connected with a tube to a machine that was pumping air into her fast and furiously.

"What is that?" I asked the nurse.

"It's a positive pressure ventilator."

"Why is it going so fast? Can you turn that down?"

"That's her. She's breathing that fast," the nurse explained. "She went into respiratory arrest a few times. This is helping her breathe. When she stabilizes, we are going to do an MRI to see what is going on that is making it hard for her to breathe and swallow."

Feeling the need for his warmth and compassion, I called our rabbi, who arrived the same day. He entered Mom's room and held her hand while she was gasping for air. Once again, I felt grateful for his support. I clung to hope as Mom clung to life.

Hours passed and finally the speed of the pumping decreased. A physician entered the room and consulted with the nurse about the MRI. The ventilator needed to be disconnected for the test to be done. I watched as the face mask was removed and the machine was turned off. Mom was breathing heavily on her own. A porter arrived and the nurse and porter began wheeling Mom's bed out of the room. I heard Mom say ever so softly, in between heaving breaths, "Okay, God, you can take me now." Then she turned to me and whispered, "Rickey, I left you a note in my dresser. Read it."

Farther down the hall, I heard the nurse say to the porter, "No wonder the daughter is so worried about her. She can barely breathe on her own."

The physician met me in Mom's intensive-care room. "The MRI shows that she has significant swelling in her airway, probably because the ventilator was in there for six days. The swelling will likely abate and we can help achieve that with medication. For now, we will keep her in intensive care and we will feed her through a nasal-gastric tube."

Our rabbi made another visit. Hearing that Angela and I were struggling to sleep in chairs in the waiting area, he left abruptly. He returned after half an hour and said, "I found you a room where you can sleep tonight." He led us to a staff surgical waiting room and told us that it would be empty overnight. "Staff only use this during the day. There is a phone in there so the intensive-care nurse can call you at any time if your mom's condition should change. You will be a lot more comfortable in here."

I thanked him profusely.

A few days later, Mom was breathing consistently on her own. She managed to sit in a chair for the first time since her operation and was speaking in a more normal voice. Mom turned to Angela and me and said, "I don't recommend this operation to anyone! It is a big operation. And someone told me that a bypass lasts for only seven years on average.

Can you believe that? That's very upsetting. Well, we have to live with hope."

When she was returned to a regular hospital room, a speech-language therapist assessed her ability to swallow. She explained to us the dangers of Mom aspirating if she tried to drink or eat anything but said that she would slowly introduce Mom to puréed food while still keeping the nasal-gastric tube in place. That way she would be sure to consume enough nutrients. The therapist explained that there would be five levels of food introduced over the next few weeks, puréed, minced, ground, chopped, and then, finally, easy-to-swallow regular food. Mom was excited to hear that she would be given puréed food.

After a few hours, a meal was delivered to Mom. She looked at the covered plate with relish, her eyes sparkling with delight. She pushed the button on her bed to enable her to sit up in front of her meal and pulled the cover off the plate. Angela and I looked at each other trying to conceal our disgust. Mom looked at the mass of pureed peas in front of her with the joy of a child looking at a big piece of cake. She was ecstatic as she put the spoon to her mouth and swallowed the peas. We had to encourage her to go slowly. She had not eaten anything for weeks and her pleasure at tasting the food brought tears of happiness to her eyes.

Mom improved slowly, enjoying every milestone that she achieved along the path back towards her normal life. She never doubted her ability to reach that goal.

Mom's attitude was a perfect blend of two opposing beliefs: She was living life as if she would live forever, without fear, and at the same time she was living every day as if it was her last.

If only I could walk along the narrow bridge without fear and, at the same time, never take a moment of life for granted.

Mom's heart attack and bypass surgery were transformative in an unexpected way when it came to our relationship. Our respective roles had shifted. While I continued to disclose my thoughts and feelings to her and to seek her advice, I was becoming her primary caregiver. I accompanied her to all her appointments and coordinated her health care. As time went on, she asked me to accompany her to the bank and asked me to look over her bank book to make sure that it was accurate. She began to call me her 'lifeline.' This sweet expression of appreciation carried with it an onerous responsibility. It wasn't so long ago when Mom had been my lifeline. *I was not prepared for this role reversal.*

I'm thinking of Carmela, a woman in her fifties, who sought treatment because she felt overwhelmed by the task of caring for her mom. Carmela was effusive, speaking loudly, orchestrating her words with her hands, shifting her body with every phrase. She brought with her an aura of warmth. When she first sat down, she smiled broadly, and thanked me for seeing her. A few soft curls from her short brown hair dangled onto her forehead.

"I'm having a real hard time dealing with my mom. She is eighty and has a bunch of health problems including heart problems, diabetes, and she just had a knee replacement. She complains all the time that I am not doing enough for her. I have a brother and he does nothing much. Sometimes I ask him to shop and he brings her some groceries. Mom depends mostly on me and I do everything for her."

"You are disappointed that your brother does not do more. You're feeling it's not fair."

"That's right. It isn't, but it's always been that way."

"What about your father?"

"He died ten years ago. Sudden stroke. He never recovered. I was close to him. He was the sweetest man, very loving, very kind. Not at all like mom."

"I am sad to hear this. You still miss him. That was a big loss."

Carmela wept softly. "I miss him. I always will."

"How is your mom different?"

"She's an authoritarian, controlling person. She has always been critical of me. I never do it right for her. I can never please her. My husband, Frank, is like that, too, but my main problem is Mom. I go over there to help and I come away in tears."

"In what ways does she expect you to help?"

"She expects me to shop for her now that she is recovering from surgery. She expects me to drive her to all her appointments and to cook for her. I cook at home and bring her meals. I make sure that she has all her prescriptions and I call her every day to remind her to take her pills. It's a thankless job."

"That is very hard. You feel the need to care for her. You're doing it for yourself and for her, Carmela. Are you also taking care of your family at the same time?"

"Yeah, my three kids. Each of them has their own problems. James is struggling at university. Carolyn is having trouble with her boyfriend. Susie gets into fights with me all the time. They all live at home even though they are in their twenties. Frank is not much help at all."

"You feel very much alone, it sounds, without much help and without emotional support. You feel that it's your job to care for everyone, your kids, your husband, your mom. It sounds exhausting. What about caring for yourself?"

"I am trying."

"Yes, you are caring for yourself by coming here, Carmela. What about taking some time every day to do something for yourself, something that gives you comfort, pleasure, or relaxation, even if it is only for a short time? You need to be at the top not at the bottom of your list. What would help you feel better on a typical day?"

"Maybe a walk. I like going out of the house. Maybe talk to a friend. It helps me to talk it out."

"I suggest you make an appointment with yourself to do something like that every day. What time of day would be best?"

"After supper."

In the sessions that followed, Carmela disclosed that she had always felt intimidated by her mother. "As a child, my mom would answer for me if anyone asked how I was doing."

"You have mixed feelings about your mom. That complicates helping her."

"I am being like a mom to her and a much better one than she was to me. It's unfair."

"It is very unfair. Your caring reflects the kind of person you are choosing to be, Carmela. You want to be a better caregiver to her than she was to you even though it is unfair. Do you talk with her and go to her home every day?"

"Yes, pretty nearly every day."

"Must be exhausting and frustrating and stressful."

Carmela laughed loudly. "All of those and more!"

"Does your mom need you to call her and come over nearly every day?"

Carmela paused for the first time before responding. "No, actually. She just likes it that way."

"How often would you like to go to your mom's each week to help her?"

"I'd say three or four times."

"And if you did that, would you feel guilty that you weren't helping her enough?"

"No. I think I would still be helping her enough unless something out of the ordinary happened."

"And about how long would you like to be with her when you visit her?"

"I suppose about one hour. But she won't be happy with my visiting her for fewer days and if I only stay for one hour."

"But didn't you tell me that she isn't happy with you even when you make daily visits and stay for longer? It sounds like whatever you do, she isn't happy. You said it yourself that you can never do enough for her."

"Yes, it has always been impossible for me to please her."

"It sounds like pleasing her is beyond your ability. Perhaps, it would be wise to give up trying to please her. I know that's hard to do. Wouldn't it be better to make your goals helping her as much as you wish and take care of yourself better?"

"It is time I give up trying to make her happy."

"And give up on trying to make her love you the way you wish she would."

"Yes, it is time after all these years."

"It is important for you to think about your well-being, Carmela. You have a full-time job and are trying to care for your husband and kids as well as your mom. Somehow along the way, your needs have gotten lost in the shuffle."

"I have been feeling like I'm burning out. I'm not used to taking care of mom and my kids—it's like I have another kid and one who is never happy with me."

In time, Carmela worked out a better schedule for herself. Her visits and phone calls with her mother became less frequent and shorter. In her sessions she rehearsed communicating her needs and feelings more assertively to her mother. She became less vulnerable to her mother's hurtful comments and practised thinking to herself, "That's just the way she chooses to be." Eventually Carmela was able to leave hurtful conversations and visits promptly without guilt and without arguing. As she became more loving and caring toward herself, she began to communicate her needs and feelings more directly to her husband and children. The focus of her treatment shifted to improving those relationships.

Carmela came to accept that she could not change her mother but that she could change the ways in which she responded to her. She began to make self-care her priority.

It took me years to learn the lessons that I taught her.

45

Of Endings

February 9, 2000. It was the fourteenth time that I had driven to the courthouse.

As I approached the building, I was filled with the dread of going inside. It was a building of pain. I had endured time and again the agony of hearing falsehoods about me broadcast to judges who believed them. I had endured the excruciating pain of witnessing someone I had once trusted and loved with all my heart tear the truth and my heart into shreds, as if he was ripping tissue paper.

The case conference that was scheduled was the first of its kind for us. David had explained that we would be in front of a judge for a long time, perhaps hours, and that this judge would see us through all the next steps up to and including the trial. All the other times different judges presided over the action. Each judge had made it clear that he knew nothing about our case when the motion was heard. He listened to the lawyers and made decisions as to which arguments were more persuasive. It appeared to me that none of them took the time to read the affidavits and factums ahead of time. What was the point of spending all the hours writing them and at enormous expense financially and emotionally? That process felt punitive.

As David and I stepped out of the elevator, I heard a commotion coming from the end of the long hallway. I could see Luke and his lawyer having a loud, heated conversation.

Luke's lawyer turned around momentarily. Seeing us, he motioned to us to wait.

After several minutes, Mr. Stone walked toward us. "We are cancelling the case conference with your client's agreement. My client has decided to settle the access and custody as well as child support issues now without further court involvement. Do I have your agreement to cancel the case conference and settle the remaining action now?"

David turned to me and looked for my agreement as a formality. He knew better than anyone the tremendous relief that I was feeling.

"First, Mr. Stone, we request that you send a letter to Mr. Bonninger, the lawyer who is representing the bank. You need to inform him that the bank does not have a chance of winning an equalization claim given the clear evidence of financial wrongdoing on your client's part. After your client declared bankruptcy and the bank assumed the equalization claim, you wrote a letter encouraging Mr. Bonninger to pursue the claim against my client. You supported the integrity of your client's claim. You need to state that after reviewing the transcripts of the nine days of discoveries, your view has changed. You will state that, in your view, any court will invalidate your client's equalization claim and expose the bank to costs. I need to see that letter before we proceed and receive confirmation that Mr. Bonninger's office has received it before we settle the remainder of the action here and now."

Mr. Stone hastily wrote the letter as David looked on. It was quickly processed by his secretary and faxed to Mr. Bonninger's office after which David asked Mr. Bonninger's legal assistant to read the letter back to him and to fax it to his office.

David began to draft the final settlement agreement. *Was this really the end? Would the letter be enough to dissuade the bank?*

A final agreement was drawn up over a few hours. I was granted sole custody. Access was to depend on Michael's readiness to spend time with his dad, but a tentative schedule was specified. Child support was set to remain the same as it had been. Since we still did not know Luke's actual income, David recommended that we consider the initial support amount to be a reasonable estimate.

The final agreement was submitted to the court for the judge's approval. David and I turned to leave. Luke had been sitting back in a chair at the end of the hall for the entire time of our deliberations with his lawyer. As I left the courthouse, I cried tears of relief mixed with sorrow for the deep wounds that Angela, Michael, and I had suffered because of the battle.

A few weeks later, a registered letter arrived from the bank. I trembled as I opened the envelope. Skipping over the opening paragraph, my eyes focused on the words that the bank "has reviewed the transcripts of the nine days of discoveries and will settle the equalization claim with you for twenty thousand dollars." As the equalization claim was initially worth over three hundred thousand dollars, this was a real victory, not a pyrrhic one. The children and I could continue to live in our home. My savings had been depleted by the litigation and the amount I would pay to the bank but remained sufficient for us to continue living as we had been. For now, there was money for Angela's music education and Michael's tutoring.

Our case became the twelfth of divorces for which an unequal claim was granted.

It is now over twenty years since I walked out of that courthouse for the last time and yet the question of means and ends continues to haunt me.

How ironic that the war that had brought me indescribable pain had become a lifeline for Darlene. She wanted to see the action through to the end, even as her body betrayed her day after day. After the final settlement, I drove to her home, following David's car. By this time Darlene was barely able to move. She was unable to talk and used a board with letters on it to communicate. Against the backdrop of a body lying almost lifeless on the bed, her eyes still sparkled with life. Caregivers were with her twenty-four hours each day, and her daughter was constantly by her side. Darlene's eyes lit up with joy as I described the events of the day. Her happiness brightened the whole room. She was proud of her work, of David's efforts, and my seeing it through. My heart sank every time I looked upwards to the ceiling hoist and lift used to move her body to the bathroom. I tried my best to refocus on the joy in her eyes. David inserted the syringe full of medication into her stomach tube, his routine for the last few months. I told Darlene how grateful I was for all that she had done—all the telephone conversations that she had transcribed, her well-organized and enormous timeline showing all of Luke's financial transactions, all the hours that she had spent with me analyzing each document that had been in the boxes from my basement, the boxes that David referred to as the key to the entire case, the many all-nighters during which she had spent typing up affidavits and factums and letters, and all her 'Oh's' and 'Look-at-this!' comments when she saw something that appeared to be pivotal. I knew Darlene appreciated my heartfelt gratitude.

One day in 2001, on a day of her choosing, Darlene gathered her three adult children around her bed, and said farewell to each of them in turn and then embraced David one last time. She had decided not to allow the disease to snuff the air out of her but rather to slip quietly into that dark, endless sleep on her terms.

I feel rage that this cruel disease took away such a cheerful, caring, and beautiful soul.

I walk around the office, my tears flowing for Darlene.

46

A Very Strange Summer Display

"You must stop college, Michael. You simply cannot do it." Angela was saying words that neither Michael nor I were prepared to hear. "Mom, you must stop. You are making yourself sick and miserable. It's not right." I knew that Angela was speaking the truth. At the same time, I didn't want to know.

Angela was completing her second year in piano performance in Ohio. We were at a hardware store looking for some items that she needed. As we walked by the lounge chairs that were part of the summer furniture display, I had started the conversation. "I'm totally exhausted. I just helped Michael complete a project for his child development course. It was assigned in February but Michael only asked me to help him two weeks before the due date. He did not know how to begin so he forgot about it. I worked with him every day for hours so that he could complete it."

"I'm sorry, Mom. I forgot all about that assignment," Michael said, as I collapsed into one of the lounge chairs. Angela and Michael sat on two chairs facing me.

"Look at Mom, Michael. She's exhausted. She can't go on like this anymore. You can't do college, Michael." Angela was adamant.

"Yes, I can!" Michael cried. "If Mom helps me, I can get my Early Childhood Education diploma."

I am thinking about the day when Michael graduated from high school. When his name was called to go up to the stage to receive his grade twelve diploma, he hesitated. Angela and I urged him to move before the next name was called. Returning to his seat with his diploma rolled up and held under his arm, Michael looked at me and said,

"Mom, I don't deserve this. You did so much of the work. I don't deserve to graduate." His comments broke my heart.

"Michael, you studied hard. You spent hours writing tests and exams and papers. I helped you and all the tutors helped you but you are the one who passed. You deserve to graduate."

Angela went on, oblivious to the customers in the store who were looking at us. "Michael, it is not okay that Mom is doing so much work for you. If you do become an early education childhood teacher, you will not know how to do that job. When you are at work, you will not be able to call Mom and ask her for help."

"But Angela, I have been a good teacher at the daycares where I have completed my practica." Michael turned to me. "Mom, you will help me, right?" It was a demand. "Like you always have."

"Look at Mom," Angela pointed my way. "She's exhausted, Michael. She can't go on helping you and working full time and doing everything else she does for you. She'll get sick for sure."

"There must be a way that Mom can help me and not get sick so that I can graduate from college. There must be a way!" I heard my mantra to never give up amplified many times over in Michael's words.

"Michael," I said softly. "If I continued to help you and you graduated, it would be a farce."

"What's a farce?" Michael asked.

"A farce is like a lie. It means that you would be holding yourself out as someone who has knowledge and skills that you do not have. Working as a teacher, your lack of knowledge would become clear and either you would get fired, or worse, make a big mistake of some kind. Your experiences in practica are not real jobs where you are expected to be in charge of the class and develop programs on your own." Michael was attentive to every word.

"It would be lying?"

"Yes, it would be lying." I said "You must withdraw. I will help you find a job as a teacher's assistant. You should be proud of yourself that you graduated from high school and completed two years of college. Angela and I are very proud of you."

The three of us hugged.

That was the end of school for Michael and the beginning of his work as a teacher's assistant in daycares. I had finally achieved the insight that moving forward sometimes requires giving up.

47

Moving Day

I was standing outside on the driveway waiting for the moving van to arrive. All of Michael's essentials and countless other memorabilia were crammed into boxes ready to go. Michael had packed his old shoes, New Year's Eve hats and decorations from years gone by, a broken hand mixer that reminded him of all the times he had licked sweet meringue and icing from the blades, old birthday and appreciation cards, torn clothes filled with memories of delightful experiences, coins he had found on streets and the floors of buildings, and numerous photos of his favourite rollercoasters and pirate-ship rides.

Michael resisted change except for this enormous one—moving into his own apartment. He was delighted at the thought of having his own home.

It was 2009, Michael was twenty-four years old. For many years I had lived in fear that he would never be able to live on his own. Yet here he was, in so many ways independent and confident. He would be moving into a one-bedroom apartment that was a short drive from my house.

The last few years living with Michael had been incredibly stressful. Michael took over the entire house, often shouting when playing video games, constantly talking out loud to himself, venting his anger by throwing objects and yelling in the basement, and engaging in control struggles with me about anything and everything.

"Michael, please don't slam the door!" I shouted with every bang.

"I didn't slam the door! Please, Mom!"

"Michael, what would it take for you to say, 'I'll close the door more softly next time'?"

"But I didn't slam it in the first place, Mom!"

There were countless times when he insisted on retelling me stories, his words flowing like a powerful stream that could not be stopped. "Michael, you told me many times about the rollercoaster ride at Cedar Point that you love." I just wanted a little silence in the car.

"Please, Mom, let me finish. I have to finish. I have to get the words out."

I laugh now when I remember how much I feared that he would never learn to talk!

Then there were the battles over food. "Michael, come for dinner."

"What did you make, Mom?"

"Chinese."

"I don't feel like that. I'm going to make lasagne for myself."

"No, I don't want to have to clean up all the mess. I don't want you in the kitchen all night. Please, just join me to eat the meal I have prepared."

"Don't worry, Mom. I promise that I will clean it all up."

There was no point in doing battle because I would inevitably lose. Many times, I wished that I had not taught Michael how to cook. Cooking brought out some of Michael's most obsessive behaviours. His lasagne was much too lovingly prepared over a span of three to four hours. It would be smothered with melted cheese with a freshly prepared tomato sauce containing spoonfuls of sugar. It was completely unpalatable to me, but to Michael, it was perfection. After his long hours of preparation and cooking, he meticulously washed the dishes, pots, and everything else that he had used, requiring more than one hour. No matter where I was in the house, there was no escape from his loud commentary, while he prepared the food, ate it, and cleaned up. The words spilling out of his mouth provided me with more than I ever wanted to know about what he was thinking. Concerned about the waste of water and my exasperation at his monologue, I always ended up taking over. Not surprisingly, there would be no control struggle about that.

When Angela was twelve years old, feeling compassion for my irritation with Michael, she wisely said, "There are worse things than annoying." I hugged her close, appreciating her wisdom. Then I wrote out her words on a slip of paper and taped it onto the refrigerator where it remained for years.

Looking back, I reflect on Michael's good heart, which was as evident as his obnoxiousness. When Angela was in graduate school and called to say how hard she was working, Michael overheard my question whether she was short on groceries. Each time, Michael picked up another phone and said, "Angela, I'll take the bus to New York and bring you the groceries you need. Give me a list. I'm all set to write it down. I have saved up enough money to buy them for you." After the phone call, I needed to stop Michael from preparing for the bus trip by explaining the reasons he should not go.

I recall Michael's excitement upon being hired at an amusement park during the summer when he was sixteen. It was his first job.

One day I went to the amusement park without telling Michael. His job was operating a game in which hammering a pad hard enough would cause a ball to ascend a tall vertical column and hit a bell at the top. A large crowd gathered around Michael as he appealed to the people in his most enthusiastic tone, "Come on, everyone. Play 'Ring the Bell!' Win an adorable, big stuffed monkey!" He pointed to a gentleman at random, "You look very strong, sir! I'm sure you can win! Come on, give it a try! Don't be afraid! You can do it!"

The man stepped forward, paid Michael, whacked the pad with the hammer, and the ball went flying up to the top and hit the bell. He was overjoyed when Michael handed him the large plush monkey, which he proudly handed to his wife. Then another man stepped up to play. Same outcome. Then another. Then another. *Wow, all these men are strong.*

Later that night when I hugged Michael good night, I asked him how many people had managed to hit the bell during his shift.

"Lots and lots of people, Mom! I made them very happy."

"What do you mean?

"I don't like it when someone walks away sad. The men especially have a really hard time facing their girlfriends or wives when they try a bunch of times and the ball only goes up halfway. I keep it on the children's setting so almost everyone wins!"

"Michael, you should not do that! You could lose your job for rigging the game like that. The park will be losing a lot of money with all those stuffed animals that you are giving out that those people do not really deserve. You must promise me to stop using that children's setting for the adults." Michael thought about my direction for a long time and finally agreed. "Promise me?" I asked.

"I promise." Michael always kept his promises.

"Are you on time for your shift, Michael? It is very important when you have a job to always be on time. If there is some important reason you have for being late, call your boss and let him or her know." Michael had heard this lecture from me on many occasions.

"Well, sometimes I am late, Mom. But there's no problem. Because I always call to let my boss know. I say, 'I'm sorry I'm going to be late,' just like you told me."

I had neglected to tell Michael that calling to say that he was going to be late didn't make it okay to be late. I later found out that Michael was late very frequently. Of course, he always called to say that he was sorry.

A few weeks later, Michael received a letter from the park thanking him for his assistance during the summer and terminating his employment. His boss wrote that Michael had been helpful, "But he is often seen swinging from the display at his booth and he doesn't always give the right change to the customers." *Swinging from the display? I had never seen him do that.* Michael admitted that he had done that when he was bored. That was the end of Michael's first job.

Michael's next job was working as a buggy boy at the neighbourhood grocery store. He was delighted when an employment agency that provides daycares and nursery schools with supply staff hired him as an assistant teacher. Michael loved helping the teachers and often played his violin for the children.

I was impressed with Michael's natural respect for those who had any kind of disability. While I sometimes shied away from approaching people with obvious disabilities and felt anxious about how to interact with them, Michael responded with ease. He was warm, respectful, and friendly to everyone.

Living with Michael was taking an enormous toll on me emotionally and physically. I had no privacy and no quiet place when he was home. My rising blood pressure was sending a clear message: Michael could not continue to live with me.

Angela encouraged me to contact Community and Social Services to see if there was any support Michael could receive to help him live independently. I was informed that if Michael's I.Q. was sixty-nine or lower, he would be eligible for supported independent living. I remembered that somewhere in the basement I had buried the report of the psychological assessment that Michael had completed when he was in grade eight.

During that year, Michael had been in a special-education class in which his teacher had spent more one-to-one time with him. I was continuing to work with him at home every day. I had also hired several high school students to tutor Michael every afternoon after school.

In the winter term, Michael's grade eight teacher, Ms. Peters, contacted me to set up an Individual Education Plan meeting to determine which high school would be best for him to attend. As a prelude to that meeting, she said that Michael needed to complete a psychological assessment. I reluctantly agreed. I anticipated the pain of hearing about Michael's problems yet again. Every criticism and complaint about Michael, every description of his deficits and problems created fresh wounds. I told Ms. Peters that I knew Michael's intellectual strengths and weaknesses better than anyone. "Why do we need another assessment? I can provide all the information you need at the meeting. I am not only his mother but a psychologist." Ms. Peters said that the assessment was required to place Michael in the most appropriate high school program.

Prior to the meeting, I decided that I needed to protect my wounded heart. I did not want anything to do with the assessment report or the assessor. The principal, Ms. Peters, and the psychometrist who had assessed Michael greeted me warmly. I felt dread.

I took control from the outset. I provided a detailed description of Michael's cognitive strengths and weaknesses and described the high school program that I thought would be best suited for him.

At this point, the psychometrist began. "Dr. Miller, I have a copy of the report of my assessment for you." She handed me the report in a large brown envelope. I dropped it on the table quickly as if it was toxic. "Here is a summary of my findings and recommendations." She said as she handed me a single page. I placed it on top of the envelope and looked up at her. The psychometrist was a young woman. She was eager to go on despite some anxiety that registered on her face. Perhaps she was concerned that I would be critical of her report. After all, she knew that I was an experienced clinical psychologist.

"No thank you." I asserted just as she drew a breath to begin her presentation. "I know all about his weaknesses and problems. I don't need to hear them again. I know that he has a verbal and nonverbal learning disability."

The psychometrist shook her head immediately to indicate that this diagnosis was incorrect. I tried my best to ignore her but I was shaken. *She must be wrong. I know my son better than anyone.*

Or do I?

The psychometrist spoke in a soft, apologetic tone. "I've also written about his strengths."

"I do not want to hear your report, thank you." I said. "Which high school does the committee recommend for Michael?"

The psychometrist slumped back in her chair, feeling rejected and frustrated.

The principal spoke next. "Thornbury Secondary. That school has an excellent special education department. Michael will be in special education for some of the day and in regular classes for other periods."

I signed the documents indicating my agreement. I was happy that they had selected the same school as Angela was attending. I reluctantly took the envelope with me when I left. As soon as I got home, I threw it into my files under the folder marked "Michael's Reports." All those reports contained painful reminders of Michael's academic difficulties. Even though I did not want to look at any of them again, my obsessive need to keep potentially important documents ensured that I would file this new unwelcome addition as well.

Eleven years later, when I needed Michael to receive assistance to live on his own, I thought about the assessment report that I had never read. I retrieved it from the basement.

After all these years of praying that he would become normal, of trying to cover up his deficits, I was now praying that this report would indicate the opposite.

With tears of joy mixed with grief, I read the psychometrist's clearly worded assessment and her conclusion that he met the criteria for the more serious diagnosis of developmental disability. His I.Q. was, indeed, in the range needed for him to receive the assistance that he required.

"I'm sorry," I said out loud, as I pictured the image of the young psychometrist in front of me. "Thank you for writing such an accurate report. I'm so sorry that that I dismissed you and your report eleven years ago. That was rude and disrespectful of me! Your report is my salvation and will help Michael."

I submitted the report along with other documents to the Ministry, and a worker came to the house to interview Michael and me. I was grateful to Angela for coming from New York to attend this important meeting. I told the worker that I could not live with Michael in the house any longer due to my health problems. I also told her that Michael did not have a relationship with his dad and that Angela was studying piano performance in New York City. There was no one else to take care of Michael and if something should happen to me, what then? The sooner he had the opportunity to manage living on his own, the better.

Shortly after that meeting, we were referred to Community Living, an agency that provided support for adults with developmental disabilities. Angela accompanied Michael and me. She was articulate as ever and able to ask questions that did not occur to me. We were told that there were two openings for supported independent living. To qualify I had to guarantee that Michael would, in fact, move out of my house. That was not difficult. I had already located an apartment and was ready to pay the first and last months' rent. I was also in the process of obtaining financial assistance from the Ontario Disability Support Program for Michael. I never take it for granted that we live in a country where such assistance is available.

A few weeks later, I received a letter from Community Living indicating that Michael had been accepted into their program. I jumped for joy. Michael and Angela were elated as well. A support worker would visit Michael in his apartment once each week to help him live as independently as he could. I would no longer be his sole support.

Prior to his move, Angela and I spent hours telling Michael that he could not yell, scream, throw things against the walls, or damage the apartment in any way or he could be thrown out. We also told him repeatedly that he must not play his violin after eleven o'clock at night so that his neighbours could sleep. Michael promised to follow these rules.

Michael was ready to begin his adventure of living on his own.

I was certain that I was, too.

I missed Angela terribly after she left home to study at university in the United States in 2003. I could not have been more supportive of her pursuing her career in piano performance. At the same time, I significantly underestimated the impact her moving out would have on me.

In her first few months, I asked Angela to set aside time every night at eleven o'clock for a phone call. Naturally, she resented the obligation. It did not take me long to come to my senses and understand that my need for daily contact was bound to drive us apart.

Adapting to my aloneness was a challenge that I had not anticipated. Since Luke moved away, I had become closer to Angela. When she departed for university, I felt intense pangs of loneliness. I had helped many of my patients cope with the life changes that occurred when their children moved out, but my knowledge did not make my adjustment any easier.

As I was driving home from my visits with Angela, I often reflected on our week-long canoe trips that we had enjoyed every summer for fifteen years while vacationing at the Errington's, a wilderness resort in Northern Ontario. From our canoe, we marvelled at the majesty of the moose, the black bears, and the bald eagles. We paddled for hours all day watching the fish jump out of the water, admiring the beauty of the thick boreal forest, straining to catch glimpses of the merganser ducks with their chicks swimming near the shore, and listening for the mesmerizing calls of the loons. All the while we shared whatever thoughts and emotions drifted through our minds.

Our relationship could not have been closer.

Or so I thought.

48

The Acid Test

Angela and I were enjoying dinner at our favourite vegetarian Chinese restaurant. I told myself that I was fully prepared for her announcement. *Would tonight be the night?* A twinge of anxiety resurfaced. *I was a loving mom. I had liberal values and was open-minded. Nothing could fracture my close relationship with Angela.*

It still surprises me that I am so naïve when it comes to knowing myself.

We had finished our meal. Angela was more quiet than usual. She told me that her friend, Chalita, who was working abroad, had entered a competition for a two-year fellowship with a company in New York City. Having already obtained a master's degree, Chalita would move back to New York and work towards a second master's degree if she won.

Angela had met Chalita at International House, a student residence in New York in 2009. At that time, Angela was beginning her studies toward a Ph.D. in piano performance. Chalita had just completed her first master's degree and was about to leave New York for her first job.

As we sat together in the restaurant sipping tea, I thought about the close, long distance relationship Angela had enjoyed with Chalita over the past four years. Angela was not dating anyone. She was spending hours every day practising for performances and competitions as well as attending classes and working on her dissertation. She had no time to date.

I asked whether Chalita had won the competition. If she had, I knew that Angela and Chalita would both be living in New York. A little voice within expressed anxiety that the two of them might become closer. Then I felt guilty for my concern.

"It's very good news," Angela began, seriously. "Chalita won and will be given a full scholarship to return to New York." The words were spoken in a sombre tone. Angela looked at me nervously.

"Good for her. You must be very happy about that." I heard myself say with genuine enthusiasm.

"You know, Mom, I love Chalita." Angela's words spilled out quickly. She looked at me with more tension in her eyes than I had ever seen before.

"That's wonderful," I said. "Does she love you too?"

"Yes. And in fact, we are engaged."

"Oh, that's fantastic."

"I thought that you would be very upset about this, Mom," she said.

"If you love Chalita and she loves you, that's all that matters. I am happy for you both."

The right words were automatic. Acceptance was not.

In the days and weeks that followed, my relationship with Angela was strained. I fuelled my distress by anticipating losses. I was grieving the loss of Angela's Jewish identity, believing that it had suddenly become a fragile part of her that was at risk for dissolving. Anticipating her becoming less Jewish threatened my identity.

I was also grieving the loss of the grandchildren that I believed I would never have. I had been counting on Angela to bless me with grandchildren. Michael would never marry. I berated myself for expecting Angela to compensate for Michael. Angela's mission in life was to make herself happy, not me. *Given fertility clinic technology perhaps she could have a child.* Even though I filled my mind with logical thoughts, I continued to grieve and rail against this reality.

I had always been passionate in my support for gay rights and my disdain for any form of prejudice. I accepted that others should be free to love whoever they chose. My failure to extend the same right to my own daughter caused me enormous dissonance.

Sitting in my office now, I think about Tina. I worked with her years before Angela's disclosure. Tina was a young woman, with dark eyes, and a serious expression. Tears were always gathering around her sad eyes, threatening to stream down her face. She expended a great deal of energy trying to hide from the intensity of her pain.

"My family rejected me when I came out. That was three years ago. I was twenty-one."

"That must have been very painful. How did you cope?"

"I was in a relationship with Linda at that time. I told my dad and he told me I better not come back home. I should stay with Linda at her place. My mom would not be able to handle it."

"That's such a hurtful rejection of the person you are. Heartbreaking."

"Yes, it was heartbreaking—to be told not to come home. Like I'm no longer part of the family. Like I'm no longer worth loving." Tina began to weep. Then she straightened up in her chair, grabbed a tissue, and wiped her eyes. She shut her eyes tightly to stop the tears.

"Tina, if it would help, you can just let your feelings be."

"I cry at home. Now, here with you, I want to explain what's going on." Tina took a few deep breaths before beginning again. "My mother is narcissistic and highly controlling. All through my childhood years whenever I had a problem, her advice to me was 'Tough it out.' I had a closer relationship with my father, but I was always afraid of him. He'd shout a lot. After he told my mother that I was gay and that I had a relationship with Linda, she called me. She said, 'You have betrayed me. You are mentally ill.' Then she went into a flurry of questions—'Where did we go wrong? What should we have done differently? How did this happen?' Then she said, 'You should never have told Dad. You should have pretended that you were normal. Don't come home. Don't call. I can't cope with this.'"

"What was the impact on you?"

"Can't put it into words, Doctor." Tina paused. "All my life I wanted to be loved unconditionally; just to be loved for the person I was. When I got good marks at school, Mom was happier but, even then she said that I could always have done better."

"Your mom has a lot of limitations when it comes to love."

"She certainly does. She was abused physically and I think sexually by her father. I shouldn't be so angry with her. But I am."

"You have a right to feel angry, disappointed, hurt, and all the other emotions flowing through you, Tina. Your mom could have done better. We all can. She has hurt you very deeply by rejecting you. Sounds like your dad hasn't done much to help."

"No. He stands by Mom. I think he actually props her up."

"That rejection happened three years ago. What's been going on since then?"

"I haven't spoken to Mom or Dad since. No contact for three years. I've been living with Linda. We are close but sometimes she doesn't come through for me when I need support. She's big into problem-solving. Most of the time, I know what to do. What I need more than anything is to be held close, or for her just to say that she understands my feelings."

Over the next few months, Tina focused on improving her relationship with Linda. Her primary goal was to communicate more assertively rather than respond in her usual quiet, passive manner when Linda failed to meet her needs. "You expect that Linda should know without your telling her exactly what you need from her. You need to ask her to hold you, to give you the support you need. When she fails to meet your needs, what happens?"

"I lose my temper I get so furious with her. And then I regret everything I said out of anger."

"Maybe your frustration with her also reflects frustration with yourself for failing to let her know what you need from her. No matter how close we are with someone, the other person can't read our minds. Sometimes you might want a hug, at other times her telling you that she understands how you feel, at other times some other supportive response. We need to ask the other person directly to respond in the way that we need at that time. When Linda comes through, you can thank her. When she doesn't, you can convey your disappointment and hope that she reconsiders. I suggest that you share these suggestions with Linda so that you come through better for her as well."

In her sessions, Tina practised communicating more assertively in roleplays. I extended this to our working relationship. "Tina, let me know when I come through for you and when I don't. Let me know when you wish to change the topics or the way we are discussing issues. Give me feedback directly so I know what you need."

As Tina worked toward communicating her needs more directly to me and Linda, she began to treat herself with more care and respect in other ways. She was taking time for lunch breaks during work rather than pushing herself through them to please her boss. She was setting aside more time for herself to enjoy outings with Linda and with other friends.

Reviewing her childhood experiences brought her learning history to light in a new way for Tina. "I understand that with a mom who was so controlling and impossible to please, as a child I could not have been assertive. I could not have said what I needed from her. I had to be quiet. That was the only way to avoid being hurt by her."

"It was a survival strategy. Now, as an adult, you have other choices. You can be quiet and passive at times when you feel that is best. You can choose to be assertive and direct at other times. Psychological health is being flexible and doing whatever most of you feels is best for you at that time."

In a later session, Tina arrived clearly tense. As soon as she sat down, she began to weep. "My aunt passed away last week."

"I'm sad to hear this, Tina."

Tina cried for a few minutes. She asked for a glass of water and sipped it as she regained emotional control.

"The funeral is next week. We were very close. She always loved me, accepted me, even when she knew that I was gay and was with Linda."

"It is wonderful that you had a loving relationship with her and that she accepted you for the person you are. I understand the grief you are feeling."

"She had cancer for a few years. You know it's coming, Doctor, but when it happens, it is always a shock. You are never prepared for the loss of someone you love."

"That's true. Losing someone we love is the hardest thing for us to accept."

"I visited her at the hospital when my parents weren't there. I saw her the day before she passed. The nurse said that she wasn't conscious, but I know that she felt my presence when I kissed her and held her hand."

"You're probably right, Tina. How loving of you to be there with her. You need to give yourself permission to grieve. Be gentle with yourself."

"The problem is the funeral. It's next week. I want to be there. I haven't spoken to my mother for the past three years. I emailed my dad and told him that I will be there."

"That was courageous, Tina. You didn't know how he would respond."

"He said, 'You better not talk to your mother. She's going through a hard time without your making it worse. You know she just lost her sister.' It sounded like a threat."

"How did you feel when he said that?"

"Hurt again."

"I understand. Attending the funeral is emotionally challenging not just because you are grieving the loss of your aunt but because it will be difficult to be in the same place as your parents. You will need to cope with whatever they say or do."

"I need to go, to honour my aunt. I've been rejected for three years, Doctor. I am used to it."

"Used to it, yes, but never at peace with that rejection. You want to be accepted for the person you are. You want to be loved unconditionally like all of us. You have always yearned for that."

"That's a very faint hope."

"After all the time that's elapsed, I don't think you can possibly predict how you will feel when you are sitting in the same room as your parents at the funeral. You might feel drawn to look at them and perhaps speak with them or maybe you won't. They may feel differently seeing you again. We don't know. You need to give yourself permission to play it by ear. Caring for yourself means that you do what most of you feels is best for you at that time."

In her next session, Tina arrived with a broad smile and eyes wide open announcing that something significant had occurred. "When I saw my mother, she looked so much older. I thought about all the time that had passed. I don't know why but I walked over to her and said, 'Hello, Mom.' Mom paused and looked at me with a puzzled expression, as if she did not know what to say. I just stood there with Linda. Mom stood up after a few moments. There was a softness in her face, Doctor. She said, "Hello, Tina. Hello, Linda." Then, Doctor, this is amazing…" Tina's face brightened. "She hugged me. It was a very quick hug, like she wanted to hug me and didn't want to hug me at the same time. She walked back to her seat without looking back. Tears were streaming down my face as I walked back to my seat. I never thought this possible after three years, Doctor. It looked like a tiny gesture, but that hug was a sign of acceptance. So was her saying hello to Linda."

"You took the first courageous step forward, Tina. You said 'Hello' first."

"That's true. I did."

"You wanted to reach out to her. You weren't ready to give up on your relationship with her. And your mother wasn't ready to give up on her relationship with you either. Perhaps, the loss of her sister brought home the message to your mom that life is precious, that you are precious. Perhaps, the loss of your aunt sent a similar message to you, giving you the courage to reach out to your mom. As long as two people are alive, there is always the potential for their relationship to improve."

At the time that I worked with Tina, I remember thinking many times that I would never reject my daughter the way her mother did.

After Angela disclosed that she was gay and was engaged to Chalita, she saw my obvious unhappiness. I felt guilty for causing her pain. No doubt she felt guilty for causing me distress. She must have also felt deeply hurt, rejected, and disappointed that I was failing to embrace her with open arms.

Was I really different from Tina's mother?

I confided in Mom. When I told her that Angela was gay and planned to marry Chalita, Mom's response was, "That's peculiar. But if they love each other, that's the only thing that matters." I felt admiration for her immediate and genuine acceptance and shame for my failure to do the same. Michael also expressed nothing but joy when I told him that Angela and Chalita would marry.

I was the only one having a problem. My love and respect for myself and for Angela demanded change.

I chose to return to my values, to move away from anticipating losses, to focus instead on the present. Standing before me was my beautiful daughter. I chose to open my heart to her joy. I asked Angela to tell me all about Chalita who I learned was also a beautiful person and clearly in love with her.

My relationship with Angela grew closer. Our friendship and respect for each other blossomed. By embracing Angela with open arms, I brought peace to my heart. And Angela forgave me.

Surrounded by family and friends, Angela and Chalita were married under a chupah. Angela created a wedding ceremony that honoured Jewish traditions, clearly reflecting the importance of her Jewish identity and beliefs. She asked Michael to play "Fields of Gold" on his violin and a friend from university to play a portion of Beethoven's opus 110. Chalita's Buddhist family were touched by the prayers and speeches and loved the klezmer music. They enthusiastically danced the Horah with all the guests. The prayers, speeches, music, and dancing transcended all superficial differences among us. Coming from different places with different beliefs, we joined together in the celebration of two people who were deeply in love.

49

The Emerging Artist

When the phone rang, I hesitated to answer. I anticipated hearing Angela's dejected tone and her words telling me that she had not placed in another competition.

Every time Angela performed in a competition and did not win first prize, she tortured herself with incessant self-criticism about the imperfections in her performance. For weeks, she would be inconsolable. "The hundreds of hours I spent practising, it's all for nothing," she would lament. Any words of comfort that I offered only provoked Angela's anger. I could only watch the devastation of her self-inflicted pain.

I waited patiently for Angela to lift herself up again and return to the piano as she always did. She often asked, "Why do artists like me continue along this agonizing journey?" Their passion for music was the answer.

At age fifteen, Angela's Suzuki teacher, with whom she had studied since age four, encouraged her to audition for Emilia Jansson, a teacher at the Royal Conservatory. I drove Angela to the audition. She prepared the first movement of the piano concerto in D major by Haydn. I waited anxiously in the parked car while Angela performed for Ms. Jansson.

Angela emerged from the building and ran to the car, "She accepted me, Mom!"

Angela was a student at the professional school for music at the same time that she attended undergraduate studies in biochemistry at university. The pressure of pursuing both careers mounted day after day. Angela spent hours every day practising the piano and then spent more hours completing her homework. After filling the house with uplifting music, Angela delighted in sharing her fascination with string theory and quantum physics, neither of which I understood. She won awards in biochemistry and achieved high marks in a nationwide chemistry competition.

Early in her second year at university, Angela began to feel ill. The stress of reaching for perfection as an artist and achieving high marks in science and mathematics courses conspired to churn her stomach. Nothing alleviated the pain in her gut, which increased as she forced herself to maintain her gruelling schedule.

"Angela, your body is telling you that you cannot reach for excellence in music and science at the same time. You must make a choice."

Having won a prize from the university as an outstanding student in chemistry, Angela had a bright future ahead as a scientist. I thought that a career in science was more practical than one as a musician. I joined her in a discussion of the pros and cons of both options. Then I simply said, "Angela, you must follow your heart."

It did not take Angela more than a few moments to answer. "I cannot live without the piano."

I respected Angela's right to choose her career path. Having worked with many patients who felt vicariously validated and gratified by their child's achievements, I worked hard to give Angela the credit for her success. I reminded myself many times that I was responsible for my choices and that Angela and Michael were responsible for theirs. It was not easy.

I still have to work to resist taking credit for my children's success and blame for their failures.

George comes to mind. He sat down and leaned toward me, his eyes aflame with anger. I immediately felt compassion for the deep pain that he must be feeling.

"I have applied to art school in New York and that's that!" he shouted as if defying me.

"You're an artist, George?" I asked softly.

George abruptly relaxed in his chair. I thought that he was seeing me for the first time.

"Yes," he began. "I am a painter. I paint portraits and landscapes. Mostly I use oil. But I also like to sketch. I have always wanted to be an artist. Now that I'm twenty-three, I am ready to leave home and move to New York where the famous art school is."

"You started off today with a lot of angry feelings and pain. What is that about, George?"

"My parents!" George took a deep breath. "They want me to become a physician. 'You're so smart,' they say. 'You got into medical school and now you want to throw that away!' They yell at me day and night. 'Don't you know that very few people become well-known artists? Very few artists make money. You won't be able to support yourself as an artist and we don't have the money to support you for the rest of your life.' They make me so angry!"

"They hurt you deeply. They don't believe in your ability. They worry about your future."

"They are worried about theirs! They are worried they will have to give me money. That I won't be able to make a living as an artist. They don't believe in me."

"You want them to believe in you."

"Yes, but they don't."

Looking into George's eyes, his anger melted into sadness, I asked "Do you think their worry about your ability to support yourself is a realistic one?"

"Well, yes and no. Some artists become art teachers or work at art galleries. Some do work outside of art to make money. I will find a way, Doctor. I won't need my parents' money."

"Have you told them that you have thought about the financial issues seriously?"

"Yes, but they don't believe me. It's not just about money. They want me to be a physician so they can be proud of me!" George snarled as he repeated "Proud—they will only be proud if I am a doctor."

"It's as if your parents are living through you. Are they not gratified enough by their own achievements?"

"No, they are not. They are both high school teachers. It's not enough for them. They want their son to be a physician. What they don't get is that I need to be true to myself. I have applied to three art schools in New York and am awaiting their answer. If I am accepted, I'm moving to New York. I have saved up enough money to rent a room there."

"It takes great courage to stand up to your parents and to stand up for yourself, George. Sounds like there's been a lot of arguing back and forth. Am I right?"

"Yes, there's been a lot of yelling."

"How does that leave you feeling?"

"Angry, disappointed, frustrated, and hurt."

"Perhaps it's time for you to stop fighting." I paused. "Why add to your pain?"

"What do you suggest?"

"Well, shouting back doesn't seem to get you anywhere. What could you do when your mom or dad starts shouting at you rather than shout back?"

George was silent for several minutes. He looked at me nervously. I read in his expression that he was reluctant to let the words escape from his tightly pursed lips. Then they slipped out.

"Weed and magic mushrooms. They both help. That's what I do after I shout back."

"Part of you was a little nervous about letting me know about your use of drugs. Why was that part nervous?"

"Because … I thought that you would not approve. My parents don't. They know. I've told them. 'You hurt me so much that I have to use drugs.' That's what I've said. That's the truth."

"It's not about my approval, George. It's about being true to yourself, caring for yourself—that's what counts. You're choosing to use weed and magic mushrooms because you are in so much pain, you don't know what else to do. And you get back at your parents by doing that, too. Right?"

"Yes."

"You tell them that it's because of their hurtful behaviour that you are turning to drugs, which they don't like."

George nodded.

"Do you wish to continue to use those drugs to cope? Are you open to exploring other ways to help yourself?"

"For now, I want to keep using. But I'm open to considering other ways as well."

With those words, George began to move toward self-care. He worked with me until he moved to New York and made the transition to another psychologist there.

Like George, Angela chose to follow her heart. I decided to support her career in every way that I could. She completed her year at university and entered competitions at three undergraduate piano performance schools in the United States. She was ecstatic when she received her acceptance letter from a university with a well-known music program. It was 2003 when I travelled to the United States to help Angela move into a house that she was renting with two other students.

I encouraged Angela to send some recordings of her performances to Claudio, the conductor of the community orchestra in which I played violin. He was impressed and invited her to perform Beethoven's third piano concerto in the following season.

I took delight in shopping with Angela for her gown and sandals. A week before Angela's rehearsal with our orchestra, Ms. Jansson arranged a dress rehearsal for Angela in her studio.

Mom and Michael took seats in the front row of the theatre on the evening of Angela's debut. I could barely play my violin during the piece. The exhilaration of hearing Angela's interpretation of the concerto was overpowering. Angela received a standing ovation and Claudio invited her to play an encore. After her last note, the hall was filled with applause again. I presented Angela with a bouquet of flowers and kissed her. "You played beautifully," I whispered in her ear.

Back stage, Michael and Mom met us and entered the green room where Angela was sitting and quietly reviewing her playing. Mom could not hold back her excitement. "Angela, you sound just like a professional!" Angela smiled. Michael hugged her for a long time.

Angela was invited to perform with other orchestras in the area. She performed Beethoven's fourth piano concerto with an orchestra just outside of Toronto and she accepted a last-minute request to perform Beethoven's third piano concerto with another symphony orchestra after the soloist suddenly became ill. Solo recitals followed.

Leading up to each performance, Angela played her pieces for Michael, Mom, and me. Each time, the three of us sat perfectly still until the last note, moved by the deep emotions that Angela shaped. After each of Angela's performances, Mom said again, "Angela, you sound just like a professional!"

In 2009, Angela's recordings qualified her to compete in the Beethoven International Sonata Competition. She made it past the first round. As a finalist, she performed two sonatas, opus 57, the Appassionata, and opus 110.

Waiting for her phone call, I could hear her performances of Beethoven sonatas in my mind. The ringing of the phone came earlier than I expected. Getting up the courage to answer it, and prepared to console her yet again, her words sang out, "Mom, I won the whole thing!"

After our conversation, I filled the house with Angela's recording of opus 110 and imagined that I was in the United States, looking on as she basked in the sunshine that was finally beaming down on her.

Angela's journey is a story of persistence, overcoming countless hurdles, being courageous and, most importantly, being true to herself. She inspires me.

50

A Most Unfortunate Lobster Dinner

In the summer of 2008, Angela returned to Toronto for a visit. She took Mom, who was ninety-two, to a restaurant for one of her favourite meals: lobster. They were gone for a very long time.

"That was the best meal that I have ever had!" This was always Mom's refrain after every meal that she enjoyed.

"She loved it." Angela said. "I watched her enjoy every morsel. It took her over two hours to finish. There was no conversation as usual."

"I was too busy eating," Mom said.

"And then she said, 'I'm not hungry anymore!' as if it was a big surprise to her" Angela added.

The next morning Mom woke up with pain in her abdomen that was so severe she could not get out of bed. I called 911. I handed the paramedics the page with her health history. They did an ECG and told her that her heart was doing fine. "Try to take deep, slow breaths, Mrs. Miller. That way you will relax. You are just experiencing a panic attack."

Mom was not a candidate for panic attacks. "Mom is experiencing severe abdominal pain," I said as calmly as I could. "Something is seriously wrong. She needs to go to the hospital."

The paramedics eventually agreed and transferred Mom into the ambulance. Angela and I drove to the hospital after calling Michael, who said that he would take the bus and meet us there.

When we arrived at emergency, I handed the nurse Mom's medical information sheet. Mom was diagnosed with gastritis. She was given some medication and sent home. By then her abdominal pain had receded.

Angela went out with friends that night. I was with Mom at her home to ensure that she was recovering from her gastritis. It soon became apparent that she was not recovering. Mom began wheezing and shaking. She was hot to the touch. The pain returned and was just as severe as before. Once again, I called 911 and alerted Angela and Michael, who met me at the hospital.

Mom underwent a series of tests. The physician informed us that she had developed pneumonia and that she had an infected gallbladder. A drainage tube was inserted into her gallbladder, which relieved her pain, and she was put on IV antibiotics.

The physician told us that when the infection in her gallbladder and her pneumonia resolved, her gallbladder would be removed. Another operation awaited her. I wondered whether she would survive.

Mom was discharged home with the drainage tube connecting her gallbladder to a bag. Hours after her discharge, back at home, Mom needed to go to the washroom. Angela was horrified when Mom emerged holding the end of the tube that had been connected to her gallbladder in her hand.

"I don't know what this thing is," she said innocently, "but it just came out."

Angela looked at the place where the tube had entered her body and saw no way of reinserting it. I called the hospital to obtain instructions and the physician who spoke with us reviewed her chart and told us not to worry. It had likely drained sufficiently. We could just leave the dressing on her abdomen and she would continue to improve.

Mom did not continue to improve. Several hours later, she had a high fever and was trembling again. The severe abdominal pain returned. I called 911 and she was taken back to the same hospital by ambulance. This time her condition rapidly deteriorated and within several hours she was admitted to the intensive care unit.

The physician met us in the waiting room and told us that Mom was suffering from toxic shock and was septic. "Her gallbladder has burst and she is in critical condition. We will treat her with intensive antibiotics and hopefully she will recover but she may not."

Angela, Michael, and I were with Mom overnight and every day and night thereafter. Mom required a feeding tube as she was unable to eat. She hung somewhere between life and death for weeks. When there was evidence of some recovery, I encouraged the nurses to help her sit up in bed and stand. However, they told me that this would be impossible for her as she had no muscle tone left after lying in bed for over three weeks. When the nurses tried to help her stand, Mom's arms and legs hung loosely like thin rubber strands that had never moved with purpose. I wondered if she was capable of surviving. *Would she be able to return to the wonderful quality of life that she had been enjoying?*

Mom's physician told us that, if she survived, she would need to undergo surgery to have her gallbladder removed in a few months.

All through this nightmare, I knew that the physicians had misdiagnosed her initially with gastritis and had failed to tell me the signs that I should look for that would signal a gallbladder blockage and a potential emergency. I decided to keep my focus on helping Mom recover rather than on the human errors that had contributed to this crisis.

When Mom arrived at the hospital the third time, when an emergency nurse heard that she had enjoyed a lobster dinner the evening before her abdominal pain set in, she told us, "You know, lobster has a lot of cholesterol. It was probably too hard for her gallbladder to manage." Her comment shot through Angela's heart. "It's my fault, Mom. I suggested that Bubby and I have that lobster meal."

"Angela, you could not possibly have known that this would happen. Don't blame yourself. None of us could have known."

Mom's zest for life and motivation to return to her normal lifestyle kept her going and, once again, she slowly climbed the mountain of recovery. On August 1, 2008, she underwent an open cholecystectomy, in which her gallbladder was removed. After that, she worked consistently at regaining her strength by standing and walking for longer and longer periods of time. Three months after the crisis, in September 2008, Mom was attending her opera, the theatre, and symphony orchestra concerts as usual and once again enjoying eating out—although she never ate lobster again.

51

Lilly

Since 2005, Mom was using Wheel-Trans to travel to her shows and appointments instead of public transportation. Wheel-Trans provided her with door-to-door service. She was allowed to have a caregiver join her. Michael quickly learned how to book Wheel-Trans trips by telephone. Just about every weekend, Michael joined Mom on Wheel-Trans trips to various locations throughout Toronto. Mom and Michael were an odd couple. She would be walking quickly with her walker and Michael would be trying to keep up with her, talking non-stop about how he located the restaurant online and the delicious food on the menu. They enjoyed each other's company immensely.

I smile as I think about the love flowing between Mom and Michael; how she had cared for him when he was little and now how he was caring for her.

I tried to meet as many of Mom's needs as possible. As time went on, this was becoming more and more challenging. Three or four visits each week became the rule. As her ability to cook for herself diminished, I made regular trips to restaurants and then to her home to deliver ready-made food as well as groceries. Sometimes I cooked her meals. I did my best to make minor repairs in her home and made appointments with experts for more complicated ones. She became unable to keep track of her bank accounts and the bills. Taking on this task required me to visit her banks and consolidate her various accounts.

In 2006, as her ninetieth birthday was approaching, I decided to plan a surprise birthday party. I rented a banquet hall that included a band playing klezmer music and invited our relatives and her friends. Angela flew in from New York.

On the evening of the party, I told Mom that I would be taking her to a lovely restaurant to celebrate her ninetieth birthday. When we entered the banquet hall, Mom took a seat at one of the round tables. Shortly after, she said with surprise, "Oh look, one of my friends from my old company is at this restaurant too!" Then after another few minutes, "I see someone else I know. One of our neighbours is here."

I said, "Mom, all these people are here to celebrate your birthday with you."

Mom's eyes welled up with tears as one person after another came up to congratulate her. She could not hold back her emotion when Angela came into view. "Angela!" she exclaimed with delight, "you came in from New York for my party!" Then we invited her to sit in the middle of the dance floor while the klezmer band played and we all danced a Hora around her. I had never seen Mom so happy.

At the end of the night, Mom turned to me and said, "Rickey, that party was more elaborate than my wedding. I have never had a party like that in my life!"

Shortly after the party, I urged Mom to have a lifeline system installed in her home. It took many months for me to convince her. I explained that pressing a button on the necklace she wore would activate the speaker in her home. "Someone will ask you if you need an ambulance."

"You worry too much," she said. "I won't have any such emergency."

Eventually Mom was so fed up with my nagging that she gave in. She felt that she was doing me a favour. *Indeed, she was.*

One day in 2007, when I was in the middle of a session with a patient, my secretary knocked on my door.

"There's an emergency call from lifeline on line one."

I excused myself from the session. "Hello, I am Rickey, Faye's daughter. What's going on?"

"We can't reach your mother. The lifeline alarm has sounded. We have been advised by the alarm company that her alarm is also going off in the house. We have dispatched emergency services."

I explained to my patient that there was a family emergency and apologized for ending our session early. I rushed to my car. It was pouring rain. I tried my best to drive safely despite my panic. I imagined Mom's lifeless body lying on the floor somewhere in her home.

When I arrived at the house, a fire truck was parked by the curb. A fireman was walking towards the front door with an axe in his hand.

"Wait!" I cried. "I'm the daughter. I have a key!"

"We tried to get a response, but the door is locked and no one has answered."

With trembling hands, I unlocked the door. *Where would her body be?* I was terrified to look.

Three firemen entered the house with their high boots caked with mud and their raincoats dripping. They left big brown puddles wherever they walked. While I turned off the alarm, they began their search. One of them rushed down to the basement. The other two went into every room on the upper level. After a few minutes, they concluded that no one was home.

"Well, then, why did the lifeline and the security alarm both go off?" I asked, expecting that they would know.

"We have no idea. But there is obviously no emergency here." With that, the firemen left.

Suddenly it occurred to me where Mom might be. I looked through her phone book under the tab for 'H' and called her hairdresser. "Hello. This is Rickey. Is Faye Miller there?"

"Yes, do you want to speak to her?" A friendly voice asked.

"No. That's okay. Just tell her that I forgot that she would be at the hairdresser today. When will she be finished?"

"In about one hour."

"Okay. Fine."

I breathed a sigh of relief, but it was cut short when I looked down and saw the huge muddy footprints lining the hall. The evidence that the firefighters had been in the house was everywhere. I had to hurry and clean up the mess completely. If Mom knew anything about what had occurred, she would certainly cancel the lifeline system. Worse than that, I knew that she would get down on her hands and knees and clean the floors herself.

I carefully scrubbed out every footprint. As I crawled through the house cleaning the floors, I reflected on how lucky it was that I had arrived before the axe had slashed through the front door.

Even though she never found out about this episode, Mom cancelled the lifeline system not long after. She insisted that it was unnecessary. My anxiety increased. I became her only lifeline.

By 2008, I was reaching my maximum coping capacity with my full-time workload, helping Michael every day, practising my violin, and taking care of Mom. For the past few years, I had recommended that Mom consider hiring a caregiver. She refused. "I don't need anyone to live with me. I can cope perfectly well on my own," she asserted each time.

Despite my pointing out to her that I was feeling overwhelmed by everything I needed to do for her, she remained adamant. "Come less often. I don't need you to come so often. I don't want to exhaust you. I can go to the store and hairdresser by myself."

Mom's indomitable, youthful spirit, which kept her going at her maximum, had a downside. She refused to accept that she had become dependent on me for many tasks that were extremely difficult, unsafe, and sometimes impossible for her to do on her own. Arguing with her only resulted in mutual agitation.

I am picturing Mr. Feldman walking into my office. From the moment he entered, grasping the handles of his walker, limping slowly forward, there was something very distinguished about him. He was wearing a navy suit with a matching tie in different shades of blue. I knew right away that it would not be appropriate to use his first name. He looked at me briefly as he slowly made his way to the chair. I hoped that he did not see the anxiety that swept across my face when he let go of the walker and transferred himself to the chair. As I closed the door, I noticed that another gentleman was sitting in the waiting room.

"That's my son, Ronald." Mr. Feldman said softly with a refined British accent. "He drove me here. Next time I'll take Wheel-Trans. He wants to talk to you afterwards."

"Well, that's entirely up to you, Mr. Feldman. I would be happy to talk to him with you if you wish."

"Yes, Doctor. I do wish. He has no idea what he's done to me, Ronald and his wife, Maggie. They put me in a damn nursing home! Took me out of my condo!"

"You feel hurt about what they did. When did this happen, Mr. Feldman?"

"I've been there for a month. Hate it. Disgusting. I managed on my own in the condo. They pushed me into their car one day and drove me there."

"Pushed you?"

Mr. Feldman took a breath. He gazed out of the window. "Well, I have to be honest with you, Doctor. They talked to me about this plan of theirs for months and months. They asked me to have an open mind. They drove me to this place and showed me around. Then one day, they told me that a room had become available there and they absolutely insisted that I get in the car and move in."

"That must have been traumatic for you. It felt like they pushed you into that place. You did not want to leave your home."

Mr. Feldman's eyes filled with tears. "No, I did not. I want to go back. But they've sold it. It's a done deal. There's no home to go back to."

"It's a big loss and hard to accept because the decision was out of your hands." I paused as Mr. Feldman collected himself. He wiped away his tears with his hands. "Why did Ronald and Maggie think this was best?"

"They said that they could not come over anymore to help me."

"What help were they giving you?"

"They were making sure I take the right pills. Sometimes, I made mistakes, Doctor, like we all do. They were shopping for me and bringing over meals that I could warm in the microwave. That was very kind of them. I appreciated their help. They had arranged homecare to help with baths. I was always afraid that I would slip and fall in the bathtub. They kept saying that they could not keep this up and that I didn't have enough money to hire someone who could come in to help me every day."

"Tell me about your accommodation in the nursing home, Mr. Feldman. What is it like?"

"It's a very small room. I have a bed and my TV from my condo. There's a dresser and a tiny kitchen area where I can make a pot of tea. I have photos of my two grandchildren. Would you like to see them?"

"Yes, please."

Mr. Feldman took out his wallet and pulled out two small photos. He smiled with pride as he went on. "That's Mary Ann and this is Joseph. She's three and he's five."

"They're beautiful, Mr. Feldman. Do they visit you?"

"Yes."

"That must lift your spirits."

"I love them. Yes, they make me feel better. But I still miss my home. I'm still mad at Ronald and Maggie."

"Have you told them how sad and angry you feel?"

"Well, I keep my control, Doctor. I tell them that they were wrong to move me. I could have managed on my own for longer. I am eighty-eight years old but very strong and independent."

"I can see that you are very strong in spirit, Mr. Feldman. That is very clear. Ronald and Maggie were helping you a lot during the week at the condo. Your body needed assistance. Ronald and Maggie said that they could not keep up. Do they work?"

"Yes, they work. I know it was hard for them."

"That's a reflection of the good heart you have, Mr. Feldman, that you feel compassion for Ronald and Maggie at the same time that you feel angry."

"Well, I'm not that tied up with myself all the time, Doctor. "

"That's a caring choice you've made, Mr. Feldman." I leaned forward. "Any move is hard but especially a move like this—one that requires accepting that as our body ages we need more help to manage. Often the help we need is more than our family can provide. Not everyone can afford to hire someone to help them at home. All your feelings are perfectly understandable."

"Thank you for saying that, Doctor. Tell my son that."

"You can do that, Mr. Feldman. Shall I ask Ronald to join us briefly? Our session is almost over."

"Yes."

I ushered Ronald into the office. He looked sheepish as if he anticipated being criticized.

"Your dad has something he'd like to tell you about his feelings."

"Ronald," Mr. Feldman looked at his son intently. "I know you and Maggie couldn't keep up. I know you feel you had no choice. I'm so sad and mad that you forced me to leave my home and sold it and put me in this nursing home."

"I know how you feel, Dad. We considered every other option. We knew it would be hard for you. We couldn't leave you there on your own. You could have fallen or forgotten to take your pills. Something bad could have happened and I would never have forgiven myself if that happened. I love you too much, Dad." Mr. Feldman reached over and touched Ronald's hand. Ronald was weeping. "I never wanted to hurt you, Dad. I didn't know what else to do." I allowed Mr. Feldman and Ronald to hold each other's hand for a few more minutes, past the end of the session.

I am thinking about how difficult it would be for me to give up my independence.

Mom and Dad had saved money and paid off the house so Mom could remain in her home and afford to hire a caregiver. Even though she was able to remain in her own home, that change required a huge adjustment.

One day in 2008 when Mom was ninety-three years old, Michael, Angela, and I attended a performance of *Hamlet* with her at the Stratford Festival. I told her that I would pick her up at nine in the morning.

When I arrived at the house, I heard Mom's house alarm screaming. I opened the door in a panic, turned the alarm off, and saw Mom sitting in the living room with her coat on, weeping. "I cannot do this anymore. It's too much. I don't know the code for the alarm."

"It's okay, Mom. We will hire a caregiver. You will be a lot happier with someone here to help you with the alarm, and the housework, and everything else you need." As I comforted her, I wondered how I would find a caregiver and when. I was booked up with patients. Michael agreed to stay with her for the week.

On the way back from Stratford, I handed Angela my cellphone and asked her to look up agencies that placed caregivers for the elderly.

As soon as I arrived back home, I called one of the companies and said that I needed a female caregiver as soon as possible. I asked for a live-in who could work Mondays through Saturdays.

The next day Angela and I interviewed three Filipino candidates with Mom. Michael was present as well. Lilly stood out immediately. She described the care that she had provided to an elderly woman in Israel. Lilly looked much younger than a woman in her mid-thirties. She had long black hair, a slim figure, and a relaxed and confident manner. During the interview, Lilly made a passing reference to attending mass every Sunday. The power of her faith came across in her tone and in the way her eyes lit up when she told us about the church that she attended. Lilly told us about her father and three sisters who lived in the Philippines and how she sent them money. She shared stories about the senior who she had assisted in Israel. It was clear that she had developed a close relationship with her and with her family. Since this woman had passed away, Lilly told us that she kept in touch with her daughter. We exchanged some Hebrew words. I laughed as I told Lilly that she could converse in Hebrew much better than I could.

Lilly took a seat on the couch beside Mom. When she reached over and touched Mom's arm, Mom recoiled as if the touch was repugnant. I cringed. I did not want Mom to put off a potential caregiver.

"I'm sorry," I said. "My mom is very independent. She is not used to having anyone help her."

Lilly smiled and said, "That's okay. I know."

Mom, Angela, and I agreed to hire Lilly and thus began our eight-year relationship that blossomed with Lilly becoming a beloved new member of our family.

Mom's adjustment to living with Lilly and accepting her help took time. Lilly was patient and respectful, allowing Mom to do all that she could independently while ensuring that she was safe.

Mom's diminished independence did not diminish her zest for life. When Lilly came into her world, we could not know that another life-and-death crisis was about to challenge Mom's fighting spirit.

52

Is There a Doctor in the House?

It was the night of July 23, 2010. The phone woke me up. "Mommy has a bad pain in her chest. It has gone on for a while now and it has not responded to nitro spray. I think we need to get her to the hospital." Lilly spoke calmy. I panicked.

"Okay. I'll come right away and drive her downtown to the hospital that has her records. Call 911 for an ambulance if her condition worsens." My words were well rehearsed. For the last ten years, I went to bed with anxiety that the phone would wake me with an emergency that I would have to manage. I was prepared intellectually but never emotionally.

As I drove downtown, I worried that Mom might pass away in the car. *Perhaps I should have called an ambulance. But then the choice of hospital would be out of my control.*

We made it to emergency. The wait was brief after I gave the triage nurse Mom's history and pointed out that she might be having another heart attack.

The emergency surgeon entered the cubicle after running some tests. "Your mom appears to have a pulmonary embolus, a blood clot in her lung. We will give her heparin and hope that this abates. We are going to keep her overnight and will move her to a regular room."

Once Mom was moved up to the regular room, the painkillers began to work. She urged Lilly and me to go home to get some sleep. I asked the nurses to call me if anything changed. Reassured that she was out of danger, I drove Lilly home. Lilly told me that she would go to the hospital in the morning to be with Mom. I told her that I would meet her there and thanked her for coming with us and offering to help Mom in the morning, which by now was only a few hours away.

When I arrived at the hospital, Lilly was already there. A physician came out of Mom's room. "We just gave your mom hydromorphone for her arthritic pain. She has been complaining of pain in her left hip."

I found this odd. I asked the physician softly by the door, "She had a total left hip replacement in 2005. Isn't it strange that she would have pain in her left hip?"

"No, that can still happen," the physician said as she began to walk down the hall towards the nursing station.

I proceeded to Mom's bedside. She slept for a period of time. When she woke up, she became extremely agitated. "I need to call 911 for a doctor!" she shouted. "This pain in my leg is unbearable. Isn't there a doctor in the house?!"

Lilly told me that this had also happened earlier. "The nurse keeps bringing her hydromorphone. She needs more now."

"Why can't I get a doctor to help me?" Mom was shouting. "Call 911 for me. Isn't there a doctor in the house?" She repeated in a panic.

Seeing Mom grabbing her left leg, I lifted the covers.

"Oh no!" I gasped. "Look at her foot! It's black!" Immediately I realized that Mom had a blood clot somewhere in her left leg and that her left foot was dying. I ran out into the hall and shouted in panic at all the nurses who were at the station. "My mom has a blood clot in her left leg. Her foot is black. Get a physician. Fast!"

A physician arrived within minutes and confirmed my diagnosis. "I have contacted a vascular surgeon to perform emergency surgery on your mom. He is attending to another patient in the hospital across the street. He will be here as soon as possible. It's so odd that your mom developed both a pulmonary embolus and a peripheral arterial thrombosis, two very different types of clots." The physician ushered me into the hall. "Your mom may lose her leg," he said. "It depends on how much damage there has been. It doesn't look good."

My horror was mixed with fury. *How could they have thought that this was arthritic pain? Why did no one look at her foot?* Then anxiety took over. *Would she lose her leg? Would she survive this operation? Mom was ninety-four. How many more life-and-death health crises was she capable of surviving?*

Within the hour, Mom was being wheeled into the operating room. Holding her hand as she moved towards those ominous double doors, I said, as usual, "Mom, I'll see you soon."

It was well after midnight. I collapsed in tears in the lonely corridor. I called Michael who took a taxi to the hospital and found me crying. He hugged me and helped me find the surgical waiting room.

Hours passed. The vascular surgeon finally entered the waiting room. "We saved her leg. Your mom will recover. She needs to be on blood thinners for the rest of her life. She had a pulmonary blood clot and then developed a peripheral arterial thrombosis." He repeated the observation of the previous physician. "It's very strange that she developed both at the same time. That's quite unusual."

I didn't care how unusual it was. "Thank you so much. Thank you for saving her leg and for saving her life. Thank you!" was all that I could say through my tears.

Once again, Mom chose to follow a rigorous rehabilitation program. Her recovery was inspiring to witness. She pushed herself to walk again and slowly but steadily climbed another mountain to reach her usual and unbelievably high quality of life. As we left the hospital weeks later, she thanked the physicians and nurses profusely. Mom chose to feel no bitterness, no recriminations, no blame for the misdiagnosis, and the increased risk caused by the delay in her receiving the operation. After she thanked the physicians and nurses, she turned to me and repeated the words I had heard since childhood. "When you have something nice to say to someone, Rickey, say it right away. Don't delay."

I asked for a copy of Mom's discharge summary. There was a brief description of the blood clots in her lung and leg and the treatments that she had received for both. There was nothing mentioned about the emergency caused by the diagnostic error. I was angry but not surprised.

Weeks later I requested an appointment with the head of cardiology who had supervised the physician taking care of Mom during this hospitalization. "Dr. Franks, I want to make sure that this error does not occur for any other patient. My mom could have died. She could have lost her leg. I should not have been the only one who noticed that her foot had turned black. She wanted to call 911 because the pain was unbearable. Somehow my mom knew that this was more than arthritis. She had undergone a total hip replacement on that side. The physician responded to her pain complaints by prescribing painkillers, which likely delayed the diagnosis. We must make sure that this does not happen again to anyone."

"I agree with you completely. I will launch a thorough investigation," Dr. Franks said.

"I only want you to educate the physician and nurses on that floor so that this error does not happen again. They need to examine a patient who complains of pain before they prescribe painkillers. No hospitalized patient should ever have to ask if there is a doctor in the house."

"I will make sure that this never happens again. I promise."

I left the hospital feeling reassured that Dr. Franks would follow through. At the same time, I reflected on the importance of trusting our own intuitions about our health. I thought about the importance of having someone we trust ask questions and advocate for us when we are unable to do that ourselves. Sadly, not everyone has such help.

All human systems are imperfect because all of us are imperfect. While I moved toward forgiving the nurses and physician for their error, this crisis added to the enormous weight already on my shoulders as Mom's lifeline. I had nightmares about what might have happened to her had I not been at the hospital that day to see that her foot had turned black. The only way to cope was to accept my own humanity, my own imperfection. I could only do my best. I would not always arrive on time. I would not always do the right thing.

The time would surely come when I would not be able to save her life.

53

Amani

In 2004, Amani and I had been in practice for fourteen years. Our children had grown up together. We had enjoyed many delicious meals at her home. Every time I had complimented her for her amazing culinary skills, Amani always said the same thing: "It doesn't mean anything." I could never understand her comment. Every dish she prepared was a work of art. It was perfectly spiced, perfectly cooked, truly the best food I had ever tasted. I marvelled at her skill every time I had the opportunity to watch her. Everyone who was fortunate enough to be a guest at her table left with great joy and treasured memories.

Sometime that year, Amani confided in me that she was having a health issue. I knew that she hated the idea of seeing a physician. She had a friend who was a physician, but she was reluctant to even ask her about health-related issues. She told me that she felt that she was subordinating herself to someone else when it came to asking a physician about a symptom. I found it difficult to understand.

Over the years I had recommended that Amani consult with a physician. She did not make an appointment. "Are you afraid that you might have some kind of illness? Is that the reason you don't want to see a physician?"

"I don't want to get undressed for a physician to examine my body. That's humiliating."

I asked Amani about her health problem and she told me that she was constipated and had been for some time. Her mother had died from colorectal cancer. I asked my family physician if she would take Amani on as a patient. After she agreed, I strongly recommended that Amani make an appointment with her.

"I will try some remedies at home first." Her terse reply clearly indicated that this was not a topic for further discussion.

After a few more months, Amani mentioned her symptom again. "I have talked to my friend and she told me what to do. The problem should resolve in a short time now."

It did not resolve.

In 2005, Sadi, Amani's husband, called. His tone was one of desperation. "I'm on the way to the emergency department. Amani is in extreme pain. Meet me there." Sadi knew that I had experience navigating through hospital systems. "You've been through this with your mom so many times. You know how to get help quickly. You know how emergency departments and hospitals work."

I did not hesitate. "I'll be there right away."

Walking through the doors to the emergency unit as if I worked there, I quickly located Amani's cubicle. "Amani has had a few tests already," Sadi said, and then a physician entered her cubicle.

"I have good news for you. It's not cancer." We all breathed a deep sigh of relief. The physician handed Amani a prescription and told her that she could go home. He told her that he had referred her to a gastroenterologist for a colonoscopy as further investigation was warranted. The abdominal pain that had triggered the emergency visit subsided.

Weeks passed. Despite the prescribed medication, Amani's abdominal pain returned. She attended the appointment for the colonoscopy.

Sadi called that evening. His voice was broken. "It is cancer."

The anticipated loss of my dear friend and partner took my breath away. I spent hours staring into space, too shocked to cry, in a fog of disbelief. I saw the faces of my dad, my funny uncle, and Darlene. Then, I heard a voice within, 'Where there is life there is hope. Surely, Amani will receive effective treatment. Surely, she will survive."

The next day at work, Amani and I saw patients as usual. At the end of the day, I went into her office, not knowing what to say. She burst into tears. "How could this happen to me?"

I cried with her. I hugged her. "We are all vulnerable. It can happen to any of us. There is no fairness in the world. There is no fairness that this happened to such a good person as you, Amani."

Despite my words, I felt outrage. What right did cancer have to threaten the life of my friend? She was in her fifties, full of life, and a good person.

Amani struggled through rounds of chemotherapy, which took a terrible toll on her. She underwent further surgeries, the last one of which left her with a colostomy. Each time, Amani fought back to recover. She continued to see patients and care for her family. I marvelled at her courage, her optimism, and her unbelievable strength.

One day after she saw her last patient, Amani rushed into my office. I was packing up, ready to go home. "I'm leaking somehow. I must go home right away."

"I'll drive you home, Amani. I'll help in whatever way I can."

As we drove the short distance to her home, I felt a great deal of anxiety. I had treated patients who were coping with colostomies, but I had never seen one nor did I know anything about maintaining it. Amani will teach me, I thought.

Amani quickly opened the door to her house and ran up the stairs. She took off her pants and went into the shower. She pointed to the ostomy supplies on the counter and removed the leaking bag that was attached to her body. She told me how to dispose of it. Then she tried to instruct me as to what to do next. When my first attempt to be her nurse failed, she told me to call her ostomy nurse. The nurse gave me clear step-by-step instructions that I was able to follow. After the procedure was complete, Amani asked me to leave so that she could wash herself. I went downstairs and breathed a sigh of relief.

I wept for Amani. Helping her with the ostomy bag and seeing the scars left by her surgeries brought home to me how much she had suffered. After that day, I was even more impressed with her smile when she greeted me each morning, by her dignity, courage, and choice to live life to the fullest. She told me on many occasions that my mom was an inspiration to her. "She has beaten the odds so many times and not only survived but went to concerts and shows and ate out. She enjoys her life. She is my role model."

I wondered if I would have the courage to make the choices that Amani and my mom had made in the face of serious illness.

One day when she was experiencing more pain than usual, Amani went home early from the office. I went to her home after my last patient. After letting me in, she lay down on the carpet in her living room. "This position is better for me," she said. I sat on the sofa and asked what I could do to help. "Just be with me," she said. We were silent for a long time. Then Amani said, "It gets you in the end."

"It is very scary but, Amani, we don't know," I began. "There is hope as long as you are here. You are getting the best treatment." The words were true and important to say but gazing into Amani's tear-filled eyes, I knew that she needed to talk about the dark cloud that was hanging over her head. Follow her lead, I reminded myself. *Each of us knows what we need.*

The conversation shifted between life and death. Amani recounted humourous episodes that had occurred in our practice. "Do you remember the time I saw the police officer who came in uniform and had a gun?"

Our intense grief and anguish suddenly transformed itself into hysterical laughter. "Yes! I remember how you went through that session thinking that you had to be careful about what you said lest he shoot you! Thank goodness we got in touch with the referral source at the police to tell their officers to attend sessions in regular clothes and without a gun!"

We both chuckled thinking about how we both jumped up with delight when the first patient called. "And, Amani, even though we rapidly became very busy with patients, you still taught me how to knit. Think about it, we've worked together for more than thirty years now."

"Yes, we have, and we are still friends."

For a few hours we travelled together through memories and emotions with Amani leading the way until she rose to her feet and offered
to give me something to eat.

54

2016

I knew that I would be helping Mom more and more every day as we approached 2016, the year of her hundredth birthday. During Chanukah in December 2015, I spent an afternoon at her house grating potatoes and onions and following her recipe to make a large pile of latkes, one of her favourite foods.

Mom's eyes lit up with delight when I placed five latkes on her plate along with spoonfuls of sour cream for dipping. She gobbled them up before I returned to the kitchen. I was jolted by her shout, "Rickey! Come back here with those latkes!" I hesitated. She wasn't supposed to have so many, given the five different diets she was told to follow: low salt, low sugar, low carbohydrate, low fat, low cholesterol. Then I thought, she's almost one hundred. She should enjoy more latkes. Quickly, I returned to the living room with another plate full of latkes. Mom ate them with relish. After her latke feast, I heard her familiar refrain, as if it was a surprise. "I'm not hungry anymore!"

I worked intensively as Mom's case manager coordinating all her medical appointments and hospitalizations. After her blood clot emergency in 2010, Mom was hospitalized briefly again for different problems including episodes of atrial fibrillation, vertigo, asthma, unstable angina, pneumonia, falls, breathing problems that were diagnosed as chronic obstructive pulmonary disorder, a gastrointestinal bleed, inflammation of the bile duct, and congestive heart failure.

Every night for six years, I went to bed with anxiety that Lilly would call with another health crisis. Each time the phone rang out its emergency call, it was usually the middle of the night. Startled each time, I listened to Lilly describe Mom's symptoms and provided whatever medical advice I could. I was always faced with the choice to call 911 and risk the ambulance taking Mom to any hospital, or to drive her to the teaching hospital downtown and risk her dying in my car. I was on my own making life-and-death decisions. It was a crushing responsibility. Whether driving behind an ambulance or driving Mom myself, I kept thinking I'm doing my best to help her. When it's her time, it probably won't matter which I choose.

Mom fought her way back to health and returned home after each crisis, but by 2015, she never fully returned to the same quality of life that she had experienced before. Still, she attended her seniors' club meetings and, with Michael or Lilly at her side, enjoyed the opera, ballet, and symphony concerts. She spent hours watching videos of her ninetieth birthday party and Angela's wedding. Every time she watched that video she commented, "Two women—that's strange." But there was not a hint of disapproval in her tone.

At each of her follow-up appointments with her family physician, Dr. Bromstein commented, "I don't know how many lives you have, Faye! You are incredible."

To which I always added, "My mom refers to our rabbi as 'my handsome rabbi,' and he says that she is a miracle."

During each of her crises, I booked off patients and spent days and sometimes weeks with Mom in the hospital. Lilly and Michael were helping but Terry was absent. In a series of emails, I asked Terry to come to Toronto to help out. "You could help a lot by taking Mom to appointments, doing some of the grocery shopping, preparing some meals, and just talking with her, keeping her company. It's very hard for me to manage as I am still working full time and need to help Michael cope on a day-to-day basis."

"I would not be of any help to you," she wrote back. "I would not do what you want me to do. Besides, I don't have a car."

I was angry with Terry's refusal to help. Having retired at age fifty-five, it was clear that Terry could afford to rent a car. Then I reflected. She resented Mom and me. She was correct. She would probably not be helpful.

I felt sad for my aloneness—no sibling to help, no husband to help. Allowing the sadness to wash over me for some time, I turned to focus on my many blessings. I thought about my loving relationships with Mom and with Angela and Michael. I thought about Mom's incredible courage and strength, her love of life, and the very special closeness that we shared. *How lucky I was to have her in my life for all these years!* Then I asked myself the question that I recommended my patients ask themselves every day: How can I help myself feel better right now?

Dr. Bromstein referred Mom for palliative care in her home. The first time the physician arrived, I was impressed not only by his knowledge about comfort measures, but by his cheerfulness, respect, and candour.

In the last week of her life, Mom was surrounded by Angela, Michael, Lilly, and me. I played recordings of Mom's favourite Yiddish songs. Our cantor visited and sang '*Raisins and Almonds*' to her. This was the lullaby that her mother often sang to her at bedtime when Mom was a little girl.

We held Mom's hands as she quietly slipped out of this world. For some time after she passed, I told her how much we loved her, hoping to send her consciousness away upon a gentle, sweet breeze.

I called the emergency phone number for synagogue, and within minutes Mom's 'handsome rabbi' entered the house. He asked us to hold hands in a circle around Mom as we said *Sh'ma Yisrael*, the watchword of our faith, an affirmation of His oneness. For me, at the time, it was a comforting affirmation of the continuity of life.

Later in the same year, Amani passed away at fifty-nine after battling cancer for eleven years. I was deeply honoured when her husband asked me to deliver the eulogy and to participate fully in her Hindu funeral. I was also traumatized.

A part of me died with Amani.

Sitting in my office now, it is easy to allow myself to become overwhelmed by the injustice of pain and illness that befalls so many good souls. I am thinking about my funny uncle, Dad, Mom, Darlene, Amani, and so many of my patients.

The crucial question isn't why God only watches the sparrow fall, rather, it is what do *we* choose to do for that little bird? If my very tenuous ever vacillating faith in a Supreme Being has any value, it is in the inspiration it gives me to make good choices to help myself and others. To reach up toward godliness through our actions enables us to walk along the narrow bridge of life without being overcome by fear.

I hear a knock at the door. I let the movers in and watch as they place the lids on the boxes and load them onto their trolleys. I wheel my psychologist's chair out into the hall, turn, lock the door for the last time, and walk away, just the ordinary person I have always been.